Counterfeit, Mis-Struck, and
Unofficial U. S. Coins

*a guide for the detection of cast and struck
counterfeits, electrotypes, and altered coins*

by Don Taxay

Introduction by John J. Ford, Jr.

Arco Publishing Company, Inc.
New York

Third Printing 1975

Published by ARCO Publishing Company, Inc.
219 Park Avenue South, New York, N.Y. 10003

Library of Congress Catalog Card Number: 62-20291
ISBN 0-668-01000-2

Printed in the United States of America

"The best investment in numismatics is knowledge."
—Wayte Raymond

PREFACE

TO the earliest moneyers, the concept of authorized (as against unauthorized) coins would have conveyed little meaning. Money, in fact, consisted of mere ingots, and the sole authority a man recognized was a pair of scales. Only after the passing of centuries, when the ingot became standardized and was punched with a guarantee of its value, did authorized coinage have its birth. But since the seal of authority, unlike the weight and purity of a coin, possessed no intrinsic or "hard cash" value, and could furthermore be easily imitated, it was soon applied where it should not have been, giving rise to what is today colloquially called the "unauthorized series."

The evolution of the monetary concept and its subsequent perversion is the theme of our present work. As we shall see, it is a theme with many variations and one which has been played for nearly three thousand years. In modern times the "unauthorized series" has been perpetuated primarily by the counterfeiting and altering of coins—evils which are daily becoming more prevalent. It was with the purpose, in fact, of providing collectors with a means by which to detect such spurious pieces that *Counterfeit, Mis-struck, and Unofficial U.S. Coins* was originally conceived; it is hoped that the reader will not lose sight of this aim in the midst of the anecdotal information.

D.T.

New York
January 3, 1963

NOTE: It should be understood that all data given in this book in regard to counterfeiting are purely schematic and will not enable anyone to manufacture false pieces; moreover, any such attempt, for whatever purpose, is punishable under the severe provisions imposed by Federal Law. (Also see end of Chapter II.)

Acknowledgments

MY DEBTS in regard to this work are manifold, and it is hardly possible to acknowledge them fully in the space of a few words. Nevertheless, I would like to thank my colleague John J. Ford Jr. for his excellent Introduction and varied assistance; Walter H. Breen of whose kindness and illimitable memory I have availed myself so often; Paul Franklin and Eric P. Newman for numerous helpful suggestions; Richard A. Miller for his assistance in preparing the drawings as well as his happy instinct for the "mot juste" which has rendered the text more fluent in many places; Miss Eva Adams, Director of the Mint; James B. Rhoads of the General Services Administration (National Archives); Ray Reute of the Medallic Art Co.; Vern W. Palen and John Croke of the Phillips Electronics Corp.; Herman Steinberg of Capitol Coin Co.; Q. David Bowers of Empire Coin Co.; Robert Bashlow; Charles M. Wormser of New Netherlands Coin Co.; Henry Grunthal and Richard Breaden of the American Numismatic Society.

Photographs are reproduced through the courtesy of John J. Ford Jr.; Charles M. Wormser; Paul Franklin; Q. David Bowers; R. S. Yeoman, editor of the Whitman Publishing Co.; Lee Hewitt, editor of the *Numismatic Scrapbook Magazine;* Elston Bradfield, editor of *The Numismatist;* Dr. J. Hewitt Judd; Herman Frank of August Frank & Co.; Phillips Electronics Corp.; Jack McKay; Harry Forman; Al Worfel; John A. Troyan Jr.; Bob Medler; Vernon Brown, Curator of the Chase Manhattan Bank's Money Museum; The American Numismatic Society; and the Smithsonian Institution.

CONTENTS

PREFACE v

INTRODUCTION by John J. Ford, Jr. xi

Chapter I
A SHORT HISTORY OF MINT TECHNIQUES AND TERMINOLOGY 3

Chapter II
ON THE ARTS OF COUNTERFEITING, CLIPPING AND ADJUSTING 19

Chapter III
ALTERED COINS 59

Chapter IV
FAMOUS FORGERIES OF THE U.S. MINT (AND OTHER
OFFICIAL ECCENTRICITIES) 75

Chapter V
NEW DIES FROM OLD—A POSTSCRIPT 119

Chapter VI
"PEDIGREED" FORGERIES 132

Chapter VII
PRIVATE COINS BY NECESSITY 162

Chapter VIII
A COMEDY OF MINT ERRORS (AND EPILOGUE) 180

APPENDIX 213

SUGGESTED READING 215

INDEX 217

INTRODUCTION

COIN collecting began to grow popular in this country about 1855. Three years later, the Numismatic Society of Philadelphia published their *Catalogue of American Store Cards,* and the famous numismatist and antiquarian, C. I. Bushnell, put into print two similar works concerned with tokens. In 1858, in Albany, J. H. Hickcox penned the valuable classic, *An Historical Account of American Coinage,* and in 1859, Dr. M. W. Dickeson, of Philadelphia, wrote his *American Numismatic Manual.* During the following year, Prime wrote on *Coins in America* for *Harper's Monthly* magazine, and J. R. Snowden (Philadelphia Mint Director) was compiling his *Description of the Medals of Washington.* These pamphlets and books (the Prime article was reprinted in book form) constituted the first numismatic literature in the U.S. Simultaneously, as the interest in coins, tokens and medals became almost a fad, auction sale catalogues and lists appeared, which were devoted entirely to numismatics. By the middle years of the Civil War, some of these contained comments and observations by the compilers, and many appeared on large paper in limited deluxe editions. In 1869, the first American sale catalogue to contain photographic plates appeared. As coin auction sale lists evolved into catalogues and were themselves saved for reference, magazines devoted to coins (either in whole or part) were also published. The first of these to be concerned entirely with numismatics, and possibly the most important American periodical ever published on the subject, was the *American Journal of Numismatics,* which collectors first read in 1866.

Early coin books and catalogues were not only interesting but provocative; in fact, many of the statements made were downright controversial, if not libelous. Much research was involved in writing these pioneer words on American numismatics, and several of the early publications are still used today and highly valued as standard works.

As the twentieth century approched, however, the number of new books on the subject slowly decreased, and the sale catalogues degenerated, by and large, into dull, monotonous lists. Authors and cataloguers did less researching, thoughts and conclusions became more stereotyped, and a sort of dependence upon the ideas and concepts of the immediate past developed. There were exceptions to the decline of imaginative numismatic writing, as S. S. Crosby showed in 1897 with his *The United States Coinage of 1793, Cents and Half Cents,* and L. H. Low proved a few years later with his comprehensive work on Hard Times tokens. Nevertheless, in spite of the efforts of these writers, and a few others, including the indefatigable Edgar H. Adams, a sort of reliance upon numismatic legend began to predominate. Writers and cataloguers would merely rehash the data and conclusions of earlier authorities, and then, as the years passed, embellish them. Rumors became inextricably bound with facts, even if the facts were originally erroneous; stories were built up around the recollections of older collectors, and a sort of American Numismatic Mythology was the result.

As the years passed, anything said or written by an earlier source, even if it had been garbled during the passage of time, was taken as gospel truth. The catalogues of the most prominent and successful coin dealers of the pre-World War II years, the Chapman brothers of Philadelphia, Tom Elder of New York, and B. Max Mehl of Fort Worth, Texas, served as reference texts to the collectors of their day, but the attributions and descriptions contained in these sale offerings were almost always stereotyped. This has been by and large true of the succeeding generations of dealers, in whose catalogues we often find statements and references long antiquated if not obviously incorrect. This fifty-year period of decadence in the written numismatic word may well be regarded as the dark ages, in so far as new ideas, new thoughts, and original research on American coins, medals, tokens and paper money are concerned. It is true that Edgar Adams wrote many refreshing articles for *The Numismatist*, but his *United States Pattern, Trial and Experimental Pieces*, based on the old R. C. Davis compilation, included everything from counterfeit coins to the most fantastic pièces de caprice.

While Adams did try to present us with a creditable reference work in his essay on privately-made California gold coins, his era was still characterized by the monographs of Beistle, Doughty, Gilbert, McGirk, McIlvaine, Venn, Wurtzbach, and other sincere but mediocre authors. It was not until the period of WW-II, that S. P. Noe tackled the complex silver series of Colonial Massachusetts, and Dr. W. H. Sheldon, expunging the entire past literature on the large coppers, 1793-1814, wrote his brilliant and original *Early American Cents*. During the post-war years, the late Dick Kenney wrote many fine articles and booklets, mostly on subjects requiring depth of thought and study, and the dedicated father-son team of Melvin and George Fuld have taken a new and unbiased look into the complicated world of tokens and medals. Others have joined these argonauts of the past decade, and today we have both collector and dealer probing, studying, questioning and, most important, giving us the tangible results of their "close look" approach.

Just as coin collecting grew popular in 1855, it has become enormously popular since 1955. During the past eight years, collectors have flocked to the hobby in increasing numbers, and the ranks of dealers, both large and small, have grown so fast that they now seem to outnumber even the collectors. As the "consumers" of numismatics—the collectors—continue to swell in number, so has the amount of coin articles, pamphlets, books, and periodicals. This radically new interest has even given birth to a weekly coin newspaper, *Coin World*, which not only managed to grow to over 100,000 paid circulation in little more than two-and-a-half years, but which has, from time to time, published really informative and accurate numismatic articles.

Despite this intense activity by avant-garde researchers, however, there still remains, among the rank and file, a tremendous amount of what can only be defined as profound if not inexplicable ignorance. Amateurs and professionals alike, while spending large sums of money for rare and unusual coins, have all too often almost no inkling of basic, detailed or scientific numismatics. Too few among the collectors found at any regional or national convention today have, for example, read Eric P. Newman's masterpiece, *The Secret of the Good Samaritan Shilling*, and fewer still have really understood it. The same might be said in reference to the splendidly conceived and executed studies of Walter H. Breen, or of the recently published Judd work on Patterns, or, in general, of the basic standard catalogues and guide books. It is impossible to fully comprehend the hobby of numismatics, not to mention the science, without understanding how coins are made (and in the process often fouled up), how they have been (and are continuing to be) counterfeited for the purpose of deceiving collectors and the public generally, and what the real story is behind many of the forgeries, "novodels," pièces de caprice, alterations, and other dishonest numismatic produce which have always been with us—often under the aegis of a distinguished pedigree.

The resurgence of interest in coin collecting and numismatics has resulted in a series of books which include not only several splendid and definitive monographs, but also a host of "beginner" and general books. Unfortunately, however, none of these answer a great many of the questions that are asked every day. Eric Newman and Kenneth Bressett can write a meticulous work like *The Fantastic 1804 Dollar,* which explodes what might be called "the B. Max Mehl school of numismatic mish-mash," but their monumental efforts cannot, for instance, be fully understood or appreciated without a great deal of fundamental knowledge. The 1804 Dollar tome concerns itself with ante-dated restrikes and novodels (alias Mint-made struck copies), official chicanery and duplicity, and with the confusion and ignorance of numerous well-known numismatic personalities. But where, except in a few specialized and almost inaccessible articles, can the new collector (or the old) locate the background data that constitute the fist in the Newman-Bressett gauntlet? Where are casts, struck U.S. counterfeits, hubbing, explosive impact copying, and the electrotype process of reproduction explained? No single article, no part of any text, no dealer's catalogue or list . . . nothing published in American Numismatics, including the standardized guides carried by every collector and referred to by every professional, provides us with the answers in a plain, practical and thorough way. And yet, without a basic primer of advanced knowledge, the efforts of the Breens and the Newmans seem almost the proverbial "pearls cast before swine."

It has been almost two years since Don Taxay first approached me with his portfolio laden with notes, and commenced his bombardment of probing questions. Taxay had worked with coins and attributed them for dealers from Boston to New York to Chicago, and in doing so, he had come up with many queries to which he could not then locate the answers. It was in discussion and conversation with collector after collector that Don decided that there should be a book containing the answers. Since such a book was certainly not available, and because one was not even on the horizon, he decided to compile and write it himself.

The results are fascinating! Don has not only managed to assemble a great many facts of importance to the most advanced student of United States Numismatics, making his book an indispensable reference work, but he has done so writing in a most lucid and provocative manner. Every collector will find his observations on the 1922 Grant half dollars, the 1943 "copper" cent, and other popular coins and coining errors refreshingly new; but it is his expositions in numismatic science which have excited the imagination of advanced researchers. No one has ever before laid bare the laboratory tests of Specific Gravity, Assaying, Spark Spectro-analysis, X-ray Diffractometry, X-Ray Spectrography, or Metallography for numismatists. And yet, the use of these procedures in determining authenticity should be familiar to every collector paying a four- or five-figure price for a coin, and certainly to the man selling such an item. Don's book is far from the last word that will be heard on these subjects. However, like a university education, the data on the following pages is not only intended to inform, but also to prepare the way for a more detailed study of old facts and new techniques. I, for instance, in reading the galley proofs for this book, became so interested in scientific coin analysis, that I investigated the subject still further, and found yet another method of analyzing coins and determining forgeries: *Neutron Activation Analysis*. This test goes beyond the surface layer (the first .0001 [1/10,000] of an inch thickness), but then, that procedure, and the implementation of possibly others, could be a subject for another work. What is important is that Taxay has created a beacon to show the way. This book is a sign of the rebirth or revival of interest in American Numismatic research. It signifies vigorous activity in numismatic thought, and should impress upon the reader the fact that we are entering a new era . . . truly the renaissance of numismatics in the United States.

John J. Ford, Jr.

Counterfeit, Mis-Struck, and Unofficial U.S. Coins

I

A SHORT HISTORY OF MINT TECHNIQUES AND TERMINOLOGY

THE first medium of exchange considered to deserve the title of · coined money was struck in or around the seventh century B.C. by King Gyges, the fabulously wealthy ruler of Lydia. This consisted of mere globular lumps of electrum (a natural alloy of gold and silver) that had been cast into a rough shape and impressed with a plain nail punch as a guarantee of their value. Prior to the invention of this elementary seal, the same ingot had to be reweighed with each transaction; thus, however crude the nail punch might appear by modern standards, it marked a great improvement in the ancient economy.[1]

Nevertheless, it was not long before the desire to create more artistic coins ushered in a period of simple aniconic patterns. This in turn was followed by the use of representational figures, some animal, some human and some divine. The most immediate effect of

---

1. The word "punch" as used in numismatics has four distinct meanings. In dealing with the earliest Greek coins it represents first the incused impression in the flan, and secondly the implement producing it; for the medieval period and later it is used to denote any of the irons that impress elements into the die, as well as the upper die itself.

3

the transition was a change from the old incuse designs to those in low relief. This meant that the punch (which was growing more elaborate all the time) had now to be cut in intaglio.

Gradually, coins began to assume a more discoid appearance and, as a corollary, the concept of front and back (obverse and reverse) was born. To the punch was thus added a bottom, or anvil, die.

Some authorities believe that the first hubs, or cameo dies, originated in Athens, around the fourth or fifth century B.C. Whatever the actual occasion, their advent was of great significance. Under the constant blows of a sledge, the ordinary working die soon broke, and when this happened, it was necessary to prepare an entirely new one. One day, however, an ingenious person conceived the idea of cutting a die in which the design appeared in relief. This could then be used to strike working dies in the same way that the latter struck off coins. In practice it was not so easy. Without first heating the die-blank (as was done with the flan) the force of the sledge could do no more than establish the central portion of the design. Since the die had to be kept hard, the engraver just "hubbed" what he could and cut the remainder by hand.

Fig. 1. A Fifteenth Century German mint. The center man hammers the metal into thin sheets which are then cut, by the man on the left, into individual flans. These, in turn, are given to the man on the right who will strike each one between the dies. The finished coins are weighed on scales to make certain that they contain their full value.

The medieval coiner, on the other hand, fashioned his dies from a series of embossed punches, each of which bore a simple geometrical form. This inelegant technique furnished not only the letters of the alphabet but the King's portrait as well!

The forging of the die into its proper shape was done by an apprentice. One end of the die was burnished until perfectly smooth, after which the die sinker laid out his design. He began by punching a small, round center indentation or guide mark. Then, with a compass, he cut a pair (or several) circles which he translated into the inner and outer beading. The remainder of the composition was fashioned by means of individual irons or punches.

More curious was the means by which he prepared his flans. Instead of casting the metal in individual molds, this early artisan hammered out thin sheets of metal on an anvil, and then, with a pair of heavy shears, cut out the blanks one by one. Towards the end of the thirteenth century, the technique was varied by casting metal in small square rods. From these, the flans were sliced and trimmed to make them round.

Modern coining methods may be said to begin about 1510 with the introduction of rollers for reducing cast bars, machines for punching out blanks, and the screw press. It is the last of these which we shall now consider.

The principle of the screw press was simple but effective. The lower die was fixed to the foundation, the upper to the base of a vertical column which could be moved up and down by rotating the two long arms to which it was attached. Each arm was possessed of a heavy weight to lend it momentum, and could be turned by means of ropes. Four men were needed to operate the press, plus a moneyer whose job it was to remove the stamped coin and replace it with a fresh planchet. One of the advantages of the screw press was that it was easier on the dies, the force being registered, not by a blow, but with a more gradual pressure. Another was the rate at which it could be made to operate. In seventeenth century England, a single press stamped out twenty-five to thirty coins a minute—nearly one every two seconds. (*Fig. 2*)

For all this, the screw press could no more "hub" on a full scale than could the ancient sledge—and for the same reason—because it relied on manpower. Not until the introduction of the steam press (in the U.S., 1834-5) was the problem finally solved.

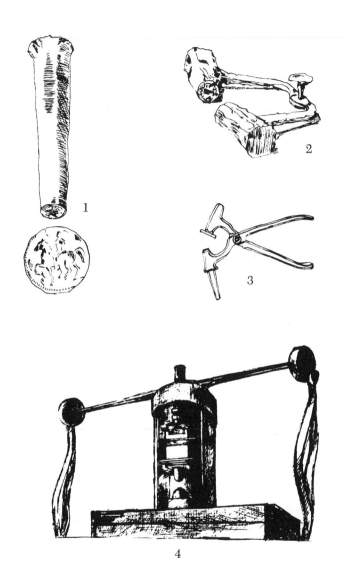

Fig. 2

Figs. 2 & 2A. Methods of striking coins from the earliest times to the present: 1) Ancient Greek die used to strike Philip II tetradrachms, ca. 350 B.C. 2) Roman hinge dies. 3) Renaissance hinge dies; the spike at bottom was imbedded in a tree stump for stability. 4) A seventeenth century screw press. 5) Modern

Fig. 2A.

steam press. Instead of the hammer-blow and recoil method of earlier presses, the two dies are moved by means of a toggle joint, and operate as part of a single motion.

The perfection of the hubbing technique meant that only one die need now be cut—the hub itself.[1] This was accomplished in the following way. The hub blank was smoothed down and perfectly covered with a layer of transfer wax. A tracing of the design was then placed over it and rubbed with a smooth instrument, impressing each line into the wax. This impression was finally gone over with a graver which cut the design into the steel. This method continued in the U.S. until the 1830's when it was superseded by the use of an ingenious instrument called the portrait lathe (the precursor of our modern reducing pantograph, which we will soon describe).

The ancient die cutter would be very much surprised to learn that his modern counterpart no longer works in steel, but in wax-like models many times actual coin size. For that matter, a Cook's tour of the Philadelphia Mint would be quite an eye-opener to most of us. Of course few of us could manage such a tour, but were we able, this is what we would see:

From the drawing board, the design is sculptured in plastilene (modeling wax) at about six to eight times actual coin size. The model is then impressed in plaster of Paris, forming a negative, or intaglio, mold. The latter is touched up in order to maintain its detail and used to cast a similar positive copy. The positive is likewise touched up, after which it will appear exactly as the original, except that it is in plaster, not wax. The reason plaster is not employed from the start is because it is too brittle to tolerate engraving.

When the positive model has been approved by the Mint Bureau it is then used to cast a second negative copy. This negative is dipped into beeswax, covered with powdered copper and electroplated with alternate layers of copper and nickel to a thickness of about one sixteenth of an inch. The electrolytic shell, or "Galvano," is then

1. With the advent of hubbing, the die variety was never the same again. The hub contained every part of the design except for the date and mintmark which were still punched separately into each of the working dies. These elements were omitted so that the hub would not become obsolete at the end of the year, nor have a limited use within the year itself. After 1840 the date was sunk by means of a multiple numeral punch called the logotype. This device insured that the date would be of more uniform size and spacing, and (aside from periodic blunders by the engravers) it rendered the dies practically indistinguishable. It is true that the logotypes themselves may vary slightly in their relation to the device, but the person who tries to assemble a collection based on such minute differences is in for an exasperating experience. Today, the only element which is punched individually into the working die is the mint mark, and consequently this little letter has now become the focal point for thousands of collectors.

separated from the plaster, trimmed, backed with lead, and mounted on a Janvier reducing machine. Here its relief will be transferred to a soft, tool steel cylinder of the diameter of the coin, this being, as we know, the hub.

At the front of the reducing machine is a fulcrum on which rests a long, rigid bar. At one end of this bar a *tracing point* has been fastened, just opposite to the electrolytic shell. On the other side, and closer to the fulcrum, a *cutting point* is attached facing the blank hub. As the shell and the hub rotate in equal, counter-clock-wise motion, the two points, each commencing at the center of their respective models, work their way gradually towards the edge. In this duet the tracing point is the leader and its motions are precisely reproduced on the hub in a smaller ratio, the proportion being established by the relative position of the two tools.

The finished hub is heated, then chilled very quickly causing it to harden. The die blank is also heated, but allowed to cool slowly with the result that it anneals. The hub is then sunk into the die blank from three to five times, and after each blow the blank is reannealed to prevent its breaking. The completed die is removed and carefully inspected for any imperfections which may have resulted from, say, a misalignment between blows. Any additional work required is done by hand-tooling, after which the excess metal is trimmed off. The hub is carefully stored away, and the die (which is actually the master die) is now hardened and used to produce "working hubs."

From a single working hub, about two hundred and fifty dies are sunk of which approximately two-thirds are "proofed," a special process which we shall describe later on. In the case of the cent, each die will then strike up to a million or a million-and-a-half coins before it is retired. Compare this performance to that of the early die, which could turn out possibly several thousand coins and sometimes broke after striking less than a dozen!

Having finished with our hubs and dies, we are ready for the second stage in the coining process which is the preparation of the blank, or coin planchet. For this we must go now to one of the three government refineries, located in San Francisco, Denver and at the U.S. Assay Office of New York City. Here the raw materials are brought and refined into the pure bullion needed for coinage. The metals are weighed in order to determine the correct proportion required for alloy, and melted in huge blast furnaces in the smelting room. The molten metal is then poured into upright molds producing ingots weighing up to several hundred pounds each. These will be shipped to the Philadelphia Mint where the process of coining will continue.

After the ingots have been annealed they are subjected to repeated passages through huge steam rollers where they are progressively broken down, thinned and gauged to the exact thickness of the desired coin. Still intact, these long ribbons of metal are reannealed and made ready for the blanking machine.

Here, each strip is carried along by two gripped rollers, and with every progression new blanks are punched out in gangs by short steel cylinders from above. In the case of the dime, as many as thirteen can be punched out in a single stroke. The attendant will weigh the first few blanks and, in the event that they are found to be too heavy, he will pass the strips once more through the last steam roller to correct the fault. When the run has been finished the blanks are sorted out on sifts, and any pieces of "shruff," i.e. edge pieces, crescents etc., which have come off the strip and been mixed in are expected to fall through, leaving only the full-sized blanks on top. The scrap metal is then returned to the furnace for remelting.

The work-hardened planchets are annealed, cooled in water and, lastly, cleaned with dilute sulfuric acid and cream of tartar to remove the discoloration caused by heating. They are now ready for what is variously called the milling, upsetting or edge-rolling machine.

Here the blanks are made to pass through a narrow groove which is bounded by two concentric rollers, one fixed and one movable. As the blank enters between the two, its edges are uniformly raised so that the finished coin will be protected from excessive wear and also stack more easily. Formerly this operation was called "marking" or "lettering" because the edges of the coin were not only thickened but also marked with an inscription contained in part on each of the rollers.

After receiving their upset, the blanks are weighed on sensitive scales, and those found to be either too heavy or too light are condemned to the furnaces for remelting. The remainder pass on to the final operation which is that of stamping.

The blanks are fed into the press by an automatic feeding device. They are then carried forward, one by one, and placed onto the lower of the two dies by the "layer-on," a mechanism simulating the action of human fingers. The die (together with the blank) drops a set distance into its "collar," and the punch, or upper die, is brought down with great force. In the case of a silver coin, the inner wall of the collar is reeded, and the blank, pushing outward under force of the blow, will receive this impression also. The machine then lifts the upper die, and the lower rises through the collar, allowing the coin to be ejected. Another blank is pushed forward and the operation continues.

In addition to its regular production, the Philadelphia Mint also strikes a number of *non-circulating coins*. The best known of these (as well as the only one currently available at the Mint) is the proof. In recent years there has been a tendency to extend the meaning of the word "proof" to include any coin with a shiny surface. Without going into a discussion of motives, we should mention that such thinking is extremely illogical, no less in fact than if we were to call iron pyrite "gold" and attempt to value it at thirty-five dollars per ounce!

We forget that a highly polished, mirror-like surface is a quality possessed also by several types of non-proof coins (not to mention mere buffed coins) and that the two truly distinctive features of a proof are its broad, polished edge and perfect relief. Unfortunately, the misconception is to a great extent perpetuated by the current proofs themselves, which are poorer in relief than even the regular-issue coins of a half century ago. Thus, when we speak of the characteristics of a proof, the reader may take it that we mean the "classical" or pre-1936 coin.

Since proofs were originally intended as presentation coins, it is only natural that, at every stage of the operation, their ingredients were carefully selected and processed. Dies, free from any imperfection, were given a high polish and then put into an hydraulic press. While an enormous pressure is exerted by this press it is quite unlike the "equal force" obtained from the impact of ordinary fast-action machines. Instead, it yields a force similar to that of a squeeze which slowly increases its pressure as it bears into the coin. The metal can thus penetrate more deeply into the delicate markings of the matrix, creating a fine, intricate embossing. If one examines a genuine proof coin under a magnifying lens one sees that the contours are very sharp and not at all rounded off like those of a regular coin. The edge is also higher for it has been built up by the displacement of metal under the extreme pressure. Lay a genuine proof coin next to a non-proof and you will see that the former is much thicker at its edge.

Ironically, there are two distinct types of proof coins which have nothing at all of the sacrosanct "proof-surface." These are the matte (also spelled matt and mat) and sandblast proofs struck at the Philadelphia Mint between 1907 and 1935. The matte finish was produced by pickling the planchets in dilute acid, the sandblast finish by pelting the planchets with a fine stream of sand projected by compressed air. The former is found, with several variations, on the copper and nickel proofs of 1909-1916, and the gold proofs 1907-12; the latter seems to have been confined to the silver proofs of 1916-35 and gold proofs of 1912-15. The silver sandblast specimens consist mostly of commemoratives manufactured to order—fifty of the Hawaiian Sesquicentennials and one to three each of certain other issues. The finishes produced by these techniques vary somewhat in texture and brilliance, although the general appearance is that of a softly lustrous, granular surface. The traditional "brilliant" proof surface is believed to have been abandoned during these years because of the increasing convexity in the fields of the dies which rendered burnishing more difficult.

In addition to proofs, there are a few other types of non-circulating coins with which the collector should be familiar. These can be grouped as follows: [1]

ESSAY

An essay is a coin *trying* out some new idea, device or mechanism. It is legally struck from official dies, not as a regular issue, nor as a proof nor restrike of a regular issue, but for one of the particular reasons given below.

---

1. The definitions employed here were compiled by John J. Ford Jr., and the author, and will be used in the forthcoming 19th edition of *The Standard Catalogue of United States Coins*. It should be noted that many coins exist which either represent a combination of the categories given here, or which cannot be specifically attributed because of insufficient information regarding their manufacture. Other definitions, employed at different times and for different purposes at the Mint, will be dealt with later on.

I. *PATTERN PIECES*
    A.   *Regular Pattern:* An essay representing a new design proposed for adoption as a regular issue, but either adopted in a modified form or not adopted at all. Patterns are struck in the same metal as that in which they are intended to circulate. *(Fig. 3)*

    A-1. *Regular Pattern Trial:* A regular pattern struck in other than its proposed metal, for the purpose of testing the dies.

    B.   *Transitional Pattern:* A pattern that is adopted *as proposed,* either in the year following its date, or subsequently. Transitional patterns are currently collected as a (more or less) separate series, and have achieved considerable popularity in recent years. *(Fig. 4)*

    B-1. *Transitional Pattern Trial:* A transitional pattern struck in other than its proposed metal, for the purpose of testing the dies.

    C.   *Experimental Pattern:* An essay which involves a fundamental change in the circulating medium, whether in representing a new shape of coin (e.g. ring dollar, A-W 118); a new precious metal (e.g. aluminum 5¢, A-W 629, goloid dollar, A-W 1606, metric gold $20., A-W 1572); a new *use* of metal (e.g. nickel 10¢, A-W 669), or a new denomination (A-W 57, 108, 395, 1498, 1578). Experimental patterns are either regular or transitional. *(Fig. 5)*

    C-1. *Experimental Pattern Trial:* An experimental pattern struck in other than its proposed metal, for the purpose of testing the dies.

II. *TRIAL PIECES*
    A.   *Regular Dies Trial:* A proof or sample of a regular issue struck in some other metal, invariably base, *for the purpose of testing the dies* (e.g. A-W 1707). Not to be confused with experimental patterns, false metal coins, Mint errors or simulated Mint errors.

    B.   *Die Trial:* A uniface impression (one side only) sometimes struck from an unfinished die. This may (but need not) be on a round planchet. *(Fig. 6)*

    B-1. *Die-Trial Splasher:* An impression made by pouring soft lead onto a piece of paper and impressing the metal by

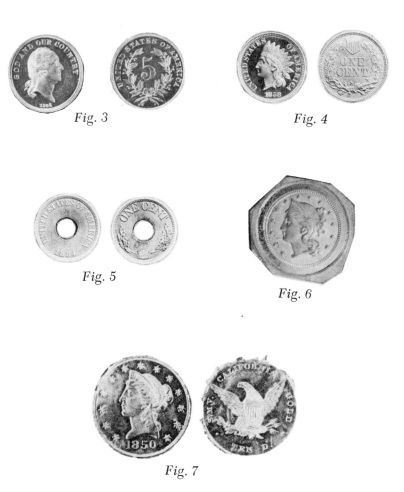

Fig. 3

Fig. 4

Fig. 5

Fig. 6

Fig. 7

Essays: Fig. 3. Pattern nickel five cents with the head of Washington; Fig. 4. Transitional pattern 1858 Indian Head cent; Fig. 5. Experimental pattern "holey" cent of 1884; Fig. 6. (1857) die trial for gold half eagle; Fig. 7. White metal die trial splasher for Dubosq & Co. gold eagle.

hand with a single die. The purpose of this technique is to get a quick positive impression from the die. Splashers are of unusual thinness, always with ragged or irregular edges, and often show paper adhering to their blank side. *(Fig. 7)*

C.   *Pattern Trials:* Trial impressions struck from pattern dies. These are included in their respective places under patterns.

D.   *Set-Up Trials:* These are the first regular impressions made from a new pair of dies before exact pressure necessary for bringing up the full relief has been determined. Since this pressure varies somewhat due to the effects of annealing and hardening (of both dies and blanks), the blows are at first registered very softly, then gradually increased until the proper adjustment has been made. Set-up trials are supposed to be withheld from regular production, but through inadvertence they occasionally find their way out of the Mint. They are generally and erroneously classed with "Mint errors."

OFFICIAL RESTRIKE

An Official Restrike is an impression from a correctly matched pair of dies, made later than the year shown, and intended for an official purpose (e.g. the 1879 Flowing Hair type $4., manufactured in 1880 to further promote the new denomination among the members of Congress). The continued use or re-use of dies during the year dated, or in immediately subsequent years, *in the regular course of business,* is not considered restriking. Both practices were common during the early years of the Mint.

Within the scope of our definition, restrikes made as normal practice by Mint officials for the Mint Cabinet or for presentation are *not* official restrikes, and will be dealt with under the next heading.

PIECE DE CAPRICE

The piece de caprice is a coin struck from official hubs or dies, or from simulated official dies, *illegally or unofficially,* in or out of the Mint, by either Mint personnel or laymen—and solely for the purpose of providing a numismatic curiosity or rarity. Included here are pieces that purport to belong to one of the previously described categories, coins allegedly of regular issue, and fanciful productions of almost any kind.

I. *RESTRIKES*

    A. *Unofficial Restrike:* An impression made from a correctly matched pair of *original* dies, but after the date shown, and without legal authority (though possibly with official sanction). Within the Mint these were struck to provide gifts for visiting dignitaries, to augment the Mint Cabinet either directly or through trading, and for reasons of personal profit. Outside the Mint they were struck from discarded dies which had been sold by the Mint as junked scrap, or which had otherwise been obtained by private persons. Unofficial restrikes may be impressions in proper or false metal and from either regular issue or essay dies. In fabricating trial pieces a single die (without the restraining collar) is generally used on a large flan.

    B. *Simulated Restrike:* An impression from a pair of dies one or both of which were manufactured after the date shown, and in a similitude of the original dies (e.g. 1801, 1802, 1803 dollar restrikes).

    C. *Fantasy Restrike:* An impression from a pair of dies one or both of which were manufactured after the date shown, but for which year no original dies or coins (of that denomination or type) ever existed (e.g. 1804 dollar).

II. *SIMULATED SERIES COIN:* An impression made from a correctly matched pair of dies in the year shown, but unofficially or illegally after the series or design has been discontinued (e.g. 1884, 1885 Trade Dollars, 1913 Liberty Head nickel, 1868 large cent, 1866 Philadelphia Mint quarter, half dollar and dollar without the motto "In God We Trust").

III. *PIECE DE CAPRICE MULE:* An impression made from *unmatched dies*, either in the year shown, or at a later date, in or outside the Mint. These may be bi-metallic (e.g. copper and silver two cents, A-W 522), bi-denominational (e.g. five cents/cent, on nickel planchet, A-W 827), bi-metallic *and* bi-denominational (e.g. two cents/Standard Silver quarter, on a copper and nickel planchet, A-W 819), with double obverse or reverse (e.g. 1858 Indian Head cent obv./1858 Flying Eagle cent obv., J-220), or from some other unusual combination of dies.

IV. *FALSE METAL COIN:* An impression from a correctly matched pair of dies, in the year shown, and struck, in a collar, on a planchet of correct diameter, but in other than the authorized metal (e.g. 1863 dollar in aluminum, A.W. 369). This should not be confused with the experimental pattern, trial piece, Mint error or simulated Mint error.

V. *FANTASY OR EPHEMERAL COIN:* An impression with appropriate (though intentionally individualistic) devices, legends etc., which is struck without legal authority, though possibly with official sanction. It may be struck at the Mint (e.g. Panama Pacific dollar and half dollar without the "s" mint mint mark), but most often is not. In the latter case, it is usually offered as a semi-official pattern.[1]

VI. *SEMI-OFFICIAL REPLICA:* An electrotype *made at the Mint* from a U.S. or other coin (e.g. copper 1804 dollar).

VII. *SIMULATED MINT ERROR:* An impression which, in some way, has been deliberately perverted so as to resemble an actual coining error. This should not be confused with (1) mules, which can never happen by mechanical malfunctioning or by error, (2) any of the trial pieces listed earlier, (3) false metal coins, (4) coins overstruck to test the die, or for the sake of economy (e.g. 1795 without pole and 1797 half cents struck over Talbot, Allum & Lee tokens).

Of the various families of American coins, patterns have always held a special place in the hearts of collectors. Many years ago, a Mint attaché, in trying to capture something of this appeal, wrote:

"Open for me your cabinet of patterns, and I open for you a record which but for these half-forgotten witnesses would have disappeared under the finger of time. Read to me their catalogue, and I read to you, in part at least, the story of an escape from the impractical schemes of visionaries and hobbyists—a tale of national deliverance from minted evil. These are to be enjoyed as by-gones, though there lingers a fear for the spark that still smolders under their ashes. Laws have been framed for them, words have been warred over them. Now only these live for 'what might have been'; only

1. Only a few coins have legitimate claim to this title, i.e. the Getz pieces, the Jefferson Head cent, and the Bouvet 1849 eagle.

these to remind us of what has been weighed, measured and set aside among the things that are not appropriate, not convenient, not artistic, in short, that are not wanted."

We cannot say that we disagree.

II

ON THE ARTS OF COUNTERFEITING, CLIPPING AND ADJUSTING

O NE of the most persistent legends which we encounter in the older philosophies is an allegory concerning the four ages of Man. It is said that in the Golden Age men walked the earth as gods and that covetousness was unknown. Life in the Silver Age suffered a decline, and with the advent of the Bronze Age a growing desire among men for private ownership gave rise to a rudimentary economy as the only basis for mutual cooperation.

Thus every object took on a certain value which was determined by its utility and also by the simple dictates of supply and demand. The interchange was known as barter.

Let us say that one of the inhabitants of our Bronze Age community—the weaver for instance—has run out of fishhooks. This presents a serious situation for it means that unless he acts fast he may go without a meal. So with a few wares under his arm, the weaver hurries off to the "maker of fishhooks" with whom he will make the necessary trade. He offers the "maker of fishhooks" a red blanket, but the latter shakes his head, "no." The weaver then brings out each of his other wares but the answer is, alas, the same. Finally, in exasperation, he asks: "Is there nothing you will take for a fish-hook?" At this, the "maker of fishhooks" becomes lost in thought. Slowly his face clears and he replies: "Yes, I will take a whale's tooth!" So now the poor weaver must locate the owner of a whale's tooth and then begin all over again.

Probably when enough people had missed a meal for want of a fishhook, they got together and decided to do something about it. Whatever the occasion, an article was chosen to act as a medium of exchange and the value of other commodities was determined by it. Naturally the medium itself had no utilitarian value like that of the fishhook, for then it would have been just one more object of barter and its purpose defeated.

After a time it was decided that gold, silver and bronze would serve as the different values. Gold could never be defiled, even by fire or by burying it in the earth. Hence it was regarded as eternal and afforded the highest place in the tri-metallic system. After gold came silver, and after silver, bronze.

Long before the advent of money, however, the ancients had already given their values to the different metals. We have seen how they applied these allegorically to the different Ages of Man. They regarded the elements not as inert matter but as symbols expressive of the basic attributes of Man and Nature. The last Age about which the ancients spoke was called the Iron Age. But so inferior did they regard its status that they could never bring themselves to use iron for actual money. The only genuine exception were the Spartans who cast their money in long iron rods—no doubt to discourage anyone from growing rich.

It should surprise no one to learn that we of today are living in the Iron Age. The present cycle, which is supposed to have com-menced a few thousand years ago, is characterized by a full flower-ing of self-aggrandizement and an ultimate reliance upon stringent Law to maintain the crumbling social order. One of the dominant corollaries of this Age is that every advance entails a recoil, that is, a misuse or perversion of the original principle. Take the case of our early economy.

We saw that prior to the invention of money, each article had its own value which was determined largely by utility. Thus a man could not hope to counterfeit an ax or a spear without actually fashioning these objects. And even if he could somehow have produced a cheap, simulated spear, the secret would soon have been out for the objects of barter did not *circulate* as did the later money. The counterfeiter does not rely so much upon an infallible reproduction as on the rapid circulation of currency whereby his own identity may remain concealed long after the objects of his craft have been exposed.

Possibly the oldest recorded law pertaining to the subject of counterfeiting derives from a monetary convention held in 400 B.C. in the city of Phocaea, in Ionia. There it was resolved that any Mint official or coiner found debasing his metal should be sentenced to death. "But," you will say, "that is only debasing, not counterfeiting, for the coiner was striking his coins under authority and using genuine dies." Yes, but what was it that gave the coin its *value*—the device, or the worth of its metal? The latter, certainly, for which reason the origin of the fraud is of little consequence.

The most notorious counterfeiter of all time was, in fact, the emperor Nero. Since Nero introduced the art of debasing (counterfeiting) to the Roman world, it would seem to follow that he is not only responsible for its perpetuation in England (where the Romans established mints in London and Colchester), but in our own present-day society as well!

Fig. 8. The world's most infamous counterfeiter—the Emperor Nero. A bronze sestertius showing his portrait.

In early England the problem of counterfeiting was aggravated by the practice of debasing among the official coiners whose mints were scattered throughout the country. Finally in the year 1125, King Henry, seeing that the coinage would no longer be tolerated at home or abroad, ordered all of the coiners of his realm to attend a Christmas Day Conference at Winchester. There he examined the produce of each and, finding the majority of coins to be highly debased, commanded the offending parties, one by one, to forfeit their right hand "et testiculis infra."

One of the reasons King Henry was so angry with his coiners was that he had learned (like all good kings) that the striking of silver and gold coins was a royal prerogative. The striking of coppers, which commenced in 1672, did not enjoy this status and, as a result, the counterfeiting of these was punished only as a misdemeanor. When, through trial and error, this fact became generally known, the number of base half-pence and farthings soon increased to a point where they outnumbered the genuine coins in circulation. Even after the suspension of copper coinage in 1775, the situation seems to have steadily worsened as we can surmise from the following correspondence of the English coiner and inventor Matthew Boulton, in 1789:

> In the course of my journeys I observe that I receive upon an average of two thirds counterfeit half-pence for change at tollgates, etc., and I believe the evil is daily increasing as the spurious money is carried into circulation by the lowest class of manufacturers who pay with it the principal part of the wages of the poor people they employ. They purchase from the subterranean coiners thirty-six shilling's worth of copper (in nominal value) for twenty shillings, so that the profit derived from the cheating is very large.

Some of the more wily counterfeiters, wishing to accomplish the same end and yet remain within the "letter of the law" substituted their own fanciful inscriptions for the royal legend. These pieces are known as "evasions" for, though they could be made to circulate undetected among the illiterate masses, they sufficiently differed from genuine coins to evade the actual charge of counterfeiting. (Fig. 9)

For the majority of persons, however, who were too indolent either to cut their own dies or fashion molds, a few simpler techniques were, perforce, introduced. One of these was melting. The reader may recall that at one point during the Middle Ages, flans were cut out, by means of heavy shears, from long cast rods. The weight of each such flan was only "fixed" in the sense that so-and-so many could be made from a single rod. As a result, most of the coins were either too heavy or too light, and the heavier pieces were soon culled from circulation and melted down. This posed a serious problem to the Crown which was already deficient in the precious metals needed for coining. Finally, the royal coffers became so depleted that local alchemists were summoned for the purpose of transmuting the base metals into silver and gold!

Another technique was that of clipping. Here the unscrupulous person would simply "clip" or file off a portion from the edge of a coin and then place it back in circulation. In time the practice became so widespread that nothing short of an entire recoinage could save the economy. This enormous task was finally undertaken by William III and, in order to defray some of the expense, the King levied a tax on, of all things, every house of six windows or more! Many persons resented the law and bricked up their excess windows to avoid payment. Even today a few of these old houses stand, airing their ageless grievance against the unpopular window tax.

In 1607 the first of the English colonists arrived in Jamestown, Virginia. These were followed, thirteen years later, by the landing of the Pilgrims at Plymouth Rock. To these early settlers, life was a constant struggle, and when Nature failed to provide their daily needs, they fell back on the ancient method of barter.

The closest thing to actual money, in fact, which the colonists found on the new continent was the suckauhock and wampum [1] (black and white beads) which the Indians fashioned from periwinkle and clam shells, and strung on fibers of hemp or on the tendons taken from their forest meat. For more than a century these functioned as an important medium of exchange. Then as the new communities began to flourish, a certain number of adventurers joined the throng and the plague of counterfeiting sprang up once more—this time in the form of spurious wampum. Since the astute and cautious Indian would refuse any but the genuine article, it was invariably the white man who sustained the loss. In order to "assay" the quality of the beads, the Indian would rub the entire thread across his nose, evidently an infallible test to the trained proboscis.

The secret of counterfeiting is to produce a likeness of the currency and yet leave out the one element that lends it value. It doesn't really matter, in fact, what that element is. In the case of a coin, the value lies in the worth of its bullion, and the forger seeks to replace as much of this as he can with base metal. In the Indian

---

1. To denote strung beads the suffix "peage" was added to the word form. Thus, strung white (wompi) beads became wampumpeage. Today the term "wampum" alone has survived and is used to denote the currency in all its various forms.

wampum, however, the value lay in the amount of *time* that was required to produce a string of beads. Since counterfeits could be manufactured with very little effort (from cheap glass cast into beads) this one element was thus left out.

The first actual coins to circulate in the New World were not American, but a potpourri of English, Spanish, French, Italian and Dutch. When it became known that a large percentage of these were debased, the colonists requested permission of the Mother country to strike their own coins. Undaunted by her refusal, the General Court of Massachusetts set up its own Mint in 1652 and authorized John Hull, the Mint Master, to strike the first series of silver coins. An entry in Hull's diary provides us with a reference to the event.

> Upon occasion of much counterfeit coin brought in the country, and much loss accruing in that respect (and that did occasion a stoppage of trade), the General Court ordered a mint to be set up, and to coin it, bringing to the sterling standard for fineness and for weight every shilling to be three pennyweight; . . .

One would think that after the colonists had taken such pains to establish their own Mint, they would at least have shown a little respect for their coins. Apparently, however, they began so furiously to clip metal from them that, within a few months, it was found necessary to select a more ambitious design. The first coins had been punched only with the letters N E (New England) on one side and the denomination on the other. The new law read:

ffor the prevention of washing or Clipping of all such peices of mony as shall be Cojned w^{th}in this Jurisdiction. It is Ordered by this Courte and the Authoritje thereof, that henceforth all peices of mony Cojned as afore sajd shall have . . . . this Inscription—Massachusetts, and a tree in the Center on the one side, and New England and the yeere of our lord on the other side . . . (Fig. 10)

It may be asked how our forefathers dealt with those who perverted the Colonial currency. The following account concerning the punishment of a young man who had been found altering five shilling notes to the appearance of five pounds, will give us some idea.

As it was his first offence, and he otherwise sustained a good character, Mr. Griswold (the King's prosecutor) granted him every indulgence which he could consistently with his duty as a public officer. Buel's punishment appears to have consisted of imprisonment, cropping and branding. The tip only of Buel's

Fig. 9. Counterfeit English ½d and "evasion." The obverse legend has been changed from GEORGIUS III. REX. to GREGORY. III. PON. On the reverse, BRITANNIA has given way to BRITISH GIRLs.

Fig. 10. The N.E. and Willow Tree shillings of 1652.

ear was cropped off: it was held against his tongue to keep it warm till it was put on the ear again, where it grew on. He was branded on the forehead as high as possible.

Today the punishment seems, to say the least, severe. And yet, from what we know of the ease with which these early administrators meted out their "justice," we can well believe in the truth of Griswold's "indulgence." As for Abel Buel, he not only survived the ordeal but learned to turn his skills to better account. He became **the principal die sinker for the Connecticut coinage and, in 1787,** was contracted to cut the dies for the Fugio cents—the first of our United States coins.

Fig. 11. 1787 Fugio cent, the first of our U.S. coins. Some of the dies were cut by Abel Buel.

One of the reasons why counterfeiting flourished on the new continent was due to the great variety of coins in circulation. In addition to the issues of each of the colonies, there were English guineas, French louis', German thalers, Dutch ducats, Spanish Pieces of Eight and a host of smaller denominations. To a population that was mostly illiterate, it must have been difficult to recognize the value of so many different coins. In all probability the colonists accepted anything unfamiliar on the basis of its general size and color, which would explain the widespread practice of silver plating French sous and passing them for British half crowns!

The most formidable problem, however, was that of the counterfeit British half-pence which were finally overflowing the mother country and reaching across the sea. A contemporary article tells us of the situation:

The coinage of copper is a subject that claims our immediate attention. From the small value of the several pieces of copper coin, this medium of exchange has been too much neglected. The more valuable metals are daily giving place to base British half-pence, and no means are used to prevent the fraud. This disease, which is neglected in the beginning, because it appears trifling, may finally prove very destructive to commerce. It is admitted that copper may at this instant, be purchased in America at one eighth of a dollar the pound.

British half-pence made at the Tower are forty-eight to the pound. Those manufactured at Birmingham, and shipped in thousands for our use, are much lighter, and they are of base metal. It can hardly be said that seventy-two of them are worth a pound of copper, hence it will follow, that we give for British half-pence about six times their value. There are no materials by which we can estimate the weight of half-pence that have been imported from Britain since the late war but we have heard of sundry shipments being ordered to the nominal amount of one thousand guineas and we are told that no packet arrives from England without some hundred weight of base half-pence. It is a moderate computation which states our loss, for the last twelve months, at $30,000 by the commerce of vile coin.

One of the reasons why the counterfeit half-pence seemed so prevalent to the colonists was that many of the coins were being struck not in Birmingham England, but at Machin's Mill, the notorious "hardware manufactory" located on the outskirts of Newburgh, N.Y. Operations at the Mill were conducted clandestinely at night; horrendous noises, caused by certain steps in the preparation of blank planchets, reverberated through the stillness, and the workers, donning hideous masks, frightened away the local children.[1]

The Mill was built in 1784 on land owned by Capt. Thomas Machin, a military engineer during the Revolutionary War. Machin associated himself with Samuel Atlee, porter brewer, a naturalized Briton, James F. Atlee, die sinker, David Brooks, James Grier, acting treasurer, and James Giles, lawyer. Their principal merchandise consisted of "imitation" British half-pence. These bear the dates 1747, 1776, 1778, 1787, 1788 and have single outlines to the crosses in Britannia's shield instead of the double outlines found on British productions.

In June 1787, Reuben Harmon, the patentee of the Vermont Mint, finding it impossible to obtain new die punches, entered into a

Fig. 12. 1787 Vermont cent. The reverse die was originally used for striking counterfeit British half-pence, which would account for the legend BRITANNIA.

1. Simms, *History of Schoharie County.*

desperate contract with the Machin's Mill coiners, James Atlee thereafter making the dies for both. It is significant that from this time on all of the Vermont coppers show hub devices identical to those found on some "British" half-pence. The bust has become that of George III, and the female "Genius of America" has replaced the device of four sheaves of grain on her shield with the British Union Jack, i.e., the combined crosses of St. George and St. Andrew. In fact, Ryder Nos. 13 and 31 are no less than out-and-out mulings made from the so-called "British" and the anglicized Vermont dies! *(Fig. 12)*

But for all this, the Newburgh project was not a success. Owing in part to the efforts of the counterfeiters, the number of copper coins in circulation had finally increased to the point where they were beginning to depreciate in value. The decline was so sharp that even a man who debased his coins felt the pinch and, as a result, in 1789-90 Machin's Mill closed its doors forever.

Two years later, the newly established Philadelphia Mint assumed responsibility for the nation's coinage. The era of the Colonial coin was over, and with new relish the counterfeiter took up the task of perverting Uncle Sam's currency.

The Act of April 21, 1806 provided, for the first time, a set of comprehensive laws and penalties for the counterfeiting of U.S. and current foreign coins.

Counterfeiting was defined as the private manufacture of coins in the similitude of those issued by the Federal government. While it was not stated, the implication was that of a *debased or devalued coin*. It should be remembered that, in those days, the concept of coined money was substantially different from what it is today. A silver dollar was exactly what it claimed to be—one dollar's worth of silver, plus the value of its alloy. To counterfeit coins at their full weight and purity would thus have been a thankless task. One could do better as a private assayer where, at least, a gratuity was involved with each transaction.

One day, however, the miracle was finally wrought by a quiet Englishman whom history records only as Mr. Peach. For some ten months in 1821, Peach counterfeited Spanish gold doubloons which had become very scarce, and sold them at a premium on Wall Street in New York City. Each day he would purchase gold ingots at sixteen dollars an ounce, roll them, punch out planchets and strike the coins, all with the aid of just one juvenile apprentice. The planchets were prepared at the corners of Burling Slip and Pearl Street; the striking took place in the basement of a home on James Street. After the coins had been struck on a drop press, they were placed in a keg of sawdust and churned by a hand crank which caused them to be bounced about and receive a few minor contusions as would result from normal circulation. Finally they were roasted over a charcoal oven which tarnished the edges, an effect resembling that caused by bilge on the genuine doubloons which were transported in the holds of Spanish ships. At the end of the day, Peach would bring his produce of about two hundred coins down to Wall Street, sell it off at seventeen to eighteen dollars per coin and then purchase more ingots for the next run. In this way he continued for some ten months after which the genuine doubloons became once more plentiful and the market adjusted itself.

Long before the ten months had passed, however, the inexhaustible supply of the Englishman's doubloons had begun to attract the curiosity of government officials. But though he was "apprehended," Peach was never indicted or even asked to desist from his employment—and for the simple reason that the bogus doubloons were worth as much, if not more than their Spanish counterparts!

Today the concept of bullion currency has given way to that of the reduced-value coin, which is why Mr. Peach would no longer be tolerated by polite society. Our present philosophy was introduced in 1853 to halt the wholesale melting of silver coins for their increasing bullion or intrinsic worth. The act, which reduced the value of all silver denominations excepting the dollar to less than their face value, also prohibited the free coinage of the metal.

Among the less heralded advances in nineteenth century economic thinking were a few in the ancient and esteemed art of coin clipping. Of course some of the old timers, undaunted by the advent of reeding, continued to round off the edges of gold coins by means of a lathe, but the amount of metal that could be removed without detection was nominal, and it was felt by most that a fresh approach was indicated.

The difficulty, it was reasoned, lay in the tacit assumption that the content of a coin could only be extracted from its edge. Thus casting aside past prejudices, the underworld economists began now on a different track.

The "new approach" consisted of four techniques which were

known respectively as sweating, plugging, scooping and filling. In the first, one put several gold coins in a box or bag and then shook them until bits of the metal had fallen off. During the process, the practitioner probably "sweated" as much as the coins, but the softness of gold was found to compensate for his labors. The possibilities of this technique can be realized when we consider that a mere moving and counting of a million dollars worth of gold in the U.S. Treasury vaults once reduced the weight of its bullion by twenty-five pounds (troy weight) or $10,500!

In later years, the advent of electrolysis gave a big boost to the votaries of sweating. The use of an electric current enabled the counterfeiter to remove the metal equally throughout the surface of the coin without incurring any of the damage to it that resulted from the incessant jostling.

In the days when gold, in its numerous forms, could be freely manipulated by individuals, it was very difficult for the authorities to contend with the evil of sweating. It is probable, in fact, that the practice continued right up to the Gold-Prohibition Act of 1934.

The second of the "techniques" was called plugging and, in reality, it was just that. The miscreant bored a hole in the coin, plugged it with lead and then plated the area with the original metal to cover the fraud. A variation on the same theme was the technique of "scooping." A tiny hole was drilled in the reeding of a gold coin and a hair-thin wire inserted and used to poke or scoop out the interior. By aiming the wire obliquely and scooping in a circle, a person could remove a far greater quantity of metal than would at first seem possible. The practice, once initiated, was received with great favor among the San Francisco Chinese to whom it afforded an apparently lucrative pastime. Since these are simple and rather pedestrian methods, however, we shall leave them and pass on to one far more ingenious. This last is the technique of "filling."

Here the counterfeiter sawed the gold coin along its edge, divided it into two halves which he hollowed out, then filled it (when he was feeling most ambitious) with platinum, this metal being not only heavy enough to substitute for gold, but in those days worth only six dollars per ounce compared to sixteen for the latter. This done, he joined together the two halves, covering the mutilated edge with a new fluted gold rim of his own making.

Such was the skill with which the alterations were wrought that the coins, which were half genuine and half counterfeit, for a long time deceived even the skilled detectors at the Philadelphia Mint. Only a slight discoloration at the edge, caused by the heat of soldering, was sometimes visible, and even then a specific gravity test was required for verification.

When, in 1860, the first of the platinumized gold pieces was discovered, the Mint officials set about in great haste to produce an unfillable coin. The planchet of the new coin was to be concave on each side, just thick enough at the rim to permit edge lettering and thin enough at the center to prevent its being sawed through. The concaving was effected by running the planchet through the milling machine a second time after the coin had been struck.

The concave coin was never adopted. It became, instead, one more among the numberless patterns or "half-forgotten witnesses" as Patterson DuBois was wont to call them. The "filled coin," which did not depend upon Congress for its existence, continued to be manufactured until World War I when the revaluation of platinum rendered its production no longer profitable.

In our kaleidoscopic journey through the ages, the human landscape has admittedly changed a great deal. Today the rider of the ancient bullock cart and quadriga mounts his rocket-powered steeds and orbits the planet in a few short hours. But for all that, Man himself has changed very little. The laborer remains a laborer; the merchant still peddles his wares; the soldier fights; the administrator governs; and Man, the anti-social being, likewise remains immutable. Indeed, the ancient counterfeiting den unearthed at Halton Chester, England, is not substantially different from many of its modern counterparts.

There comes a time then, in every collector's life, when he must put away his history and begin talking current events. Counterfeit coins are, after all, still very much with us, and there is little evidence that their production is going to cease in the foreseeable future.

The problem for us is learning how to *detect* them. This is, admittedly, not always easy and even the expert may get fooled once in a while. Nevertheless, it is better to avail oneself of the knowledge at hand than bemoan the fact that we may not all become infallible.

Besides, in the realm of counterfeit detection, the difference between knowing *almost* everything and almost nothing is about the same as going into battle with or without one's gun.

The reader will recall that in Chapter I, we observed the various means by which genuine coins have been manufactured over the centuries. It is interesting to note, in the face of the obvious dissimilarities of each of these techniques, one aspect which is common to all: the *striking* of a previously prepared flan (or planchet or blank) with a die or pair of dies.[1]

Most counterfeit coins, on the other hand, are *cast* in molds, an inferior but much less difficult method of production. Here is the simplest of the means:

A coin which has been waxed or greased is placed in a crucible of very fine casting sand (sand and silica) so that an impression is formed. By means of rods, three additional hollows are made for a central flue and two narrower air ducts. A wax sheet is then placed over the crucible, covering the sand but permitting the upward side of the coin and the rods to protrude through snug-fitting apertures. Additional sand is poured over the entire area. The molds are separated to allow the coin, rods and sheet to be removed, and then joined again. Molten metal is poured through the flue and into the mold where it is allowed to harden. When this has been done the facsimile is removed and, if made from false metal, usually electroplated.

In this last and most interesting step we have as our constituents two electric cells (supplied by a low voltage D.C. energy source), a plating bath containing a silver salt solution (if this metal is the desired plate), a silver anode, and the base metal facsimile, or cathode. When anode and cathode are suspended in the plating bath, a current is produced which draws silver from the solution and deposits it in even layers over the surface of the coin. Simultaneously the anode is broken down, replenishing the solution with silver in the exact amount of its loss. The operation is now complete.

Despite its simplicity, however, the sand cast is seldom employed any longer for purposes of counterfeiting. There are several reasons for this. In the first place the mold, being, after all, mere casting sand, cannot survive many operations. Secondly, the gritty texture of

---

1. A few genuine exceptions exist as in the cast bronzes of early China and Italy.

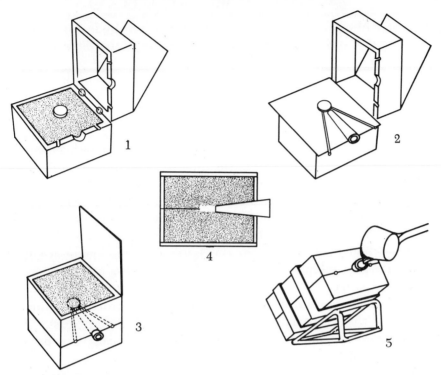

Fig. 13. How a simple sand cast is made: 1) The reverse of the coin is impressed in sand; 2) A flue and two ducts are formed in the mold; 3) Additional sand is added for the obverse impression; 4) How the mold would appear from a side view; 5) Molten metal is poured through the flue and into the mold where it is allowed to harden.

sand tends to blunt the finer definition of the copy, rendering it more easily detectable. A superior technique is known as the *lost wax method*. Here, molten rubber is employed instead of casting sand. When a mold has been prepared in a way similar to that of the previous example, molten wax is shot in and allowed to harden. Numerous wax replicas of the coin are produced in this way and imbedded in soft plaster of Paris. Before the plaster has had a chance to harden, it is placed in a vacuum where any air bubbles which would render it more porous, are sucked out. After it has completely dried it is then heated causing the wax to melt and escape. The result is a series of perfect molds.

The more durable quality of the plaster enables the lost wax method to yield multiple molds which can be worked in the manner of an assembly line. Its comparative fineness results in a smoother, more regular surface and a greater definition in the details of the composition.

Whereas, in the case of a sand cast, the molten metal had to be *poured* into the mold, the greater consistency of plaster allows that it be "shot in" by means of centrifugal force. It is thus enabled to penetrate more deeply into the crevices, enhancing the definition over that of its predecessor. Since pressure casting also effects a greater density in the metal, the modern counterfeit will more nearly approximate the weight of a genuine coin.

There are a few basic rules for detecting cast copies which every collector should know. These apply to all kinds of casts—from those poured into a mold fifteen hundred years ago to yesterday's reproduction—though, of course, in the latter case the symptoms will be a little less telling.[1]

1. If a coin has a soft and greasy "feel" to it, like that of graphite, it should at once arouse your suspicion. Such a texture normally indicates a cast (especially a white metal, or a lead-base, cast).

2. Close your hand over the coin and hold it briefly. The porous texture of cast lead will cause it to warm up rapidly.

3. Because the plating on a counterfeit coin cannot be very heavy without blunting the definition, it will tend to wear through, even after a short time, lending the piece an ugly, grey, and often spotty appearance.

4. Even if it has been cast under considerable pressure, the counterfeit will show a certain grittiness as a result of the plaster mold. The effect will be most pronounced in the intricate areas of the coin, and especially between the denticles.

5. If the coin has been cast from a mold which was not "evacuated" properly, it will often show tiny globules where the metal penetrated the broken air bubbles in the plaster.

6. A cast coin—being after all a copy of a copy—and often plated in the bargain, will lack the finer definition of the original. This will be most evident in the stars, denticles and the inner composition of the device where the metal will have been slower to penetrate.

7. Since the two molds have been prepared separately, the metal, on being poured (or shot) in, will flow into the crevice where they

---

1. Rules 2, 3, 8a and 9 pertain specifically to lead base forgeries.

meet, forming a thin line along the entire edge of the coin. Counterfeiters take great pains to remove this tell-tale line by filing and buffing it down. Invariably, however, a scrutiny of the edge will disclose traces of the filing and/or flattening of certain areas of the metal.

8. If the coin has a reeded edge, the tell-tale line will, of course, not be visible. Nevertheless the reeding has its own compensations in that it is difficult to reproduce with any degree of precision. The reeding on a genuine coin will observe an evenness of length, width, depth and direction. Counterfeits (other than those of gold coins) usually show a lack of uniformity in all these respects. Parts of the edge may be unreeded, or the corrugation simulated by mere cuts, causing the raised areas to appear unorthodoxly wide.

8 (a). In addition, the reeding on a counterfeit coin will wear much more rapidly owing to the softness of the base metal.

9. This softness will also result in a disproportionate amount of nicks, dents, scratches and general wear on the coin considering the length of its circulation.

10. A cast copy will ordinarily have a slightly reduced diameter due to the contraction of metal as it cools in the mold. This is difficult to detect from the coin itself, but it becomes evident when one compares an enlarged transparency of the counterfeit with that of a genuine specimen.

11. Tap the coin with a pencil while it is freely balanced on your finger. *It is not enough for a coin to merely ring*—many base metals do as much. The difference is one of timbre, that is, the quality of the sound.

Gold coins (90% gold, 10% copper and silver), when struck, produce the longest,[1] fullest, most satisfying of the metallic sounds. They possess few discernible overtones.

Silver coins (90% silver, 10% copper), maintain the same general characteristics of gold, but in a slightly less degree. The overtones are a trifle more pronounced though not yet jarring.

German Silver coins (about 55% copper, 30% zinc and 15% nickel), produce a very musical ring, but it is more jarring, and with higher overtones, than genuine silver. The tone is also lacking in the

---

1. In any given metal the time of resonance (as well as the pitch) varies with the ratio of the thickness of the coin to its diameter. A very small, thick coin, in any metal, will ring briefly, if at all.

"richness" that is conveyed in the sonorities of the noble metals.

Nickel coins (75% copper, 25% nickel), possess a distinctly softer, less metallic, less ringing sound than when combined with a high proportion of zinc (German silver).

Brass (70% copper, 30% zinc), produces a higher, thinner, more jarring sound than that of either silver or German silver.

Bronze (95% copper, 5% tin and zinc) is similar to brass, but more subdued in sonority.

Lead or *lead alloy*. The vast majority of counterfeit coins are cast in lead alloy and will produce a dull, flat, inert, almost non-metallic sound.

Learn to recognize these different sonorities and you will reap dividends later on.

12. Weigh the coin. A cast lead-base copy will not generally exceed three fourths the weight of its genuine counterpart. Copper and brass-filled coins (usually struck) show an additional weight of about ten per cent over lead-base ones, leaving them still almost twenty per cent shy of a silver equivalent. Gold is, of course, the heaviest. A gold coin will weigh some twenty-five per cent more than a silver one of the same size and forty per cent more than its lead-base facsimile.

When you weigh a suspicious coin, always verify that it is no more than its accustomed thickness. Counterfeiters will often increase the amount of metal in order to lessen the disparity in weight.

The following table will show you the weights to which U.S. coins conform. Coins failing to closely approximate these figures, barring an excessive amount of wear, are almost certainly forgeries.

Denomination	Date of Issue	Weight in Grains
Half Cent	1793-95	104
Half Cent	1796-1857	84
Large Cent	1793-95	208
Large Cent	1796-1857	168
Small Cent	1856-64	72
Small Cent	1864-1942	48
Small Cent	1943-	42.5
Small Cent	1944-	48
Two Cents	1864-73	96
Three Cents (Nickel)	1865-89	30
Three Cents (Silver)	1851-53	12⅜
Three Cents (Silver)	1854-73	11.52
Five Cents (Nickel)	1866-1942	77.16

Denomination	Date of Issue	Weight in Grains
Five Cents (Silver)	1942-45	77.16
Five Cents (Nickel)	1946-	77.16
Half Dime	1794-1837	20.8
Half Dime	1837-53	20⅝
Half Dime	1853-73	19.2
Dime	1796-1837	41.6
Dime	1837-53	41¼
Dime	1853-73	38.4
Dime	1873-	38.58
Twenty Cents	1875-78	77.16
Quarter Dollar	1796-1836	104
Quarter Dollar	1837-52	103⅛
Quarter Dollar	1853-73	96
Quarter Dollar	1873-	96.45
Half Dollar	1795-1836	208
Half Dollar	1837-52	206¼
Half Dollar	1853-73	192
Half Dollar	1873-	192.9
Silver Dollar	1794-1803	416
Silver Dollar	1836-1935	412½
Trade Dollar	1873-1883	420
Gold Dollar	1849-1889	25.8
Gold 2½ Dollars	1796-1834	67.5
Gold 2½ Dollars	1834-1929	64.5
Gold Three Dollars	1854-89	77.4
Gold Four Dollars	1879-1880	108
Gold Five Dollars	1795-1834	135
Gold Five Dollars	1834-1929	129
Gold Ten Dollars	1795-1804	270
Gold Ten Dollars	1838-1933	258
Gold Twenty Dollars	1850-1933	516
Gold Fifty Dollars	1915	1,290

13. When dealing with silver, one may test for the purity of the metal with the following solution:

Silver Nitrate	24 grains
Nitric Acid	30 drops
Distilled Water	1 ounce

With gold:

Nitric Acid	6½ drams
Mur. Acid	¼ dram (15 drops)
Distilled Water	5 drams

A drop of the above preparations on silver or gold plated base metal will, in each case, cause discoloration. Test on or near the edge where the coin will be most worn.

We should also note a few more or less exceptional circumstances which may endow a genuine coin with some of the properties of the counterfeit.

1. A coin which has been badly burned will appear blistered and otherwise ill-defined. In these respects it will resemble a cast copy of inferior quality. Such a coin will produce an inert, non-metallic sound when struck.

2. A coin which has been cut even slightly, or in which there is a fissure in the metal due to improper casting of the original ingot, will ring improperly or not at all. This applies also to holed or plugged coins.

3. A coin which has received excessive wear will be lacking in weight.

4. A coin which has been struck on an irregularly thin planchet, or which has been "pickled," will be lacking in detail and show a weight discrepancy.

5. A silver or gold coin which has become badly tarnished may superficially resemble lead or copper. An application of bicarbonate of soda, however (done properly by swishing the coin in a heated solution) will remove any discoloration that is not indigenous to the metal.

6. A coin that has been improperly cleaned through "scrubbing" will disclose a minutely "pitted" or pock-marked surface (not unlike that of a cast) owing to the fine hairlines of the brush. Unlike a cast copy, however, such a coin will show its marks on the fields and other unprotected surfaces, and not in the intricate areas of the dentils, etc.

It should be noted that the above exceptions are all based on "resemblances." An intelligent examination of the questionable coin should easily determine whether or not they are applicable.

After the collector has been sleuthing a while he will notice that, for each denomination, the majority of counterfeits are concentrated in a mere handful of dates. These are encountered so often in accumulations of old coins that he would do well to commit them to memory.

CAST COUNTERFEITS OF U.S. COINS

Half and Large Cents. Due to the expense involved in manufacturing these early coppers, cast counterfeits are rather exceptional. "Rare-date" forgeries are another story, but as these are seldom the result of casting we shall deal with them elsewhere.

Small Cents. Rare. Probably the largest confiscation on record was made in a small Philadelphia bakery in 1894. The coins in question were gingersnaps which had been stamped with an enlarged device similar to that of the one cent piece. The cookies together with the molds were seized, and the baker threatened with a five thousand dollar penalty and ten years in jail should the offense be repeated. The account of the confiscation regrettably omits any reference to the fate of the coin-cookies. We can only guess.

Two Cents. Rare.

Three Cents, Nickel. Occasionally seen for the dates 1865 and 1866.

Five Cents, Nickel. These have been found in surprising profusion from the earliest shield type to date. A few years ago, counterfeit 1944 nickels were detected by the absence of their reverse mint mark.[1] The maker evidently prepared his mold from coins of two different dates, producing, as a result, a non-existent combination. Similar faux pas as a 1909-S nickel and 1923-D (struck) dime have also been reported.

Half Dimes. Rare.

Dimes. Concentrations: 1891, 1892, 1907 and 1911.

Twenty Cents. Rare. Usually dated 1876 CC.

Quarter Dollars. Concentrations: 1853, 1858, 1861, 1877, 1907-09, 1920-29 and 1934-35.

Half Dollars. Concentrations: 1858, 1861, 1876, 1877, 1895, 1907, 1918 and 1920 (also see struck counterfeits).

Silver Dollars. Largest concentration: 1878-1900.

Trade Dollars. Concentrations: 1877-S and 1878-S. Struck for use in the Orient, these coins undoubtedly posed a great attraction to counterfeiters abroad. Most copies are of an inferior order.

Gold Dollars. Concentrations: type I viz. 1849-1854. Owing to the high premium which has accrued to these coins, modern fabrications

---

1. From 1942 to 1945 five-cent coins struck at the Philadelphia Mint bore a large P on the reverse. This is the only instance of a mint mark being employed on Philadelphia issues.

will usually show their full weight (if not more) and purity. The collector should particularly heed the following areas:

1. *The surface of the coin:* Many of these counterfeits will have a peculiarly shiny, granular surface, not unlike that of a matte proof.

2. *The L on the truncation:* This initial is present on all type I gold dollars with the exception of one variety of the 1849 issue, and will always appear well defined on a genuine coin.

3. *The edge:* Since the reeding on a fine cast is applied to the finished coin by means of a lathe or upsetting machine, the edge will often appear to be abnormally wide or built up. The reeding is generally less sharp than that of a genuine coin, and often with a peculiar lens-shaped appearance.

4. *The beading:* On a counterfeit coin this will be flat and less perfectly defined. This is true also, and in an even more pronounced degree, in the beads on top of Liberty's coronet. *(Fig. 14)* Gold $2½, $5, $10. Modern centrifugally cast quarter-eagles are most often found for the years 1843, 1854, 1856, 1909, 1910, 1911-D, 1912, 1913, 1914, 1915, 1927; half eagles for 1842, 1844, 1846, 1908-S, 1915-D; eagles for 1889, 1916, 1933.

STRUCK COUNTERFEITS OF U.S. COINS

Aside from gold,[1] there are only a few major exceptions to cast counterfeiting. These are predominantly early coins, mostly Bust Type half dollars which have generally been struck in German silver, a yellow-white alloy of about 55% copper, 30% zinc and 15% nickel.[2]

A few examples: If ever a black list were compiled for the entirety of the fraudulent half dollar series, it would probably outvie the *Haseltine Type Table* [3] for sheer bulk. The dies themselves are so curious one almost wishes they were genuine so that a place might be made for them in the standard albums. We shall describe a few of the more common types—partly as a precaution, but also for the sake of numismatic interest.

1. The most prevalent gold counterfeit struck from false dies is the 1921 Double Eagle (Twenty dollars).

2. In rare instances (mostly early) where the alloy is copper and silver, a superficially good color is given to the coin by pickling the blank planchet; the surface copper is thus dissolved, leaving only the fine silver.

3. A catalogue of the varieties of early U.S. silver dollars, half dollars and quarter dollars compiled, in 1881, by Capt. John W. Haseltine.

Fig. 14. 1) Counterfeit 1853 gold dollar; 2) genuine 1854 gold dollar; 3) counterfeit 1854 gold dollar (cast from same coin as the last). Compare the relief between the genuine and counterfeit coins, especially in the milling and coronet beads.

(1.) 1830. This one might be called the "tough old lady of the bust type halves." Perhaps the counterfeiter was thinking of his sweet old mother as he wielded the cutter. The 3 and 0 of the date and the fourth star on the left have all been recut. *(Fig. 15)*

(2.) 1830. A low brow type if there ever were one! The frontal curl is overly thick and the personification appears to be pouting. Date and lettering are very crude, the stars uneven. Along the rim the denomination reads FIFTV CENTS. *(Fig. 16)*

(3.) 1832. The portrait tends to be masculine with a bulbous nose. The eye also is not quite right, extending down too sharply. What is left of the composition is adequate except for the stars which are, as usual, crude. The horizontal tops of the T's are frequently missing from the reverse lettering. *(Fig. 17)*

(4.) 1832. This is one of several incredibly poor copies which must be seen to be believed. The entire head is absurdly elongated. The features are gross and undetailed, a mere triangle serving for the eye. The date is much too large and, in the reverse motto, the word UNUM reads UИUM. *(Fig. 18)*

(5.) 1833 (Contains an unusually high copper content). A slight improvement over No. 4 above, but the chin and nose are much too bulbous. Moreover the hair hangs down touching the eye, and Liberty looks as though she were in a stupor. Date and stars are very small. *(Fig. 19)*

(6.) 1833, 1837,[1] 1838. Probably the finest all-around copy of the lot, this die has been adopted from the reduced bust (type of '35) variety of the 1834 issue. The nose is somewhat too large and the shoulder-strap button a trifle more so, but otherwise it is a faithful and well-executed reproduction. The 1837 issue appears to be more weakly struck than the others and is often lacking the PLU of PLURIBUS. *(Fig. 20)*

(7.) 1833. A big, foolish looking Liberty, surrounded by a large date and stars, all very crude. *(Fig. 21)*

(8.) 1833. A liberty and eagle so perfectly executed as to necessitate their having been "hubbed" into the die. The border areas, by contrast, are very crude, and the entire date, plus two stars, is heavily

---

1. Genuine Bust Type half dollars of 1837-38 always show the denomination as 50 CENTS, never 50 c.

recut. This is the only example of "hubbing" which we have seen among the counterfeits of this series. *(Fig. 22)*

(9.) 1833. Here a suspicious looking Liberty peers up at us with a beady eye, while we regard her with equal apprehension. The date appears to have been punched in for a change, but the rest of the composition is no better than usual. *(Fig. 23)*

(10.) 1835 (Contains an unusually high copper content). Another big-headed Liberty, lacking most of her features. The LI have been omitted from the headband so that it reads BERTY, a name well suited to the composition. *(Fig. 24)*

(11.) 1837 (Reduced size). In this issue we have a high-nosed Liberty with a more than generous Adam's apple. The small frontal curl is poorly executed and gives the impression of a miner's lamp. The coin is generally well engraved; the stars are excellent but the reeding is only fair. *(Fig. 25)*

(12.) 1838. A pop-eyed Liberty! The stars are ill-shapen and mere cuts do service for the reeding. *(Fig. 26)*

(13.) 1840 (Type of 1836-39). The head is too long, too thin, the nose aquiline. The obverse shows but twelve stars. *(Fig. 27)*

(14.) 1842. This is a clumsy attempt to duplicate the earlier Bust Type which ended in 1836. The coin is very thick, very light and without its edge device. *(Fig. 28)*

(15.) 1826 (Silver plated copper planchet). The date and stars are entirely recut. Otherwise a passable copy and in many respects superior to its successors. *(Fig. 29)*

German silver counterfeits are occasionally found in other denominations also. Among the nickels, one should pay particular attention to the dates 1870, 1871 and 1875; among the silver trimes (three cent pieces), to 1860 and 1861.

The counterfeit nickels of 1875 are especially dangerous since they are not only the most plentiful, but command a good price. The piece illustrated here is apparently from the same dies as the counterfeit described in the July 1876 issue of the *American Journal of Numismatics,* from which we quote:

> A counterfeit five-cent piece is in circulation in New York and probably elsewhere, which is worthless only because not made at the Government Mint. Some of the counterfeits were recently sent to the Superintendent of the Mint in Philadelphia by the Treasurer for the

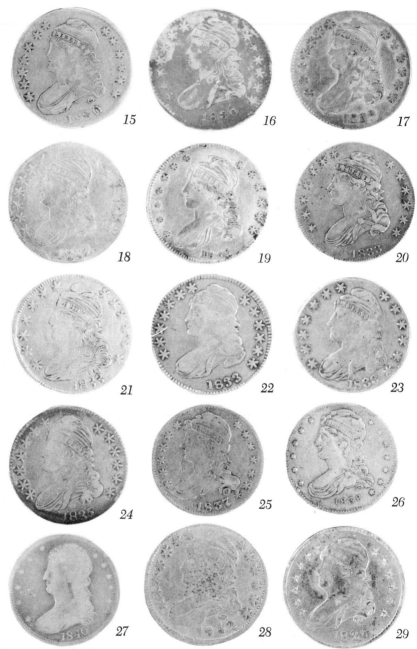

Figs. 15-29. The "Rogues' Gallery." Though struck in German silver, the workmanship on these early counterfeit half dollars would suggest that they emanated from Mexico.

purpose of making inquiries and to test their value. The Superintendent says the counterfeits have been assayed and found to contain copper and nickel in the legal proportion, that the coins are of proper weight, size, and finish, and just as valuable as good coin. The execution of the work is poorly done. The circle beneath the cross in the genuine is well defined; in the counterfeit it is indistinct and touches the scroll work. The cross is entirely out of line, and the words, "In God We Trust," are very irregular. The dates are nearly all 1875; a few are 1874. It is noticed that most of the coins are received from the west side of the city of New York, giving the impression that the factory is in that neighborhood or in New Jersey. Many come through the car conductors, and a number from the ferries.

Fig. 30. Struck counterfeits such as the above five-cent piece are still being sold to collectors as patterns or rare varieties. They can almost always be identified, however, by their unusually high relief and crude workmanship. One should bear in mind that all dies after 1836 were made from hubs, and are thus virtually identical (within their type) except for the date and mint mark.

If we are to be faithful to history, we should also mention a series of very dangerous struck counterfeits which first became known in the 1840's. From the description of these pieces given by the U.S. assayers Eckfeldt and DuBois in their *Coins, Coinage and Bullion, 1851*, it is obvious (despite the plaintive denials of the authors) that the spurious dies were sunk from hubs which, in turn, had been made from *genuine U.S. dies*, secreted or otherwise removed from the Mint.[1] The Assayers write:

1. We have already seen a counterfeit 1833 half dollar with the devices "hubbed" in. For the story behind these early Mint emissions of hubs and dies, see Chapter 5.

. . . A much more important counterfeit, or class of counterfeits, to us, is the imitation of our gold coin, lately brought to light; and which is as interesting to the man of science as it is dangerous to the commercial dealer. The varieties include the eagle, half-eagle, and quarter eagle; there is not much danger of a false gold dollar of that manufacture, for reasons which will be obvious in the examination.

These various counterfeits began to make their appearance in 1847, although some of them bear earlier dates; and they perfectly agree in character. They are of so perfect execution, that strong apprehension was at first entertained of the surreptitious procurement of genuine dies, notwithstanding all precaution in that matter. However, upon a minute inspection, the impression, although entirely "brought up," is not so sharp and decided as in the genuine coin, and from that circumstance they have exteriorly a family character by which a practised eye may perhaps single them out. The details of impression correspond to those of the genuine, to the last microscopic particular. The most skilful and deliberate artist in the world could not take up the graver and make such a fac-simile; their dies must have been transferred from our coin by a mechanical process.

The coins have a rather dull sound in ringing, but not as if flawed, although they are actually each in three distinct pieces of metal. Some few of them, where the weight is kept up, are thicker than the genuine, and necessarily so; but generally the half-eagles run, as in the gold pieces, from 55 to 60 thousandths of an inch, within the raised rim. The diameter is sometimes rather too great. The composition is as follows. A thin planchet of silver (of Spanish standard, as we found by assay) is prepared, so nearly of the right diameter that the subsequent overlaying of the gold plate at the edge will make it exact. Two other planchets, of gold, whose quality will be stated directly, are also prepared; one of them is of the right diameter of the projected coin, the other is about a quarter of an inch larger in diameter. Here are the three pieces which make up the coin. The two gold plates are then soldered upon the silver, the projecting rim of the larger disk of gold is bent up to meet the smaller, and to constitute the edge of the coin, and then the whole is finished by a blow in a coining-press. The suggestion that the coin may have been perfected in an electrotype battery is disproved by several considerations, especially by the conclusive one, that the effects of the *blow* are visible upon the silver planchet, when the gold is lifted off; and the process of *sawing out* a good coin, so as to make use of its two faces to cover a piece of silver, could not have been employed in this case, because the edge of the coin actually appertains to one of the gold surfaces; and besides, the gold is sometimes of a higher fineness than our standard.

The eagle, of which we have had but one sample, was not particularly noted, as it came after some others of the lower denominations.

Of the half-eagle counterfeits, we have had the dates of 1844, 1845, and 1847. Of the quarter-eagle, only the date of 1843 has been shown, and this had the mint-mark, O, of the branch at New Orleans . . .

Fig. 31. Fantasies of U.S. gold coins. (Above) These gilt facsimiles were originally struck as gaming counters by Kettle & Son of Birmingham, England, but
were soon brought to the U.S. where they were passed as two-and-a-half and
five-dollar gold pieces. Except when it has been surreptitiously removed, the
name KETTLE always appears to the right of the date. (Below) Of more than
full weight and purity, these fantasy ten- and twenty-dollar gold pieces may well
be called "the elite of merchant's tokens." The chopmarks would seem to indicate that they actually enjoyed a limited circulation in the Orient.

EXPLOSIVE IMPACT COPYING

Eckfeldt and DuBois, unable to account for the perfection of detail in the above counterfeits, assumed that the dies had been transferred from genuine U.S. coins by means of some mechanical process. They did not venture to explain the process, and it is just as well, since no transfer-engraving machine, either in their time or in our own, could reproduce models at a one-to-one ratio without a great deal of fine detail being lost. This is the reason that models many times actual coin size are used on the Janvier to produce a hub.

A second possibility in "hubbing" would be to make the working die *directly* from a coin in the same way in which it is produced from a hub. But this is only possible if the coin can be made more renitent than the die blank—as in the case of the 1943 steel cent (see Chapter 3). Otherwise the coin will spread at the moment of impact, producing an enlarged and ill-defined incuse impression. A recent attempt to overcome this difficulty has been to use a detonating capsule which drives the press by means of an exploding force. The time that elapses between the impact and the impression is thus reduced from milliseconds to microseconds. A counterfeit made by "explosive impact copying" will show all the diagnostic marks of the die that produced the original. Its detail will be a little weaker because it has been twice transferred, and the "spreading effect," though negligible, will probably still be slightly visible throughout (and to a more pronounced degree at the peripheries).

THE ELECTROTYPE

There is one last technique which, though ill-suited to the task of mass-counterfeiting, may be employed with a high degree of excellence in replicating individual coins. This is the process which results in the well known electrotype.

Here, obverse and reverse impressions are taken in wax or a similar substance and coated with an electrical conductor such as copper or graphite. The impressions are immersed in an electrolytic solution producing two shells of copper or the desired metal. These are trimmed, filled (usually with lead) and joined.

The electrotype represents the only basic technique of coin reproduction having its provenance in modern times. Credit for the invention, or for its application to numismatics, is given to the 19th century British antiquarian Robert Cooper Ready who, with his sons August and Charles, produced the famous British Museum collection of replica coins, medals, seals, gems, and other works of art. The Ready's were at liberty to reproduce any coin in the British national collection, and when Charles died, his own effects included more than twenty-two thousand electrotypes among which were numerous copies of U.S. and American colonial coins. To obviate the possibility of the reproductions being sold as genuine, Charles (the metal worker of the trio), stamped the initials R, RR, or MB on the edge of each, a rather poor safeguard since the letters could be easily effaced. Somewhat belatedly, the Museum recognized the dangers in releasing such deceptive copies, and deemed that all further electrotypes should consist of separate obverse and reverse shells. Before long, however, unscrupulous persons were completing the operation by filling the shells with base metal, joining them, and burnishing the edge. As a result of these practices, many of the Ready electrotypes (not to mention those of other artisans), are still in numismatic circulation where they are all too often sold as genuine coins.

The beauty of the electrotype (from the standpoint of reproduction), lies in the fact that, unlike a cast coin, it is only once removed from the original and hence very well defined. Electrotypes are most often encountered for the following coins:

1. Colonial coppers, especially those in the Washington series.
2. U.S. pattern coins of 1792.
3. Half cents: 1793, 1794, 1796, 1811, 1831, 1836, 1840-49, 1852.
4. Large cents: 1793, 1795 (Jefferson head),[1] 1799, 1804.
5. Half dimes: 1796, 1797, 1802, 1803.
6. Dimes: 1797, 1798.
7. Half dollars: 1794, 1796.
8. Silver dollars: 1794, 1804.

Since numismatic forgeries are certain to receive a more rigorous scrutiny than mere circulating coins, it is only reasonable to expect that they will be correspondingly more astute and difficult to detect. Always examine the edge for the tell-tale line or traces of filing and unevenness. It is comparatively easy to remove the line but (in the

---

1. Most of the electrotypes of the 1795 Jefferson Head cent were made by Ebenezer Mason from the "Randall" cent (ca. 1868-72), and originally sold for 50c apiece.

ordinary electrotype) next to impossible to entirely conceal having done so. Rotate the coin slowly as you regard the edge so that any flat or scraped areas will be more easily discernible. Observe the surface to see if it is entirely level. Electrotypes sometimes show also a slight concavity or waviness of surface. Examine the high points of the coin for any traces of the under-metal which might be wearing through. Ring the piece and weigh it as you would a cast but, remember, the electrotype will *resemble* a struck coin.

A still subtler and more deceptive means of fabrication is called the *drop-in electrotype.* Here, one of the halves is made in such a way as to include the entire edge, while the other is left as a mere disc to be "dropped in" after the former has been filled. The tell-tale line will now run between the outer rim and the mill, and after receiving an alternate burnishing and plating, it becomes virtually impossible to detect.

Fig. 32. A drop-in electrotype of a French Louis XVI medal. The impression can be seen in the soft metal within the shell.

A third variation is the *simulated hub trial.* The hub, as we know, is a cameo die, and a trial taken from it will therefore be in intaglio. Simulated hub trials are made by allowing an electrolytic shell to build up on the relief side, and *simulated die trials,* by building up the intaglio. Such fabrications will present a tolerably good weight and perfect sonority, and will require specific gravity or x-ray diffractometry tests for detection. Furthermore, by using two built-up and case hardened intaglio impressions as dies, a solid lead flan could be impressed on both sides and then plated.

LABORATORY TESTS

No responsible vendor will offer for sale a coin of purported "great rarity," but of questionable appearance or pedigree, until he has had it authenticated by laboratory tests. The collector, for his part, should become acquainted with each of these tests, and request that those appropriate be made when no other certificate of authenticity can be offered.

Specific gravity: This is a test to determine the density of a coin. Density, as we know, is the ratio between the mass of a substance (that is, the amount of matter it contains) and its volume (the space which it displaces). When we weigh a coin we are actually measuring its mass; but weight alone is not sufficient to prove anything unless we know for certain the exact volume of the coin. We mentioned earlier that a counterfeiter may add metal to a coin to bring it up to its proper weight. Since ninety-nine per cent of us appraise the thickness of a coin by the breadth of its edge, and not by that of its surface, the counterfeiter will sometimes build up the latter in order to promote his deception. When dealing with base metal forgeries the ruse can usually be detected by the trained eye or by a caliper, but with gold coins which have been centrifugally cast in their proper metal, a more accurate method is demanded. (It should be recalled that a cast coin will invariably be less dense than its struck counterpart and will therefore require a slightly greater volume to equal the same weight).

In testing for specific gravity, the coin is weighed first in air and then in water at the temperature of its maximum density (4° centigrade). The difference between the two figures is the weight of a volume of water which the coin displaces. The weight of the coin in air is then divided by the water displacement weight, the quotient being the specific gravity.[1]

In order to make your own specific gravity test you need only

---

1. The specific gravity of standard (coined) gold is taken at 17.2 (or 17.3 in the case of pre-1860 coinage), of standard silver at 10.3.

obtain a pair of balance scales. The rest of the equipment you will find in your own home. First weigh the coin as you normally would and note the figure. This will be your air weight. Then remove both the coin and weights, and replace one of the shallow pans with a wire coil (which can be shaped from a clothing hanger), and at the end of that, a length of thread. All that is required is that the wire and thread *exactly* balance the weight of the pan, and this can be managed by a judicious filing of the wire. The coin is now attached to the thread and suspended in water. Weights are again added to the other balance and the new figure will represent the water weight. From this, the specific gravity can be easily computed by means of the aforementioned formula.

While the value of the specific gravity test can hardly be overestimated, its results should not be taken as infallible since they neither make a distinction between an alloy which is homogeneous and one which is not, nor can they discern the substitution of one metal for another so long as the weight and volume of the coin remain unchanged. If, for example, a drop of gold were mixed with white metal, the weight and volume of an electrotype could possibly be adjusted so as to show an over-all correct weight and specific gravity.

Assaying: The traditional method of determining, by quantitative analysis, the composition of gold and silver coins is called *cupellation.* While this is a remarkably accurate test, it is seldom resorted to by the collector since it can only be effected through the ultimate destruction of the coin. At the Mint, cupellation is generally used to test a sample of a large number of coins, all of which are, presumably, of the same weight and fineness. In the first operation a coin is placed in a porous bone-ash cupel, or shallow cup, and deposited in a muffle furnace. As the temperature is increased the base metal alloy gradually becomes oxidized and, in this gaseous state, is absorbed by the cupel. The gold and silver remain fused together in the form of a soft bead which is removed from the container and weighed. In the next operation, which is called "parting," the bead is placed in a platinum evaporating dish containing dilute nitric acid, and heated once again. At a temperature slightly below boiling, the acid ceases to act on the metal and the "parting" is considered finished. The pure gold bead is removed, cleaned and then weighed. The loss of weight from the last computation will determine the percentage of silver, and from the previous computation, that of the base metals.

Spark spectro-analysis: This is the investigation of substances through an analysis of the light emitted by their atoms and molecules when in a gaseous state. A minute area—a single grain or less —is scraped from the edge of the coin and placed in the lower of two electrically wired carbon rods of an arc lamp which has been impregnated with a volatile metallic salt. When a 110-volt direct current has been applied, the two rods are brought into contact and immediately separated, forming an instantaneous bridge, or arc, of flaming carbon between anode and cathode. In the 3000° to 4000° K. heat generated by the arc lamp, the sample, which is vaporized, gives off numerous light waves. The waves are focused through a lens, or collimater, where they are rendered parallel, and then made to pass through a prism. Each wave is resolved into its component colors and directed, by means of a second lens, onto a photo-sensitive plate. Since each different element has its own characteristic spectral pattern, the composition of any given sample can be easily identified. Quantitative or proportional analysis can be determined by a microphotometer or microdensitometer from the spectral line intensities and densities of the image on the photo-plate; but because of the complexity of the optical spectrum as well as the limited area which can be examined without overt destruction to the coin, the results here are not necessarily conclusive.

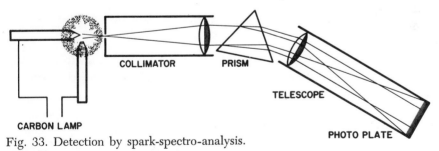

Fig. 33. Detection by spark-spectro-analysis.

X-ray diffractometry: The function of X-ray diffractometry in numismatics is two-fold: first, to make a nondestructive qualitative analysis of the composition of the coin; second, to ascertain the amount of stress which the metal has undergone, i.e., the pressure under which it was struck or cast. X rays are radiation of the same nature as "ordinary" light, but of an extremely short wavelength, emitted as a result of a sudden change in the velocity of a moving electric charge, as in the deflection of high voltage cathode rays in a vacuum tube. When an X-ray beam strikes the surface of an object at an oblique angle, its rays are diffracted by the crystals of the object at angles determined by the distance between the atomic planes, and by the angle between the atomic planes and the beam. By rotating the object, angles of reflection are obtained from each set of atomic layers so that the entire atomic arrangement in the crystal can be determined. Stated more simply, when an X-ray beam strikes the object, rays are diffracted or reflected by the atoms in the material, and they come off at angles which are always the same for a particular substance. The object is mounted on a goniometer which regulates the angle of incidence of the X-ray beam through a rotation of ninety degrees. Simultaneously, a detector moves around the object, picking up the diffracted rays at different angles which are read on a scale. While X-ray diffractometry, like spark spectro-analysis, cannot provide us with a precisely accurate quantitative analysis, it is nevertheless useful in detecting the presence of any adulterant metals, even in traces, which have resulted from imperfect refining. Moreover (and this is most important), since the amount of pressure used to stamp the planchet will affect the density or atomic spacing of the metal, a comparison of the pattern with one produced by a coin known to have been struck at the Mint, can often detect an otherwise "flawless" counterfeit.

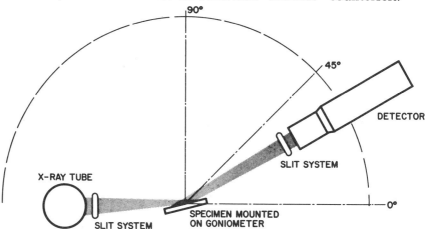

Fig. 34. Detection by X-ray diffractometry.

Numismatists who have heard the term "diffraction" used in connection with crystal analysis may wonder in what way the technique
varies from diffractometry. The answer is that while the principle
involved in each is exactly the same, the modus operandi is a little
different. In X-ray diffraction a circular camera is used instead of a
detector, or proportional counter, and the diffracted rays are recorded on film. But as only a minute sample can be examined here,
the test is by necessity somewhat destructive and less suitable for
coin analysis.

X-ray spectrography: This, to some extent, combines the techniques of the two preceding tests since it involves both X-ray bombardment and spectro-analysis. The X-rays are used here for their
ability to excite in the atoms and molecules an emission from the
substance itself. As in the test for diffraction, a collimated or parallel
beam of rays is made to strike the surface of the coin. When the
energy radiation has attained a sufficient intensity, it is absorbed by
the atoms and molecules of the specimen, which become activated
and, on returning to their normal state, emit an X-ray radiation of
their own. This excitation emission, or fluorescence, is of two kinds.
The first shows a continuous spectrum which is distributed over a
wide range of wave lengths with an intensity maximum and upper
frequency limit dependent on the speed of the bombarding X rays.
While this constitutes the greater part of the measurable radiation,
it provides us with no particular knowledge of the radiating object.

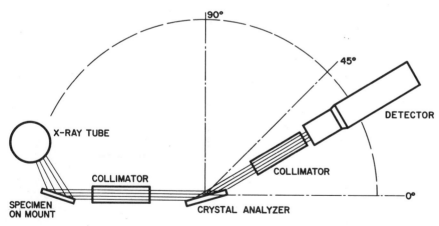

Fig. 35. Detection by X-ray spectrography.

Superimposed on the continuous spectrum, however, are various line spectra which have much sharper maxima, and these are characteristic both qualitatively and quantitatively of the composition of the specimen. The fluorescence is measured by an X-ray spectrograph which is very similar to the diffractometer, except that an analyzing crystal has been added to isolate the various wavelengths and reflect them towards the X-ray detector. By registering and counting the voltage pulses of each radiation quanta, the detector can provide us with an accurate quantitative analysis of the alloy of a coin to within one tenth of one per cent. *(Fig. 36)*

Metallography: Here the surface structure of the coin is explored under a metallographic (binocular) microscope. The microscope is illuminated by a horizontal beam of light which is reflected downward and through the microscopic objective to the surface of the coin. In this way the maximum number of rays are directed back to the observer. The coin is cleaned, washed in alcohol and dried, then etched very lightly with an acid solution. If the relief has not been tampered with, the reaction will be uniform throughout, but if a figure has been removed, and another soldered onto the surface of the coin, slight changes in color and texture will become evident.

Unfortunately, the most deceiving alterations are those wrought not by soldering, but by "chasing" the metal already present, and for the detection of this technique, an intimate knowledge of the surface of the coin may be required. If etching is to be of any use here, it must be applied diligently, in which case the missing numeral or other element can be "brought out." This is due to the fact that the relief of a coin is less dense than the fields (having been struck under less pressure), and therefore responds more quickly to the action of the acid. Since etching to this degree, however, is somewhat destructive, it is not likely to be resorted to by collectors, except in the current fad of restoring dates to illegible Buffalo nickels.

An alternative to "chasing" was introduced around the turn of the last century, for the purpose of fabricating 1804 silver dollars. The last numeral of an 1800-03 dollar was carefully removed, and the entire obverse surface of the coin, except for a small area in the shape of a 4, was covered with wax. A new digit was then built up by means of electroplating, a process we have already described.

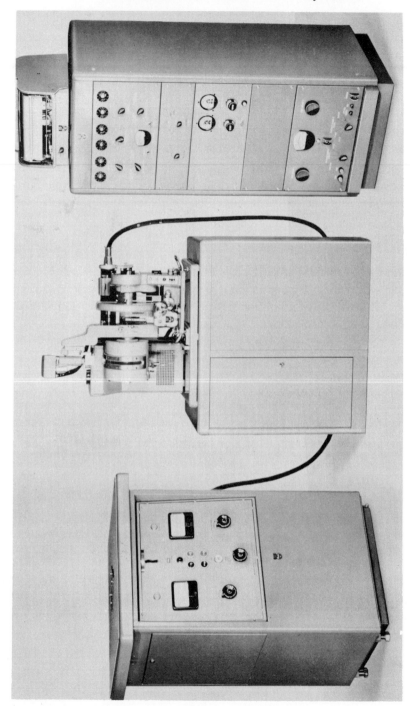

Fig. 36. A Norelco X-ray spectrograph. With the above unit, it is possible to determine the composition of a coin to within one tenth of one percent.

A summing up

The art of counterfeit detection is one which should be cultivated by every person who handles money. If this is true for the layman then it must also hold, and in a hundred-fold degree, for the collector of rare coins. An important rule to remember is never to allow your judgment to be unduly swayed by any one factor we have discussed. For example, a coin may have a distinctly *cast* appearance and yet ring well and even approximate the correct weight. This results when silica is mixed with molten lead. The product will then not only "tinkle" but be less porous.

Of course we cannot all be like the legendary Roman money changer who "could see the brass through the silver," but if, in our novitiate days, we will profit by the rules of experience, we may fare nearly as well. To put it succinctly: be cautious, view each coin with the sum total of your knowledge and—if you don't know your coins, then know your coin dealer!

We would hardly be doing our duty if we failed to mention the Federal laws regarding the acquisition of counterfeit coins: *It is absolutely illegal to collect, accumulate or display any spurious copies of United States coins, regardless of their fabric or method of manufacture.* Collectors of "replicana" run the risk of a fine; a year in jail, or both. Any counterfeit coin or paper currency over which you have control or custody must be surrendered to the Treasury Department or to one of its authorized agents, which includes your nearest bank.

III

ALTERED COINS

I N the first chapter we examined several techniques which have been used to counterfeit or pervert metallic currency. Within the last century, as a result of the tremendous upsurge of numismatic interest, a new kind of alteration has appeared wherein coins of little "collecting value" are made to resemble others of considerable rarity and worth. Among these are a few perennials which we will first note, and then describe in detail (the bracketed dates indicating, in each case, the period in which most of the fabrications were wrought):

      1¢ 1799, 1804 (1855-1858)
      1¢ 1856 (Flying Eagle) (1920-1925)
      1¢ 1914-D, 1922 Plain, 1943 "copper" (1947-present)
      5¢ 1937-D, Three Legged Buffalo (1950-present)
      50¢ Grant Memorial (with star) (1936-present)

The 1799 Large Cent. This is, for all practical purposes, the earliest date American coin to be altered for the specific purpose of numismatic deception. Fortunately the entire border areas of the early dies were hand-cut, resulting in a good many varieties for each year of issue. The most masterly date alteration must therefore leave its tell-tale signs behind.

Of genuine 1799 cents, only two obverse and three reverse dies are known to exist, together with two additional die states for these varieties. Our point d'appui, in each case, will be the relationship between two pairs of leaves (the inner of which touch the base of the T in the word CENT) and the stem of the wreath which runs between them. In the first reverse the stem is clearly visible between the pairs of leaves; in the second it dissolves into the outer pair about one third from the top; in the third it can be seen to run along the edge of the outer pair.

If the coin in question answers the description of number one, that is, if the stem can be clearly seen between the inner and outer leaves, there should also exist a center dot above the upper left serif of the N in CENT, and a second very minute dot slightly above and to the right of the first dot.[1] If this is the case, turn the coin over and examine the obverse in regard to the following points:

1. A genuine 1799 cent of the above reverse will show an *overdate*, i.e., the second 9 will appear to be recut over an 8. (Since this same reverse, however, was used in 1798, an alteration of the earlier variety might superficially have the same appearance.)

2. The bottom of the 7 will extend no further (in relation to the curve of the date) than the 1 and the 9. If the coin has been altered from the 1798 date of this reverse, the 7 will be longer than the surrounding numerals.

3. The word LIBERTY is situated so that a perpendicular drawn from the junction of the hair and forehead will extend just slightly to the left of the bottom left serif of the Y. On all 1798 obverses LIBERTY is farther to the left.

The variety which we have just described is the rarest of the three known, being, in fact, nearly unique. Both obverse and reverse sides are free from any die imperfections, whereas the 1798 coin of this reverse usually shows a heavy obverse rim break touching the letters RTY. (*Fig. 37*)

---

1. The latter dot may require a magnifying lens to see.

If the coin in your possession, however, answers to the description of reverse number two, that is, if the stem dissolves in the outer pair of leaves, about one third from the top, it should also show:

1. A small dot right above the left vertical of the N in CENT.

2. That the third inside and outside pairs of leaves on the right (counting from the top) are stemless and do not connect to the wreath.

3. The same obverse as in example one. (The remarks made thereanent will also apply here.) In this union the obverse has been found in a few instances with a heavy triple break through RTY. (*Fig. 38*)

But if your coin has reverse C, that is, if the stem runs along the edge of the outer leaves, it should also show:

1. A recut crosslet in the E of CENT which joins the upper serif of the letter.

2. That in the F (in OF) the crosslet and the left extremes of the upper and lower serifs are recut; and the M (in AMERICA) is recut to the left of its right vertical.

3. A small bump between the E of ONE and the T of CENT. (On early strikes the bump is very faint and difficult to detect without the aid of a glass.) (*Fig. 39*)

If your coin agrees with one of the above, it is, barring electrotypes and other such copies, undoubtedly genuine.

The 1804 Large Cent. For more than a century the prescribed method of authenticating an 1804 cent has been to ascertain whether or not the O in the date and the O in OF (in the reverse legend) line up. This can be done by folding a piece of paper over the edge of the coin (through the figures in question), and is generally considered an infallible test since, with the exception of 1804, no date is supposed to line up correctly. Nevertheless it is always possible for one of the dies to rotate, and while no out-of-line 1804's are known to exist, the writer has seen a few coins of both earlier and later dates [1] which align in the prescribed manner. An additional diagnostic, therefore, will not be out of order. (*Fig. 40*)

---

1. This is especially true of 1807, S-276.

Fig. 37. 1799 over 98 cent, Sheldon NC-1.

Fig. 38. 1799 over 98 cent, S-188.

Fig. 39. 1799 perfect date cent, S-189.

Fig. 40. 1804 cent, perfect dies.

The genuine 1804 cent has a very large fraction which is shared by only a handful of varieties from the previous year. Only in the 1804, however, does the second berry on the right extend *below* the right top vertical of the letter E in ONE.

The 1856 Flying Eagle Cent. On all genuine issues the 5 is a slanting numeral and the ball on its tail extends behind the upright. On the 1858, the 5 is vertical and it will appear thus on coins altered from this date.[1] *(Fig. 41)*

The 1914-D Lincoln Head Cent. On any genuine coin of this date and mint mark the bust truncation will be plain. If, however, the date has been cut down from 1944 or any other date after 1917, the truncation will disclose, instead, the initials V.D.B. (unless these have been surreptitiously removed).

A comparison between the mint mark on genuine 1914-D cents and coins of succeeding decades (1924-D, 1934-D, 1944-D and 1954-D) reveals, in each instance, that the former is smaller, and situated lower (it is in fact completely free from the tail of the 9) and farther to the left. Coins cut down from each of these dates will thus show corresponding discrepancies. *(Fig. 42)*

Now examine the date itself. If it has been altered from 1944, as most are, an extra wide space will result between the 9 and the 1; if from 1954, the second 1 will appear truncated and stand too high. In either case the mint mark will appear larger than normal.

The reshaping of mint marks (as from an S to a D) by metal "chasing," or by the addition of an original where previously there was none at all, is occasionally encountered not only on 1914-D cents, but on 1909-S VDB cents, 1916-D dimes and many other of the scarcer U.S. coins.[2] It is not easy, however, to reproduce the fineness of a genuine mint mark and, as a rule, a strong glass will suffice for detection. Whenever you are in doubt, always compare the dubious mint mark with one that you know to be genuine. Also look for any trace of discoloration around the letter as would result from the application of heat.

1. The other so-called "diagnostic" differences, i.e., crosslets of E's connecting with upper and lower serifs of the letters, angular junction of AM, square O in OF, all have exceptions for which reason they are omitted above.

2. On coins where the date and mint mark appear on opposite sides, one should always scrutinize the edge to make certain that a "muling" has not been made from the obverse and reverse of different years. Such forgeries are becoming alarmingly common, and they can be very deceptive.

Fig. 41. 1856 Flying Eagle cent, genuine and altered dates. On all genuine specimens, the upright of the 5 connects with the center of the ball, and on more than 95% of these, the E's in the legend have large, connecting serifs.

Fig. 42. Four 1914-D cents. 1) genuine; 2) addition of D to 1914 Philadelphia Mint coin; 3) alteration of 1944-D cent; 4) alteration of 1954-D cent.

The 1922 Plain Cent is the result of nothing more than a worn die in which the D punch filled in. It is undoubtedly the easiest of all coins to alter and the only wonder is that it has not been altered more often. The collector should examine the area for any traces of filing or other mutilation. If the area appears to be depressed, the coin is definitely suspect. *Remember that on a genuine 1922 plain cent, there should still remain a shadow of the D which can best be seen by tilting the coin.* Counterfeiters in their zeal often forget this fact.

Most genuine specimens show an irregularity in the letters LRTY and a die break from the O of ONE to the rim.

As the 1922 plain cent becomes more generally accepted as a part of the regular Lincoln cent series (and valuations adjust themselves) we may anticipate a new concentration of forgeries for this date. Let us be forewarned.

The 1943 Bronze Cent. It may come as a surprise to some that, after more than a decade of repudiation by the initiates of numismatics, a few genuine 1943 "copper" or bronze cents have been duly authenticated. Coins struck in other than their proper metal are not without precedent. Silver cents, for example, are known for a variety of dates—including 1943! It has been argued that no bronze planchets were used in the Mint during that year, but this does not eliminate the possibility of a few having been left in the recesses of the feeding chutes from the preceding issue. This theory is substantiated somewhat by the fact that a few steel cents with the date 1944 have likewise been found.

Now supposing that we have before us what *appears* to be a 1943 "copper" cent, we should conduct our investigation along the following lines:

1. Test the coin with a magnet. If it is an ordinary steel cent, plated with copper (as are ninety-nine per cent of these forgeries) it will at once be attracted.

2. If your coin passes the first test, then examine the date itself for any evidence of alteration. Compare the last two numerals to those on a regular 1943 steel cent and scrutinize them under the strongest magnification available.

3. If the date shows no sign of alteration and is in every particular identical to that of the steel cent, examine the coin to ascertain that

it is not an electrotype or cast reproduction. (We have already dealt with these techniques in Chapter Two.) Note in particular the tiny V.D.B. on the truncation. If the coin has been produced by either means, the initials will appear faint and indistinct. On a genuine 1943 bronze cent they will be *extremely* sharp.

Struck copies of 1943 cents are also known and these can be the most difficult of all to detect. The counterfeiter, working with a genuine steel cent which has been hardened to act as the hub, sinks the impression into an annealed die blank of the same metal. A blank bronze cent planchet (which can be easily obtained for a few dollars—see Chapter VIII) is then struck from it in a press.[1] A coin which has been produced in this way will, to all intents and purposes, appear genuine, except that its detail will be somewhat less sharp for having been twice transferred. The best place to observe this loss is again in the V.D.B. which, even on a somewhat used coin, is not subject to the normal amount of wear or abrasion.

It should be mentioned that all of the struck counterfeits which the writer has had the opportunity to examine show uneven centering.

One important fact which is generally overlooked in the discussion of 1943 bronze cents is that any such genuine coin, having been struck under a pressure intended for steel, will have its edges built up like the most perfect proof. From the standpoint of visual detection this is the most crucial test.

Confirmation might be obtained through X-ray diffractometry which would determine whether or not the coin had been struck under the same pressure as used in the Mint. If your specimen passes this final test, it is almost certainly genuine.

The 1937-D Three-legged Buffalo Nickel. The vanishing leg of the old bison, as well as the other peculiarities native to this coin, resulted when the die was ground down to remove injuries sustained

---

1. Every so often we read about a Lincoln head cent "overstruck with the dies of 1943." If all of these specimens were genuine, we would have more overstruck coins for this date than for all others put together! The truth is, however, that they can be easily produced by out-of-the-Mint hubbing, the technique just described. It should be remembered that any copper coin overstruck at pressures intended for stamping steel blanks will have its original impression practically (if not completely) obliterated.

during its "clash" with the obverse die.[1] Several other details have been reduced in size, which is why no alteration of the leg, *however perfect*, need deceive us. The differences which thus distinguish a genuine Three-Legged Buffalo Nickel may be outlined as follows:

1. The motto E PLURIBUS UNUM is lightly struck and appears smaller. The P of PLURIBUS and the U of UNUM are farther away from the back of the bison. On an altered coin they will appear to be touching.

2. The last leg is distinctly flatter. Owing to the loss of detail, it appears to join with the bison's third leg at a higher point, being more distant from the knee upward.

3. The tip at the animal's belly is longer (due partly to optical illusion and partly to the flow of metal) and thinner, and a jagged die break or series of tiny dots extends from it to the mound.

4. The beard is thinner; the left tussock is cut short.

5. Between the third and fourth legs, the mound is thinner, being, in fact, almost a straight line.

6. On a genuine coin the first leg begins to thin out before disappearing, and the hoof is always visible. Counterfeiters, as a rule, shave the leg clean, occasionally removing the hoof as well.

7. The obverse die shows roughness on the face, neck and elsewhere, the degree varying from coin to coin.

8. On some specimens, a slight doubling is apparent at the bases of LIBE.

Any coin professing to be a genuine "Three-Legged Buffalo nickel," but which deviates from the above description is undoubtedly spurious. *(Fig. 43)*

The Grant Memorial Half Dollar (with star punch). This is probably the most difficult of the group to detect, but with a little perseverance there is no reason why we should not be able to do so.

Historically the star has no significance whatsoever beyond the desire of Mint officials to create a second and rare variety for this coin.

---

1. See Chapter VIII. The persistent myth which would attribute this coin to a mere die clogging fails to explain, among other things, why the rest of the relief has been reduced in circumference as well as in height. The above explanation is semi-official having been related to Walter Breen by a Mint worker who had witnessed the accident.

Fig. 43. 1937-D Buffalo nickels, normal and "three-legged" variety. Note the diagnostics.

The star was present in each of the original dies and later removed by polishing. At the same time, the field of one of the dies, which was very rough, and marked by several abrasions, was smoothed down. The majority of the starred coins were struck from this imperfect die and, as a result, can be easily authenticated. These are the tell-tale signs *(Fig. 44)*:

1. A rough, raised, rectangular area extending from the chin to the G of GRANT. This is the most familiar of the defects and the one which is generally referred to as the "die break" on the starred variety.

2. A pointed, almost spear-like projection extending outward from the tie.

3. A small, raised square, protruding from Grant's head, opposite to the IT in the word UNITED. This is usually very faint.

4. A tiny raised projection at the center of Grant's nose.

5. A die break extending from the A of HALF through the O of DOLLAR.

6. A jagged die break between the top and upper left rays of the star, best seen by tilting the coin downwards.

At one time it was believed that all of the starred coins resulted from the above mentioned die (which we shall call die A), a theory which, had it been true, would have greatly simplified the task of detection. Instead, two other starred varieties have turned up without the customary die defects.

The first has no distinguishing marks whatsoever; on the second, the G of GRANT has been heavily recut. (We shall refer to these dies as B and C respectively.) There is some evidence that die B represents only an interregnum period in the alteration of A; that is to say, after the die defects had been polished down, a few pieces were struck to observe the effects which, being satisfactory, were followed by the removal of the star itself. This would account for the dearth of *unstarred* Grant half dollars except for those with the recut G. Assuming that each of the dies was used for approximately the same length of time, we should be obliged to reason that (1) die A, which struck off the great majority of starred coins would be least in evidence among the coins without stars, and that dies B and C which, together, probably constitute no more than five per cent of the starred coins, would be generally responsible for the unstarred issue. Since so few of the unstarred variety are found

Fig. 44. The Grant Memorial half dollar. This is the commonest of the three varieties with the star. Note the die defects 1) between the G and chin; 2) protruding from the tie; 3) at the center of the nose. Others are also described in the text.

Fig. 45. A close up of the star. Note the "creases" in the lower two rays.

except from die *C* (with the recut *G*), it would appear that die *B* was retired rather prematurely, unless we assume that die *A* and die *B* are the same. However interesting as a conjecture, this sheds little light on the problem at hand which is, after all, the star itself. *(Fig. 45)*

Study the exact size and position of the star on a genuine coin. Regardless of the variety on which it appears, the star will always show the following characteristics:

The lower right ray is slightly shorter and blunter than the lower left. In addition it is not cut as deeply as the rest of the star and the place at which it tapers off gives the appearance of a horizontal line. Another, shorter line begins to likewise cut off the lower left ray.

Spurious stars, aside from lacking the above features, will be surrounded by a bulge due to the displacement of metal from the punch. Another bulge, on the reverse side and directly opposite to the star, can sometimes be detected also.

Postscript

The use of money for other than its intended purpose is, perhaps, as old as the invention of currency itself. Even today, shells and annulets serve, in certain parts of the world, as both a unit of exchange and a means of personal adornment.

In our own country, the practice dates back to the earliest years of coinage when bevies of panic-stricken Puritans, seeing the shadow of witches everywhere, bent their shillings, six and threepenny coins, and wore them as amulets.[1] While most of these have since been straightened, the three-hundred-year-old creases and teethmarks still bring to mind the old nursery rhyme:

> *There was a crooked man*
> *And he walked a crooked mile.*
> *He found a crooked sixpence*
> *Against a crooked stile.*

In the last decade we have seen a tremendous revival of interest in "coin jewelry." Under existing laws we are, of course, no longer

---

1. For further information on these "witch pieces" see *The Pine Tree Coinage of Massachusetts* by Sydney P. Noe.

Fig. 46

What *not* to do with Uncle Sam's money! Fig. 46. All of the strangely attired persons whom you see above are none other than the familiar Indian Chief on our Buffalo nickel. Fig. 47. Below from l. to r., a Trade Dollar locket, quar. dollar and dime tie-tacks, an "embossed" Indian Head cent, and a "store-card" quarter.

Fig. 47

free to treat Uncle Sam's money as we please, and any mutilation or alteration, regardless of intent, may today be construed as an interference with the right of Congress to regulate its currency. The engraving of "love tokens," or the alteration of coins into rings, charms, lockets, tietacks, store cards or for any other purpose is strictly prohibited. (*Figs. 46 and 47*)

On the other hand, there are a few "altered" coins which are not only collectible, but have attained considerable value, having been counterstamped by the governments of other countries in order to render them current there.

The Chinese merchants used formerly to impress every silver dollar that passed through their hands with their own individual stamp. These are known as chopmarks and are frequently found on the U.S. Trade Dollars which circulated in the Orient. The crudeness of this technique enabled the less scrupulous merchants to simultaneously gouge out a little extra silver, a practice which resulted in our Government's refusal to accept any but "clean," or unchopped, dollars for redemption.

Fig. 48. 1875 Trade Dollar, heavily "chopped."

IV

FAMOUS FORGERIES OF THE U.S. MINT
(AND OTHER OFFICIAL ECCENTRICITIES)

WHILE it is not ordinarily remembered, except by historians and perhaps a few numismatists, the date of July 18th, 1792 marks the birth of our Philadelphia Mint. Tradition has it that owing to a lack of bullion, the first coins to be struck at the Mint—silver half dimes—were wrought from sterling teaspoons donated by President

Fig. 49. 1792 pattern half dime. Tradition has it that the Liberty Head is actually Martha Washington.

Washington. It is said also that, a year later, Washington contributed "an excellent copper tea-kettle as well as two pairs of tongs" to begin the manufacture of cents and half cents.[1]

The early history of the Mint was, in fact, marked by continual struggle and growing pains. The manufacture of a single pair of dies involved weeks of labor, and sometimes one of the pair broke after striking no more than a dozen coins. To make matters worse, Philadelphia was subject to an annual epidemic of yellow fever, and the Mint had often to shut down during the summer months just when the dies for the following year would normally be prepared. Thus, despite the fact that all of the employees worked eleven hours a day, six days a week, production at the Mint was very slow. By 1800 it was generally conceded that the project was a failure. In that year, and again in 1802, bills introduced into Congress to abolish the Mint were defeated only after a long and vigorous debate.

In 1832 the Mint relocated, and four years later, steam power, which had hitherto been employed only for certain heavy work, was introduced into the stamping itself. For the first time a pressure requisite for the sinking of an entire die from a hub could be obtained, and as a result a certain element of leisure now crept into the Mint schedule. Director Robert Patterson developed an extra-curricular interest in numismatics and, in June 1838, he inaugurated the Mint Cabinet in which coins of all nations were displayed. William DuBois, the assistant assayer, to whose care Patterson entrusted the embryonic collection, notes in his *Coins, Coinage and Bullion, 1851:* ". . . it was not our purpose to amass an immense store of coins, the very multitude of which might deter from its examination. We are rather willing to be the first to set an example of moderation in a pursuit which has its temptations to extravagance and excess." This brief concluding statement in DuBois' summary of the Mint Cabinet seems to hint at much it does not say. Indeed, it is a model of the "Freudian" conscience which cannot quite restrain itself from some intimation, however casual or disguised, of misconduct. But perhaps we are being too uncharitable in our interpretation. Let us rather begin in the right spirit, seeing wisdom in wise words and believing noble aspirations.

1. Sheldon, W. H., *Early American Cents.*

It is known that for many years prior to the inception of the Mint Cabinet, Adam Eckfeldt, second of the Mint's Chief Coiners (and first of its many Eckfeldts), had been preparing for the "great day" by amassing a reserve of "master coins" or proofs. "With this nucleus, and a few other valuable pieces from Mr. Eckfeldt," [1] the collection was officially begun. To enhance the infant Cabinet every deposit was now examined, and the better coins, which would normally be relegated to the melting pot, were retained. DuBois tells us that the "great majority of the coins—almost all of those not over three hundred years old—have been culled from deposits, and consequently have cost us no more than their bullion value." Since the weight of gold coins had been reduced in 1834, and since those pieces of earlier years could be redeemed at the Mint for their full bullion value, a steady influx continued, providing the Cabinet with duplicates and triplicates of the various rare dates. To Patterson and DuBois, it was clearly a "golden" opportunity!

Among the earliest data which we find pertaining to this subject is a letter from Director Patterson to the prominent Boston attorney, William G. Stearns. It should be added that Stearns, one of the foremost collectors of his day, had originally written to Patterson to ascertain why coins of certain dates, supposedly struck in large quantities, could not be found. A rather formidable correspondence ensued during the course of which it became apparent to both parties that they might be of mutual assistance. Thus, on August 15, 1838, Patterson writes:

> Our assistant Assayer, Mr. DuBois, has undertaken to make as far as practical, the collection of gold coins which you ask for, and has already laid aside for you the following:
> Eagles of 1797, 1799, 1800, 1801, 1803.
> Half Eagles of 1795, 1800 and from 1802 to 1813 both included.
> As to the Silver and copper coins, the opportunity of making collections is not presented at the mint as no such coins are ever received here on deposit. If, however, any of the coins you ask (for) should come into our hands, you shall not be forgotten.
> It will give me great pleasure to aid you in your interesting design, and whenever you think it may be in my power to do so, I pray you to call on me freely.

The following notation, in Patterson's handwriting soon follows: "But as the appropriation will not be more than $800 (if that much)

---

1. Evans, *History of the U.S. Mint and Coinage.* 1885

the deficiency is intended to be met by selling off some of the superfluous pieces to Roper, Morris and others."

On the face of it all this seems innocent enough. We can hardly blame the Director for selling or trading off whatever duplicate pieces were on hand rather than allowing them to be melted.

The first evidence that DuBois' "example of moderation" had begun to flag under the "temptations," was provided by the sudden discharge of the Chief Coiner, Franklin Peale, in December 1854.

Peale, a gifted mechanic, entered the Mint service in 1833 and was appointed Melter and Refiner in 1836. In the same year he developed an improved steam-powered coining press to replace the old screw press in the Mint. He also introduced the milling machine and other improvements in Mint machinery. In 1839 he was recommended for the position of Chief Coiner by Adam Eckfeldt who resigned in the same year.

How is it that a man who contributed so much to the Mint should suddenly be discharged after more than twenty years' service? In consulting Evans' *History of the U.S. Mint and Coinage,* we further learn of Peale only that: "Being specially fitted, by natural genius as well as education, for the position which he adorned, his mildness, integrity, gentlemanly bearing and high moral and mental culture constituted him a model officer. His connection with the service lasted until 1854."

What Evans fails to tell us, however, we can perhaps infer from the following letters written by the Director of the Mint to Secretary of the Treasury, James Guthrie. On August 30, 1853, the Director writes:

> I have your favors of the 27th 28th and 29th inst. in reference to making medals at the Mint for Repn. Adams & Co. for exhibition at the World's Fair at New York, and for the Massachusetts Mechanic Association. It is proper that I should call your attention to the fact that the making of medals in the Mint has heretofore occasioned unpleasant remarks. It has been objected to, because the material and machinery of the government has been used for private purposes and made a source of profit to some of the persons employed in the Coining department. I have myself very great doubts whether it is legal or proper to make medals except such as may be ordered by the government. If they are made for other purposes I am of (the) opinion that no charge should be made except for the intrinsic value of the metals used. Heretofore considerable profits have been made by the persons who have executed the medals. It seems doubtful also whether the

government ought to interfere with private enterprise by manufacturing free of charge or otherwise any work of a private character. I may further remark that in order to meet the public demands for gold and silver coin I am running the coining department twenty hours a day, and it would be inconvenient at this time to make these medals. If however it is your wish, after considering the objections I have presented, that they should be made I will make every possible effort to comply with your request.

A few months later, another curious incident seems to have occurred at the Mint. The Director, in describing it to the Secretary of the Treasury (April 15, 1854) writes:

No provision by law has heretofore been made for the preservation of the dies from which medals were ordered to be struck, nor for taking or preserving copies of them. In fact the dies have by some of the recipients of the honor of a public medal been regarded as their property and not that of the government. But through the personal efforts of some of the officers of the Mint assisted and encouraged by several of the Secretaries of the Treasury, most of the dies have been retained or recovered, and they are now in the custody of the Chief Coiner of the Mint.

The Director does not tell us by what means the "recipients of the honor of a public medal" contrived to obtain these dies, which were under the jurisdiction of Chief Coiner Franklin Peale, but the contents of the earlier letter, together with the dismissal of Peale, would seem to answer any pertinent questions.

Nevertheless, there remain two minor inquiries which might be made in connection with the Peale incident, viz: who the Director of the Mint was during this period, and whether the administration under this Director might have, in any way, encouraged such a spirit of private enterprise.

The first question is easily answered. On June 3, 1853, the Hon. James Ross Snowden was appointed ninth Director of the Mint, a position which he maintained for eight years. Snowden, a fervent perpetuator of Robert Patterson's work, fortunately bequeathed to us many records of his own numismatic activities while associated with the Mint. Perhaps the most reliable answer to the second question then may be found through a scrutiny of these records as they appear in the National Archives. *(Fig. 50)*

The first is a letter dated January 22, 1859 from Snowden to the Secretary of the Treasury, Howell Cobb. Snowden writes:

Sir,

We are daily pressed upon, by Collectors of Coins from all parts of
the Country either by letter or in person, for specimens of pattern
pieces of coin, and rare types. A few of these have been in every case
issued—some of them got into the hands of dealers and are sold at
excessive prices. I propose with your approbation, to check this traffic,
and at the same time gratify a taste which has lately increased in this
country, and seems to be increasing every day, namely by striking some
of each kind and affixing a price to them, so that the profits may enure
to the benefit of the Mint Cabinet of Coins and ores which is the
property of the U. States; an exact amount of which will be kept and
rendered to the Department.

What a revealing letter this is! It not only states that patterns and
other rare coins have "in every case" been restruck for the purpose
of obliging solicitors, but also that there have been no regulations
of any kind governing distribution. Snowden, who had previously
expressed grave doubts over the legality and propriety of striking
medals other than those ordered by the government, now finds the
distribution of *unauthorized coins* not only proper, but worthy of
every consideration. The only thing that troubles the Director is that
the numismatic department is not taking in a large enough slice of
the profits!

It may be asked how the all-bountiful Snowden was able "in each
case" to oblige the collector who appealed to him. The answer lies
in the fact that both Franklin Peale and his successor, George K.
Childs, had prophetically taken to collecting the old hubs and dies,
and had amassed a representative stock dating back to about 1800.
Thus, when John K. Curtis wrote to Director Snowden, early in
January 1859, regarding the possibility of obtaining an 1851 dollar,
Snowden replied that "one could be struck from the dies of that
year.[1]

Another interchange which is of considerable interest begins with
a letter from one P. Clayton to Director Snowden.[2] It is dated January 22, 1859.

1. Walter Breen, *The United States Half Cents.*
2. Walter Breen, *The Hundred Year Vendetta.*

Dear Sir,

If you have specimens in copper of the new $20, also model half & quarter dollars & specimen cents struck last year before sett(l)ing on the new device now used—& can spare them without detriment to the public interest, I would like to have them—My object is to give them to a friend who seems to have a passion for specimens of coins.

Snowden's reply is dated Jan. 24, 1859. . . . It begins with the provocative caption *"Unofficial,"* and then goes on to say:

Dear Sir,

I have rec'd your note of the 22nd inst. and learn from it that you are acquiring a personal knowledge of the "passion for specimen coins" which possesses so many people in our country. On Saturday I had nine applications of a similar character—today (now 12 o'clock) I have had three. It was in view of this increasing, as well as troublesome, taste that I made the request mentioned in my official letter of last Saturday (22nd inst.) which I hope will deserve the sanction of the department. In reference to the specimens you ask for I have to state that the trial piece in copper of the Double eagle of 1859 which I left at the Department is the only one I had: I have a few of the specimen cents but not all the varieties. I could send you two or three of these, but perhaps it will be best to defer sending them until the new arrangement is made, when your friend, and all other collectors of Coins, AND THEIR NAME IS LEGION, can be supplied to their heart's content.

Since the Director specifically requests permission to enlarge his numismatic sideline, we can assume that he did not consider the proposal entirely beyond reproach. Possibly, in the back of his mind, he recalled the terse statements in the laws of 1792 and 1837 which specified that *all coins bear the year of their issue!* Thus, if permission *had* been granted, we can be sure that Snowden would have preserved it as he did other important records. Furthermore, the "new arrangement" was to establish rules and regulations for the distribution of the restrikes, "an exact amount of which (would) be kept and rendered to the department." The absence of any such records must therefore be taken as conclusive evidence that Snowden's proposal did *not* meet with the approbation of the Secretary of the Treasury. We can well imagine the Director's discomfiture at the refusal of his harmless request. News of the "great dispensation" had already been bruited about by Clayton and others who were waiting on tenterhooks for the fateful hour. In such a situation what could poor James Ross do?

The best answer can, perhaps, be found in a correspondence between the Philadelphia coin dealer Edward Cogan and Director Snowden. On June 14, 1859, Cogan writes:

> I have been applied to by a great many collectors of American coins wishing to be informed whether the report now current—that there are many of the Pattern Cents being restruck at the Mint for the purpose of exchanging them for Washington pieces is true—the only answer I can give is that the many pieces shown me lately would tend to confirm the report. A rumour of this kind uncontradicted will tend to depreciate the value of every fine piece in whatever collection it may be found and I should be glad if you would give it the most unqualified denial.

Snowden replied:

> It is quite true that I have caused a number of pattern or specimen cents to be struck for the purpose of exchanging them for Washington pieces whenever opportunities to do so occur. If you possess any Washington pieces I would be much obliged if you will send me a list of them, and if there are any among them which I desire for the Cabinet I would be pleased to procure them by giving you in exchange other interesting medals or coins.

The above letter, as frank as it is accommodating, unravels the "Gordian knot" in a multitude of Mint mysteries. It solves for one thing the enigma of why the 1856 flying eagle cent, which W. C. Prime listed in 1861 as "rarity 5" of six categories, is today far more common than any other single pattern. It explains also the sudden appearance of a dozen different varieties of this famous cent in the collections of prominent Philadelphia numismatists, and the conspicuous absence of all but the original from the Cabinet of the Mint.

There is but little doubt that behind much of Snowden's complacency lay the belief that he was only acting in the long line of Mint tradition. Just where this "tradition" actually began will soon become evident.

In 1842, the four-year-old Mint collection appeared in the first numismatic edition published in the United States, *A manual of Gold & Silver Coins of All Nations,* by Jacob Eckfeldt and William DuBois —"assayers of the Mint of the U.S." One curious feature of the Eckfeldt-DuBois book was an engraving of an 1804 silver dollar, *a coin which, a few years earlier, was unknown either in the Mint Cabinet or in any other U.S. collection.*

In 1843, Matthew Stickney discovered not one but two 1804 dollars at the Philadelphia Mint and obtained one of the pieces in trade for an Immune Columbia cent struck in gold, together with several smaller coins from his own collection. The transaction is described by Stickney in a letter to Edward Cogan, July 2, 1867:

> Of the genuineness of my U.S. dollar of 1804 I think there cannot be entertained a doubt, as it was handed me directly from the cabinet of the U.S. Mint in Philadelphia on the 9th of May, 1843, by one of its officers (William E. DuBois) who still holds the same situation there and can testify to it. It was not then considered any more valuable than any other of the series, and I only desired it to help make up the chronological series, which I perhaps was the first to attempt to make of U.S. coins. *(Fig. 51)*

Within the next quarter of a century two other 1804 dollars were allegedly culled from circulation, one in a Philadelphia bank, the other, in 1865, in a Richmond, Virginia exchange office. These became known as the Mickley and Cohen dollars after the cabinets in which they resided.

In 1868 a fifth specimen was purchased by E. H. Sanford from an elderly lady who claimed to have obtained it (for the price of one dollar) from the Mint during Polk's administration. This subsequently became known as the Parmelee specimen. In 1884, a sixth identical dollar was purchased in Berlin from the Adolph Weyl collection by Messrs. S. H. and H. Chapman of Philadelphia. A seventh 1804 dollar turned up in England, and was purchased at a Glendining sale in 1917.

Two years after the discovery of the Mickley dollar, Stickney, in cataloguing his collection, wrote, "As regards the authenticity of other specimens of the U.S. dollar of 1804, I have no knowledge. Those having dollars of that date (Cohen and Mickley) were not then known to the Mint as collectors as appears by the list of which I send you a copy, then obtained, 1843, from Mr. DuBois, which remains, in his handwriting, in my possession . . ."

Before long, a vehement discussion arose over the merits of each of the seven 1804 dollars. Stickney and Parmelee regarded as conclusive evidence of authenticity the fact that their pieces could be traced directly to the Mint. Cohen and Mickley, as would be expected, argued with an opposite logic.

Modern scholars, however, are of the opinion that *none of the alleged "originals" could have been struck before the renovation of Mint machinery, 1832-36*. There are several reasons for this. First of all, the coins show indisputable evidence of having been struck in a tightly fitting collar, of the type not used at the Mint prior to that time.[1] The edge lettering, which was applied previous to the striking, is flattened—a result of the planchet being forced against the collar under pressure of the blow. Secondly, the beaded border present on all specimens was introduced on silver coins in 1828, and not noted on the dollar prior to 1836. This border, with a raised blank rim around it, was specifically mentioned by the Mint Director, Samuel Moore, in a letter of August 8, 1829, to Secretary of the Treasury, S. D. Ingham, relating to the half dimes of 1829, "like the Di(s)mes this year, *superior to any coins heretofore issued.*" Thirdly, it was not until 1817 that facilities for making proofs (such as the Stickney and Mint Cabinet specimens) were introduced in the United States. Fourthly, the top-most curl of Liberty's hair is cropped off in a manner unlike that on any genuine silver dollars of the 1795-1803 period, though it is identical to that on the proof restrike dollars of "1801." Fifthly, the date and letter punches are almost identical to those on the 1804 (plain 4) restrike eagle, and the reverse is the same as that of the restrike dollars of 1801, 1802 and 1803. And finally, the 1804's are first recorded as being extant, in 1842. Furthermore, the missing top curl and modern letter punches indicate that the dies for the 1804 dollar are not much older than the coins themselves! [2]

In 1858, a second chapter was added to the confusion when the son of George Eckfeldt, who had charge of the dies in the engraver's department, surreptitiously struck off several plain edge specimens using a new reverse die.[3] Ebenezer Mason, in reminiscing about his early days as a coin dealer on 2nd Street, Philadelphia,[4] further tells us that: "Here was offered by young Eckfeldt three genuine U.S. 1804 dollars at $70 each, and nearly all the rare ½ cents in dozens of duplicates were purchased." *(Fig. 52)*

It should be pointed out, however, that the cutting of a new reverse die was a project not likely to have been undertaken without an order from the Director. Snowden, as we have learned, was preparing for "the new arrangement" when he would begin restriking on a grand scale. In all probability, "young Eckfeldt" gained pos-

---

1. This collar was first noted in connection with the Gobrecht dollars and halves of 1836, when it was said "to give a mathematical equality to the diameters."
2. See Appendix, Page 213.
3. Newman-Bressett, *The Fantastic 1804 dollar.*
4. Mason's *Coin Collector's Magazine,* June 1882.

Fig. 50

Fig. 51

Fig. 52

Fig. 50. The Hon. James Ross Snowden, from a medal designed and executed by Paquet (center); Fig. 51. 1804 dollar, Class I (The first S in STATES is over the first two clouds). This is the Stickney specimen; Fig. 52. 1804 dollar, Class II (The first S in STATES is over only the first cloud). This is the notorious "Eckfeldt restrike." The planchet was a cut-down 1857 Swiss Shooting Thaler.

session of the 1804 dollar dies and clandestinely struck off several pieces ahead of schedule. Snowden may have been waiting for an opportune time to sound out Secretary Cobb, but Eckfeldt waited for nothing!

It seems strange to us today that such overt chicanery could soon be forgotten. And yet, in May 1868, the *American Journal of Numismatics* reported: "It is perhaps not generally known that in 1858 certain dollars of 1804, re-struck from the original dies, without collars, and therefore having plain edges, found their way out of the Mint. Major Nichols, of Springfield, had one of these at the cost of $75 and Mr. Cogan had one, but both were on solicitation returned to their source."

We may ask how the Hon. James Ross Snowden reacted on learning that another of his restless protégés had gone into business for himself. Did the Director make a clean breast of the whole affair? Did he arrange for better security measures? Did he dispose of young Eckfeldt?

For the first answer we need only examine the contents of a few letters now preserved in the National Archives. The first letter dated July 19, 1860 reads: "Will you please inform me if the 1804 Dollar has been restruck at the Mint as I have heard that several have been seen and offered for sale . . ." Snowden replied: "In response to your inquiry I have to state that no specimen of the dollar of 1804 has been struck at the Mint; and I am informed by the foreman of the dies that there are no means of doing so."

Another correspondence between Director Snowden and a Mr. Jeremiah Colburn of the appraiser's office in Boston is highly provocative. On July 18, 1860 Mr. Colburn writes:

> I have just received from your city a dollar of 1804 the price of which is $75.00, the person who sends it says—I feel perfectly satisfied that if not an original that it is from the original die. I shall be greatly obliged if you will inform me if the die is in the Mint and if any specimens have been struck from it.
>
> My opinion is that the die of this dollar is by the same hand that cut the die of a famous Washington Half Dollar which appeared a few months ago.

While no reply by Snowden can now be located, another letter from Mr. Colburn, three days later, reads that "it seems to be the general opinion that the 1804 dollar was struck from the Mint die lately."

The next letter, dated July 23 and written by Director Snowden, requests that "the Dollar of 1804 which is supposed to have been struck from the Mint Dies" be sent to him, to which Mr. Colburn, on the 25th, replies: "1 have returned the dollar of 1804 to the person from whom I received it. I was not willing to pay the price he wanted for it. I think without a doubt that it was struck from the die now at the Mint."

As we have already learned, the Director retrieved three of the coins "that never were" from persons who had purchased them from young Eckfeldt for $75 each. William DuBois, assayer and Curator of Numismatics at the Philadelphia Mint, later testified that all but one of the restrikes were then destroyed in his presence, and that the lone exception (a bizarre creation struck over a cut-down Swiss shooting thaler [Bern, 1857]) was retained for the Mint Cabinet.

As a result of the "Eckfeldt incident," a series of controls (heaven forbid there should be reforms!) were now introduced, one of which required that all dies not in use be sealed up, and a list of these filed with the Director of the Mint. The words "in use," however, meant not only business use (an antiquated concept proper to a Mint whose only function is to provide the country with a circulating medium), but also numismatic use. All orders for "cabinet coins" were to be submitted with a description of the pieces, the number struck, and the recipient.

This would have been a disastrous rule if actually enforced, but such was the ingenuity of young Eckfeldt that any such danger was averted. Thus we read in the catalogue of the Ferguson Haines collection (Oct. 1880), prepared by W. E. Woodward:

Judging from my own experience, I believe that the purchaser of an 1804 dollar, or any one of many of the rarest American coins, has no guarantee that the son of some future director or chief coiner of the Mint will not, at an unexpected moment, place a quantity on the market. 'What man has done man may do'; and the ways of the Mint are past finding out, though transactions, such as restriking 1804 dollars, 1827 quarter dollars, and rare half cents, and speculations in rare experimental coins designed, engraved, and struck at the expense of the government, have become too frequent not to be well understood. What the lords of the treasury will do next is 'what no feller can find out.' We will wait and see. In these days of investigation, an inquiry into past operations of the Mint at Philadelphia or rather into the past conduct of some of its officials, would, if properly conducted, be fruitful in results; and if properly reported, would furnish what Horace Greeley used to call 'mighty interesting reading.' As the government is fond of illustrating its reports, as a frontispiece is suggested a view of a son of a late official of the Mint, as he appeared at the store of the writer, when, on a peddling expedition from Philadelphia to Boston, he drew from his pocket rolls of (1861) 'God our Trust' patterns, and urged their purchase at wholesale, after sundry sets had been disposed of at one hundred dollars each to collectors of rare coins, with the assurance that only a very few had been struck, and that the dies were destroyed . . .

Fig. 53. This is the first U.S. half dollar to bear a motto. According to Woodward, distribution was handled clandestinely by the son of a Mint official.

Nevertheless, on May 18, 1867, a new Director, Henry R. Linderman, discovered two sealed boxes of dies but was unable to locate their respective inventory sheets.[1] Linderman writes:

On the 8th of July 1859 several experimental Dies were boxed, sealed, and placed in the Vault in the Cabinet by the then Director of the Mint and a list thereof was filed in the Director's Office. Another sealed box of experimental Dies was placed in said vault July 30, 1860, and a list filed in the same office. Neither of these papers can now be found, and the Director deems it proper to have the boxes opened and again sealed up. It is ordered that the boxes referred to shall be opened this day in the presence of the Director, Chief Coiner & Engraver. A list of the Dies shall then be made, immediately after which the dies shall be replaced in the boxes and sealed up under the official seals of the Director & Engraver.

The first die described in Linderman's inventory is none other than the obverse of an 1804 dollar! The fact that the later Director referred to the lot as "experimental dies" is of considerable interest, since he was undoubtedly reiterating the description given in Snowden's records. If there had been *no* records, Linderman would hardly have known the exact dates on which both groups of dies had been impounded. The Hon. Director Snowden would have been well

1. Walter Thompson, "The 1804 Dollar Die and Others Found at the Mint in 1867." *Numismatic Scrapbook Magazine*, Dec., 1961.

acquainted with the history of the 1804 dollar die, since a few employees whose services dated beyond the inception of the Coin Cabinet were still associated with the Mint. Nevertheless, documentation must always be welcomed and in the present circumstance it establishes, without recourse to any further proof, the true status of the 1804 dollar.

In 1861, James Pollock was appointed by President Lincoln to succeed J. R. Snowden as Director of the Philadelphia Mint. Pollock had served three terms in Congress, was elected Governor of Pennsylvania in 1854, and, in 1860, as a peace delegate from his state, he was sent to Washington "to counsel with representatives from different parts of the Union as to the possibility of amicably adjusting our unhappy national troubles." [1] In Feb. 1861, war broke out, and Pollock, having failed to reform the bulk of his countrymen, was given charge of the lesser turmoil at Chestnut St., Philadelphia.

In order to start the incumbent off on the right foot, members of the Boston Numismatic Society, in a letter dated Nov. 12, 1861, dutifully related certain recent events:

> The undersigned, a committee of the Boston Numismatic Society, were instructed to call your attention to the abuses which have of late years been practiced at the Mint of the United States whereby a number of pattern pieces and coins from dies of former years have been freely struck and disposed of by Employees of the Mint to dealers who have in turn disposed of them at great prices. Two years since Members of this Society were offered specimens of the Dollar of 1804 of which, previously, only three or four examples were known; on applying to the Director of the Mint, he peremptorily replied that none had been struck; further investigation resulted in the fact being proven that three specimens had been struck, two of which had been sold for $75.00 each; various pattern pieces, in large numbers, have also been issued without the sanction of the proper officers. Under these circumstances, we respectfully urge the expediency of destroying the dies of the current coin, and also of pattern pieces at the close of each year.

On the 21st, Pollock replied:

> Gentlemen,
> Yours of the 12 inst. has been rec'd. The abuses to which you refer, if they have ever had an existence, can no longer be practiced in this Institution. The practice of striking pattern pieces and coins from dies of former years cannot be too strongly condemned, and great care is

1. Evans, *History of the United States Mint and American Coinage.*

now taken to prevent the re-currence of any such abuse. All the dies
of former years are secured in such a manner that it is impossible for
any one to obtain possession of them without the knowledge of the
Director. The dies of the current coins and of pattern pieces will be
destroyed at the close of the year. The dies of the past few years
have also been destroyed.

The members of the Boston Numismatic Society may have won-
dered how care could be "taken to prevent the re-currence" of
abuses which were not acknowledged as ever having existed, but
possibly they thought it wise to leave well enough alone.

In 1840, the 1804 dollars were unknown and unsought. Three
decades later their fame had become such that the creative daemon
stirred once more in the hearts of the Mint officers. The third
distribution is said to have occurred in 1869 when they were offered
for sale by one of the officials at six hundred dollars each, the going
price at that time. The editor of *Numisma*, writing about the 1804
dollar in December 1885, tells us: "J. N. T. Levick authorizes us to
say that one was offered him in 1869, but he 'took no stock in it'
because he saw at a glance that it was a restrike."

It is not without significance that a similar restrike later
turned up among the effects of Henry R. Linderman, Director of
the Mint from 1867 to 1869. There is, unfortunately, no record as
to how Dr. Linderman came by his "rara avis," although a few
interesting conjectures have been made from time to time.

Since the distribution of the "original" (i.e. circa 1834-35) 1804
dollars had now passed beyond the memory of most collectors, we
should not be surprised to learn that, on at least one occasion, official
affidavits were issued, confirming the genuineness of a particular specimen. That such affidavits, however, should have been issued for the
latter day restrikes (which were known to be such!) is an alarming testimony of the moral tone which then prevailed over the Mint.

The Ellsworth dollar now reposes in the world famous "Money
Museum" of the Chase Manhattan Bank in New York City. It is
accompanied by a certificate written in longhand by Mint Superintendent O. C. Bosbyshell, an "agent" in the transaction. (*Fig. 54*)

The Mint of the United States at Philadelphia
Superintendent's Office
Feb'y 15, 1894

James W. Ellsworth Esq.
Chicago, Ill.
My dear Sir:
   The 1804 Silver Dollar purchased by me for you today, from W.
Isaac Rosenthal of 190 Berks Street, this City, came into his possession
in the following manner: A Mr. Julius Driefus, Nos. 3 & 4 South
Wharves, Alexandria Va., does business for Mr. Rosenthal, and borrowed money from him. Mr. Driefus met with a colored man who had
the dollar for forty years—that he received it from his father, who was
a freedman—the father kept the dollar because it either was the date
of his birth, or the date he became a freedman—Mr. Rosenthal cannot
remember which. I am promised a more circumstantial account, and
will transmit it to you as soon as I receive it. This dollar has been
subjected to the most severe scrutiny in the Mint, and all of (the)
experts are entirely satisfied that it is (a) genuine dollar struck in the
year 1804. Our Curator, Mr. Robert A. McClure is thoroughly convinced of this as is also our Engraver, Mr. Charles E. Barber—Mr.
Jacob B. Eckfeldt, Assayer, is a Numismatist of experience, and is
entirely satisfied of its genuineness. Hon A. Louden Snowden has also
added the weight of his opinion to those already granted. Personally
I have not the slightest doubt in the world regarding the genuine
character of this coin and I heartily congratulate you upon possessing
so rare a numismatic treasure.
                    Very truly yours,
                         (Signed) O. C. Bosbyshell
                                   Superintendent
I critically examined the above coin and pronounce it genuine and an
original dollar of 1804. (Signed) R. A. McClure, Curator
I examined the above coin and quite agree with all that is said in the
letter. (Signed) Chas. E. Barber, Engraver.

   We come now to the celebrated Haseltine-R. Coulton Davis specimen for which, "curiously," no older pedigree can be provided.
The affidavit reads:

UNITED STATES MINT, PHILADELPHIA, PENN.,
ASSAY DEPARTMENT.
                              Septr. 17, 1878.
   In compliance with the request of Mr. R. Coulton Davis, I have
made a critical examination of the Dollar of 1804, in his collection.
   Upon comparison with the specimens in the Cabinet of the U.S.
Mint, I have no doubt that this Dollar is one of the original issue—
and not a "restrike" from Mint dies.
                         (Signed) Wm. E. DuBois
                                   assayer & in charge of the
                                   Mint Cabinet.

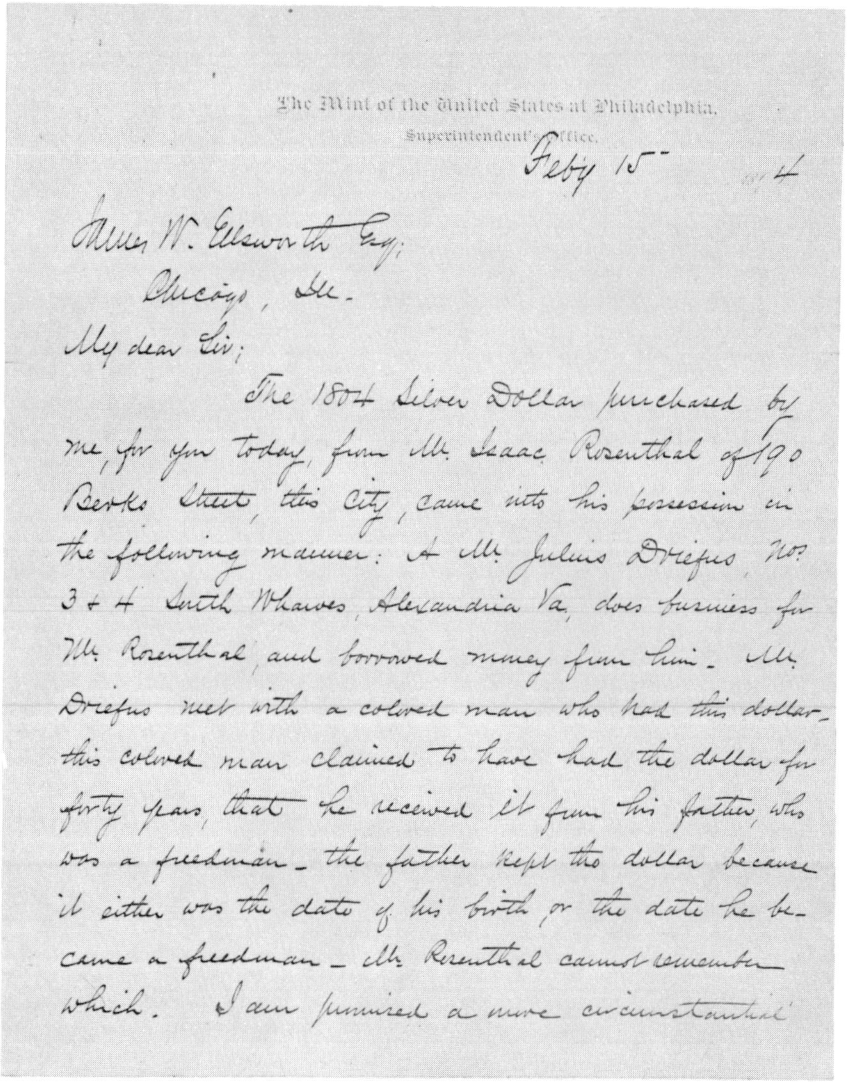

The Mint of the United States at Philadelphia,
Superintendent's Office.

Feby 15

James W. Ellsworth Esq,
    Chicago, Ill.
My dear Sir,

    The 1804 Silver Dollar purchased by
me, for you today, from Mr. Isaac Rosenthal of 190
Berks Street, this City, came into his possession in
the following manner: A Mr. Julius Driefus, Nos.
3 & 4 South Wharves, Alexandria Va, does business for
Mr. Rosenthal, and borrowed money from him. Mr.
Driefus met with a colored man who had this dollar—
this colored man claimed to have had the dollar for
forty years, that he received it from his father, who
was a freedman— the father kept this dollar because
it either was the date of his birth, or the date he became a freedman — Mr. Rosenthal cannot remember
which. I am promised a more circumstantial

Fig. 54. Mint certificate "authenticating" the Rosenthal 1804 dollar (Class III restrike). *Courtesy of the Chase Manhattan Bank Money Museum.*

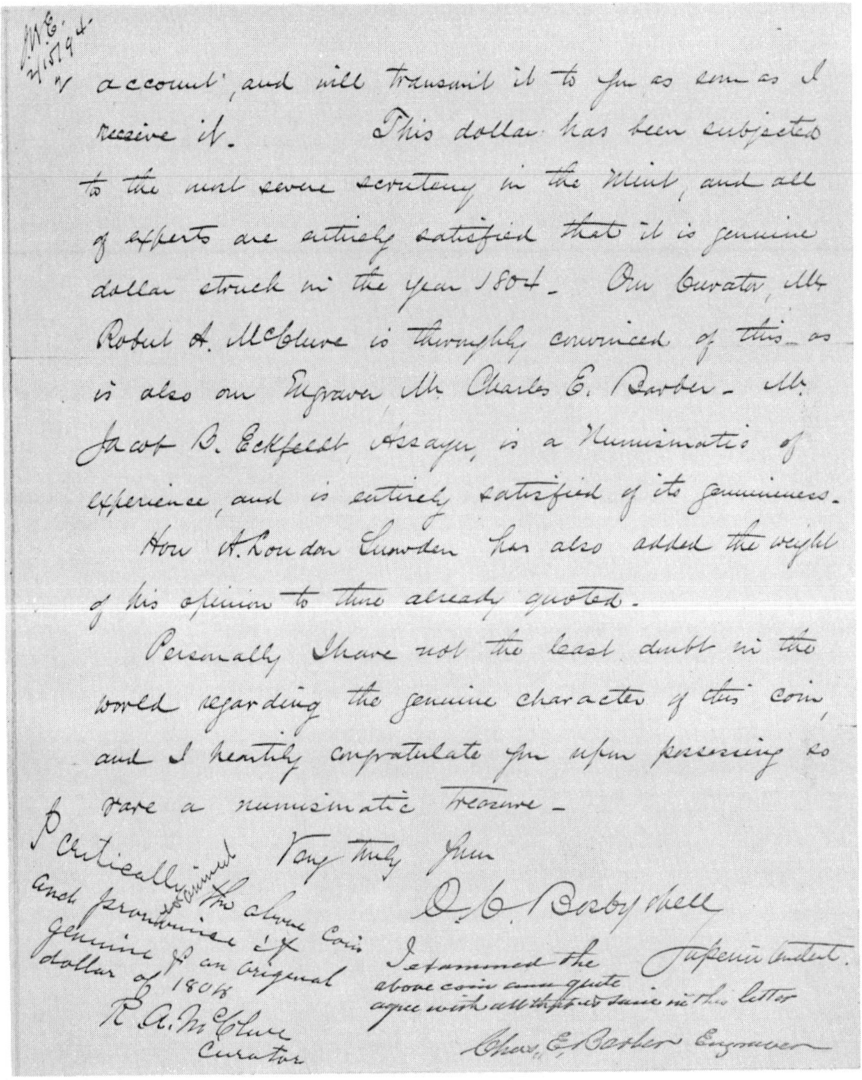

account, and will transmit it to you as soon as I receive it. This dollar has been subjected to the most severe scrutiny in the Mint, and all of experts are entirely satisfied that it is genuine dollar struck in the year 1804. Our Curator, Mr Robert A. McClure is thoroughly convinced of this, as is also our Engraver, Mr Charles E. Barber. Mr Jacob B. Eckfeldt, Assayer, is a Numismatist of experience, and is entirely satisfied of its genuineness.

Hon A. London Snowden has also added the weight of his opinion to those already quoted.

Personally I have not the least doubt in the world regarding the genuine character of this coin, and I heartily congratulate you upon possessing so rare a numismatic treasure —

Very truly yours

O. C. Bosbyshell
Superintendent.

I Critically examined the above coin and found the same to be a genuine if an original dollar of 1804

R. A. McClure
Curator

I examined the above coin and quite agree with all that is said in this letter

Chas. E. Barber Engraver

Fig. 54 (Continued).

This latter affidavit is, perhaps, the most curious of all since it is from the pen of William E. DuBois, curator of the Mint Cabinet for over forty years. DuBois, the Nestor of all the Mint's employees, had witnessed the striking of the first 1804 dollars in 1834-35, and was undoubtedly familiar with the events that followed. Furthermore, being a proficient numismatist, and having both issues at his disposal, he could undoubtedly detect the marked differences between the reverse dies of each. He must also have known that whereas the edge lettering on the 1834-35 "originals" had been applied to the planchets prior to their striking, and was subsequently defaced by the die collar, the opposite was true with regard to the later "restrikes." And yet he does not merely authenticate the R. Coulton Davis specimen, but he asserts that it "is one of the *original issue*—and not a 'restrike' from Mint dies."

It was to be expected that such official nonsense would soon insinuate itself into the great auctions of the day. Thus, in the description of the Linderman specimen by Scott & Co., Feb. 28, 1888, we read: "The latest impressions are said to have plain edges, and the others have muddled inscriptions, but this is of neither sort. At previous sales, inferior specimens have sold for $1,000 and $2,000. The perfection of the one now offered should command a large advance on all preceding offers."

And again in the May 21, 1888 Woodward sale of the aforementioned R. Coulton Davis restrike: "REV., sharp and equal to obv., head and breast of eagle also slightly worn by circulation, the edge bears the usual incused description "HUNDRED CENTS ONE DOLLAR OR UNIT," plainly visible and not partly destroyed as in the restrikes. Extremely fine, the finest original dollar of this date ever offered at auction. Entirely different in appearance from the brilliant proof restrikes of which several specimens have within a few years made their appearance in the market."

Thus the argument, which had, anyway, never been settled to anyone's satisfaction, was given the impetus of six new contestants. The owners of the so-called "originals" naturally looked askance at the interlopers who, in turn, castigated the former with sophistries which were ingenious if not altogether convincing.

At this critical juncture an even more challenging question was put to the numismatic fraternity: Aside from the dozen or so known specimens which might or might not be genuine, what had become of the near twenty thousand dollars said to have actually been coined in 1804 according to the duplicate reports of the Director and the Bullion ledger?

Over the past century numerous conjectures (most of them highly fanciful) have been advanced to account for this strange contradiction. It is known that in 1804 Director Boudinot halted the coinage of silver dollars because the majority were being exported for their foreign trade value. As a result of this fact it has often been inferred that the entire issue was thrown back into the melting pot. The difficulty with this theory is that of the 19,570 coins said to have been struck, only 14,070 pieces were deposited in the Bank of the U.S. where they could be easily retrieved. The remaining 5,500 went into "sundry accounts" which were scattered throughout the country.

The first clue to the mystery came in a surprising way. In 1913, S. H. Chapman pointed out that the early Mint ledgers showed only the *amount* of coins turned over during the year by the cashier or the treasurer of the Mint, without any reference to actual dates. By way of a supplement, a study of coin varieties revealed that dies, in the early days of the Mint, were generally used until worn out, even when they survived beyond the length of a given year. Thus, the absence of all but a dozen or so rather questionable 1804 dollars becomes intelligible. For despite three different attempts at the Mint to create this rarity, and the hundreds of thousands of words which have been written on the subject—despite even the records which tell you in black and white that 19,570 silver dollars were struck in that year, the fact remains that no genuine 1804 dollar ever existed. All that were made in that year were dated 1803!

In addition to the Directorship, the Hon. James Pollock inherited from his predecessor an incorrigible love of numismatics. The *grande passion*, in fact, sometimes found expression in his annual report which would close with a plaintive appeal for more appropriations for the Mint Cabinet.

Unlike Snowden, however, the new Director seems to have been keenly sensitive to the growing animadversions against the private and select distribution of patterns, and the restriking of earlier dates which were subsequently used to deceive credulous collectors.

As a result, on July 1, 1866, he issued a "circular letter" [1] providing a set of rules and regulations governing the public distribution of "Cabinet Coins," a euphemism adopted to cover the category of patterns in its new extended meaning. It read in part as follows:

. . . To aid in the execution of Medal and Coin dies, the Mint, nearly thirty years ago, imported the French Machine, the Tour à Portrait of Contamine, for making dies from models. The Mint has recently contracted for, and is daily expecting, Hill's Engraving Machine, purchased under authority of Hon. Hugh McCulloch, Secretary of the Treasury, an English invention, for which it is claimed, that for its superior powers, and singular ingenuity, it will supersede the other apparatus. We therefore expect to do justice to any orders, at a less expense, and in less time, than under the former system.

The occasion calls for a revision of our operations in this line, and for some reduction of prices, as will be found in the annexed schedule. And as cognate branches, it is proposed to unite therewith, the annual issue of proof or master coins of the regular series, as heretofore; and the specimen or "pattern" coins which are not adopted, or do not become so, within the year of their date. (The term "pattern" is used here, out of deference to the technicalities of collectors, not because of its peculiar fitness; for if the piece fails to be adopted, it is not properly a pattern. "Experimental" is a better term.) These last have hitherto been given out, or withheld by no rule whatsoever; although they have by degrees attained to a very considerable importance, on account of the eagerness of many collectors to obtain them. There is, indeed, a pretty strong reason, why these should be used only for their special purpose; namely to aid the Treasury Department, or a Congressional Committee, in forming an idea of the size, appearance and practicability of any newly proposed coin, or of any change of devices in an old one. But it has been found impossible to put this rigid limit upon them. If we strike only a few, the ambitious collector will have one at any price; and a competition is created, out of all proportions to the merits of the prize. It seems better, therefore, avoiding the error of making such pieces too plentiful, to give some scope to the acquisition of them.

This whole department will be under the supervision of the DIRECTOR OF THE MINT, and all inquiries and requests, with or without money, must be addressed to him. The medals and coins will be in the responsible custody of one of his clerks, who will also attend to the orders, reply to letters, and keep the accounts. The making of dies and the striking of medals, proofs and patterns, will be in the charge of the ENGRAVER, and at his responsibility; other officers of the Mint rendering such aid of materials and machinery as may fall within their province. These arrangements, though internal, are here openly stated, with a view to assure the public that there is a system of suitable checks and guards, against undue or secret issues. . . .

The ensuing Rules are in plain terms, and hardly require a statement of reasons. It may be said, however, in regard to the Rule against striking a coin or pattern after its proper date, that while it seemed desirable that some patterns of former years, which are very scarce or curious should be repeated,

1. Original document in the library of John J. Ford Jr.

yet we could not issue them impartially, without giving out an indefinite number. And if some kinds are thus struck, there would be a call for other kinds; there would be no knowing where to begin or end.

Pieces struck out of date, bear a falsity on their face, and have not the interest or value of a synchronous issue. An uncertainty is also kept up, as to the extent of the supply. And in the case of regular coinage, they so far falsify the Mint Records and Tables, as to the amount of coinage and delivery, or as to the very fact of such and such pieces having been coined in any given year.

On the whole, therefore, it seemed a plain course, to let the past go, and begin afresh. And it is a satisfaction to be able to assure all parties, that there has been no resurgent striking in the present Directorship.

The striking of specimens in other than their proper metal, never much practiced, is to be discontinued. This irregularity has, of course, never been with unlawful intent, and never would have happened, but for the importunate desire to possess something odd, or to avoid the outlay of gold or silver. Such pieces have been struck, as patterns, from the dime of 1792 down to our day; but the united voice now is against using dies meant for gold or silver upon copper or other base metal.

It is proper to say, that before these Rules were matured, advice was sought of several Numismatic Societies, and gentlemen skilled in this branch of study. There has not been an entire unanimity of opinion as to details, but the general tendency was towards the result as herein indicated; and it is hoped that a general approbation will be accorded . . .

RULES

1. No coins, nor pattern pieces, shall be struck after the year of their date; and to insure this, the dies shall be rendered unfit for that use.

2. No coins, nor patterns, are to be issued in any but their proper metal.

3. Any experimental or pattern piece can be obtained at the Mint, within the year of its date, but not after. Standing orders for such pieces will be registered, and attended to. Any patterns that remain on hand, at the end of the year, must be defaced: It is not desirable to make them as common as the proofs of regular coinage. If any sets of regular proofs remain over, they may be sold in the next year, but not later.

4. The price of a pattern coin, in any but precious metal, will be three dollars in currency; if in gold or silver, the value of the metal is to be added. But when a pattern piece is adopted and used in the regular coinage, in the same year, it will then be issued as a proof, at a price near its current value; or if it comes out early in the year, it will be placed in the regular proof set. The Director reserves the right to send a pattern piece, without charge, to any incorporated Numismatic Society in the United States. In such cases, if the pattern is in gold or silver, the value of the metal will be expected.

5. The price of the regular proof set of gold, will be forty-three dollars in gold; the proof set of silver and copper, three dollars in silver as heretofore.

To suit the convenience of many, payment may be made in the currency equivalent.[1]

6. The profits of this whole department are reserved to the Medal Fund, which is a part of the public moneys; and are not to be perquisite to any person holding a place in the MINT. All such persons are expected to refrain from dealings in this line, or affording aid to friends or dealers outside. If this expectation is counteracted, it will call for serious notice.

The tenor of Pollock's "rebuke" of former administrations is just what we might expect. No law (?) has been offended by the misdating of coins or the use of dies for striking false metal pieces, or even by the illicit contracts between Mint officials and private parties— no law, but merely public opinion. The revision has thus been undertaken from common consent—for numismatical reasons and for the sake of keeping more accurate ledgers. The profession of equal opportunity is especially touching. This would no doubt explain the emission of two silver dollars, a quarter and a half dollar of 1866, all without the newly adopted motto "In God We Trust." The Act of March 3, 1865 permitted the Director to append this motto, and patterns for each of the aforesaid denominations, all bearing the new design, were struck during the same year.

How is it then that in the *following* year four proof coins, all in the "old style," were struck at the Philadelphia Mint [2]—and that *all four* found their way into the cabinet of William H. Woodin, later Secretary of the Treasury, and an ardent collector of "pattern" coins? *(Fig. 55)*

Edgar Adams, in cataloguing the Woodin collection, described the quartet as transitional patterns, an appellation curiously retained by Dr. Judd in his 1959 volume. It is curious because it would imply that they represent something in the way of a new design, struck

1. Not long ago, the author had the opportunity to examine a quantity of proof sets (still in their original wrappings) which dated from 1866 to 1876. In several of the sets a single proof had been replaced by a coin of regular issue—the range of years indicating, furthermore, that this was common practice. Evidently a little adulteration made the proof sets go a longer way!

2. The existence of the 1866-S half dollars, half eagles, eagles and double eagles is, of course, a different matter. As Lynn Glaser points out in his article in the *Numismatic Scrapbook Magazine*, Nov. 1961, these issues "can be explained by the fact that due to primitive transportation facilities the new dies did not arrive (in San Francisco) until April 14, 1866. By that time a number of each denomination had been struck with the old reverse."

prior to its adoption, when, in fact, the opposite is true. Genuine transitional patterns for this issue were indeed struck, but, as we have said, in the year 1865, and showing the motto as it would henceforth appear.

Pollock, who retired from the Directorship in 1866, was re-assigned to the post in 1869. When Dr. Henry Linderman took charge in 1867, however, the dies which were to be "rendered unfit" were still very much in working condition.

The new Director found himself torn between two allegiances.[1] While, on the one hand, he felt bound to some sort of adherence to the rules of 1866, the prospect of destroying all of the old dies was a painful one. Finally, as a compromise, he ordered more than seven hundred experimental dies, together with numerous others which had been stored up in the Mint—some since 1800—to be destroyed by sledge and fire *after four or five impressions had been taken from each!* Indeed, the winds of chicanery were still blowing.[2]

1. Dr. Linderman himself was an active numismatist. When, in 1887, his estate was being settled, several patterns of an "unusual character" were seized by Treasury agents at the order of Director Kimball. The incident appears the more curious for the fact that Dr. Linderman was author of the Revised Statutes of 1873 which specifically prohibited the striking and emission of such pieces. These are the items which were withdrawn from auction because of government objection: #55) Complete set of sixteen pieces, 1¢ to $20 struck in aluminum from regular 1868 dies. #76) 1868 3¢ piece in aluminum. #90) 1868 half dime in nickel. #96 1868 dime in aluminum. #116) 1875 20¢ pattern in copper. #117 1875 20¢ pattern in copper. #126) 1861 half dollars with motto in copper (D-148, 149). #127) 1862 half dollar in copper (D-157). #128) 1863 half dollars in copper (D-168, 169). #162) 1861 $10 in copper (D-152, 153). #163) 1863 $10 in copper (D-172). #171) 1859 $20 in silver (D-139).

Breen points out that Linderman may have been as much a moving force behind the early Mint chicanery as was his friend and neighbor J. R. Snowden. Linderman, through the political influence of his uncle, Senator Richard Brodhead, obtained the appointment of Chief Clerk in 1853, the year in which Snowden became Mint Director. Both Linderman and Snowden came from the Delaware Water Gap region of Pennsylvania where Joseph Wharton operated the only nickel mine in the United States. It is not without interest that *the two peaks of agitation over a nickel coinage coincide with the periods in which Linderman wielded power at the Mint.* In June 1878, he was accused of official misconduct by a Congressional sub-committee. Seven months later he died without the issue having been settled one way or the other.

2. The then Chief Coiner, A. L. Snowden, in later writing of the incident, remarked that whilst there had been no law (?) against the restrikings, the practice was liable to abuse and that it was perhaps well that all of the old dies had been destroyed *as a precaution.* Considering the extent of the private enterprise which, for the years 1859 and 1860 alone, has been estimated at $50,000, one may well ponder over the volume which would have been required, in the conservative opinion of this gentleman, to *constitute an abuse.*

Furthermore, both A. L. Snowden and Dr. Linderman neglected to mention that *while the working dies had been destroyed, the hubs, and in most cases the date logotypes, were preserved so that new dies might be made at any time*. Thus, despite plaintive denials by the Mint authorities, we find among the latter-day goodies several pattern silver dollars of 1875 and 1876—struck from an 1857-8-9 reverse die, without the motto "In God We Trust." *(Fig. 56)*

In addition to Snowden's Washington collection, which he was compiling in duplicate, there was Franklin Peale's proof and pattern collection, and for the enhancement of the two no opportunity was lost to create some new rarity of trade-value. Restrikes were one thing, but after a time, when the savor of chronological collecting began to pall, it was found expedient to strike a certain number of "original" pieces—the more original, in fact, the better. Consequently, we find from this period mulings not only of different denominations, but even a few struck on bi-metallic planchets, half silver and half copper! Indeed, the "pattern" had become elastic enough to meet the demands of any occasion. *(Fig. 57)*

In Snowden's Description of Ancient and Modern Coins, published in 1860, there is a chapter entitled "Unauthorized Coins of the U.S.," wherein it is written: "Since the establishment of the United States Mint, many coins have made their appearance therefrom which do not belong to the national authorized series, being of an experimental character, and not intended for general circulation."

Within the last few years, many collectors have been startled to learn of the existence of a genuine 1868 large cent. The history of this strange anachronism, eleven years after the regular series had ended, is at once complete and incomplete. It is known, for instance, that a ten-cent coin of similar design had previously been struck as part of an experimental coinage. The obverse die was prepared from a large cent hub, the current date then being punched in. A new reverse die had to be cut owing to the change of denomination (to ten cents), but it was made in every other particular to resemble that of a large cent. What happened then was, perhaps, inevitable. By some inscrutable means, the regular reverse die of the large cent which had been stored away, suddenly appeared together with —of all things—a dozen or so large cent planchets of exact size and

Fig. 55

Fig. 56

Fig. 55. The unique 1866 no motto half dollar: a so-called "transitional pattern."
Fig. 56. 1876 silver dollar with the pre-1866 (no motto) reverse: One of the dies that Linderman missed.

Fig. 57. Here are a few of the more unusual "patterns" of the last century: 1) Muling of 1869 cent and five cents on nickel planchet (Judd 691); 2) 2¢ 1865, struck from regular dies. The planchets were formed from layers of silver and copper, compressed with rollers, so as to show one metal on each side (J-407); 3) Muling of the regular 2¢ obverse of 1869 with the obverse of the Standard Silver pattern quarter. Bi-metallic as previous (J-675).

weight and perfectly proofed! After these wondrous events—which we can only construe as being providential—there was nothing left to do but strike the coins! *(Fig. 58)*

The destruction of the dies had, by and large, little effect on the private enterprises of the Mint. (It only meant that the officials would henceforth have to look forwards instead of backwards for their inspiration.) Nor was business curbed by the injunction forbidding the striking of base metal coins from dies intended for gold and silver—a law which had been in effect since 1825! [1] The indulgence, therefore, which Pollock briefly granted to the statute, can hardly afford him much credit.

But, after all, it is only the "little people" who break laws; the big ones merely make exceptions! One of the most flagrant exceptions was perpetrated, in fact, by none other than the Secretary of the Treasury, on whose order (Oct. 22, 1863) a set of "experimental coins" for the years 1862 and 1863 was furnished to the Hon. George Opdyke, Mayor of New York. These consisted of half dollars and quarter dollars in silver and a series of gold coins struck in copper, all bearing the legend "In God We Trust," a mere two years in advance of its adoption. *(Fig. 59)*

Another archive in the office of the Secretary of the Treasury, dated May 13, 1868 (two years after Pollock's "Rules"), reveals that four complete sets of the year's coinage, from one cent to twenty dollars, were struck in aluminum at the Philadelphia Mint, for the Secretary, and at his own instance and expense. Three years later, one of the above sets was advertised for sale by Mason & Co., Philadelphia dealers, for the price of one hundred dollars.

Whatever the officers of the Mint failed to comprehend in the previous monetary laws of the United States was rendered implacably clear for them by the Revised Statutes of 1873. This law, after stating the precise requirements of our coinage, in regard to metal, fineness, weight, device etc., clearly tells us that no coins, either of gold, silver, or minor coinage shall hereafter be issued from the mint other than those of the denominations set forth in that title.

A further elucidation was provided by the "General Instructions and Regulations in Relation to the Transaction of Business at the

1. The only genuine exceptions were die trials which were to be destroyed as soon as the purpose for which they had been struck was subserved.

Mints and Assay Offices of the United States," published under date of May 14, 1874, which stated: "When a pattern is adopted and used in the regular coinage in the same year, it will *then* be issued, as a proof, at a price near its current value, or if it comes out early in the year, it will be placed in the regular proof set." [1]

This obviously is a little removed from our familiar usage of the term "pattern" in numismatics; certainly, it is worlds apart from the definition conjured by Snowden, Pollock & Co. For, as Director Kimball noted in his annual report of 1887: "The truth is . . . that there is nothing to distinguish a pattern, as an authorized issue, from the U.S. Mint, from a proof coin; a pattern piece being simply an earlier specimen or proof from a newly adopted coinage die or dies as already defined." . . . And again, "The specific provisions above cited (i.e., the "Instructions and Regulations etc."), inhibiting the issue, and prescribing the narrow limits for the striking, of pieces from coinage and experimental dies, contained in all subsequent editions of Instructions and Regulations, were in that (1874) edition first prescribed."

In 1910, the Director of the Mint summed up the case against patterns as follows: "Since the passage of this act in 1873 there has been no authority of law for the distribution of experimental or pattern pieces, and any such pieces as have been removed from the mint have been taken without authority. No title has been passed to any individual and the pieces are still the property of the United States."

That the distribution of "patterns"—and false metal patterns at that—nevertheless continued within the circle of the elect, is a fact well documented by the archives.

On December 13, 1877, nine experimental silver dollars were struck in copper for officers of the Mint, on the "general verbal authority" of the Director.[2] Four days later, the "specific authority" of the Director was cited for the production of twelve experimental silver dollars in silver and two in copper, also struck for the officers of that institution. Even more curious is a communication on the same date from the Director of the Mint (then in Washington) to the Superintendent, referring to the latter's correspondence of the 13th,

1. Italics are the author's.
2. Report of the Director of the Mint, 1887.

and revoking the "verbal authority." After stating that "in the future such specimens will only be struck after application to this office," the letter concludes as follows: "I deem it necessary that the strictest regulations and care should be observed in reference to striking specimens in any other metals than gold and silver, it being sure to lead to criticism and complaint on the part of coin collectors."

To Director Pollock, the discussion of false metal coins was of little moment, the striking of these having anyway been "never much practiced." In actual fact, however, the number of these illegitimate pieces comprised more than one half of the "essays" in numismatic circulation, as evinced by the catalogue of R. Coulton Davis, published in 1885. Davis, who was known for having more "patterns" than were in the Mint Cabinet, acquired during the 1870's a brass restrike of the unique 1849 twenty-dollar gold piece! Here was not only a false metal emission par excellence, but one more die which had magically contrived to escape the ordeal of "fire and sledge" undertaken by Dr. Linderman.

In 1887, the Director of the Mint, writing on the subject of false metal emissions, stated: "How far the sanction of this Bureau may be presumed to have been found for the production and private issue of trial and experimental pieces in soft metal and otherwise since 1873—in direct contravention of the instructions and regulations prescribed by the Director of the Mint and approved by the Secretary of the Treasury—the files and records of this Bureau disclose. Not even this degree of sanction can be found for the production of pieces in soft metal other than trial or experimental pieces—properly so called. No false metal pieces seem ever to have been required by this Bureau since its organization in 1873, or to have been sanctioned, if at all, as a matter of record. Indeed, it can hardly be believed that any useful or important purpose could ever have been subserved by the production of such extremely illegitimate pieces."

As we have seen, the Revised Statutes of 1873 left little room for doubt as to the status of the so-called "cabinet coins." The public distribution, which had been conceived and fostered under the affectionate care of Director Pollock, thus came to an abrupt end. As for the private distribution—it went on as usual, with the one difference that it required now a certain element of discretion. As a result, some of the most interesting transactions of this period remained undisclosed for many years thereafter.

As late as 1909, for example, two unique twenty-dollar gold patterns of 1876 were promulgated by John Haseltine, the famous Philadelphia dealer. Haseltine, who was the son-in-law of William Idler—one of the most favored individuals ever to have had dealings with the Mint—revealed during his disposition of the latter's collection a startling number of coins and essay pieces which had hitherto been unknown. A letter from Haseltine to Farran Zerbe, then president of the American Numismatic Association, speaks for itself:

> My dear Mr. Zerbe,
>
> You have in very complimentary terms referred to me as a "Numismatic Refrigerator." I have therefore withdrawn from "Cold Storage" two unique Double Eagles in Gold, which I now present to the Numismatic fraternity for their consideration.
>
> In 1876 the mint authorities desired to improve the design of the Double Eagle. In the old design the point of the Diadem, in the head of "Liberty" seemed too near the star and the whole appearance of the head seemed misplaced, not being in the center. In the two unique pieces the point of the diadem is placed directly between the two stars, all the stars are better arranged and the heads of Liberty are larger and placed more directly in the center. In the second type the numeral "1" is nearer the bust and the "6" is farther from it, than in type one.
>
> The reverse of type two is entirely different from type one, the T & W in "Twenty" nearly touch the scroll or label inscribed "E Pluribus," and there are other slight variations which can be noticed in the cuts. The whole heraldic design is larger and "Twenty Dollars" below, in fact, an entirely different die. *(Fig. 60)*
>
> In presenting these two important discoveries to the Numismatists of the world, I claim that both are unique and for the benefit of our science, I would respectfully desire and request anyone who thinks he has a duplicate to correspond with me and publish it with proof in the NUMISMATIST.
>
> At your request I now present these two Double Eagles in gold, in beautiful condition, for the information of all interested. I delayed sending you this until the coins were sold, as I didn't wish you to think I wanted some free advertising.
>
> Yours truly,
(Signed) John W. Haseltine.

Under the provisions of the Revised Statutes, the Mint Department became a Bureau with its Director located in Washington. The heads of each of the mints were henceforth known as Superintendents.

When James Pollock thus resumed charge of the Philadelphia Mint, it was in a diminished role, shorn, as it were, of the former imperial liberties. As a result, the carping of the habitual critics

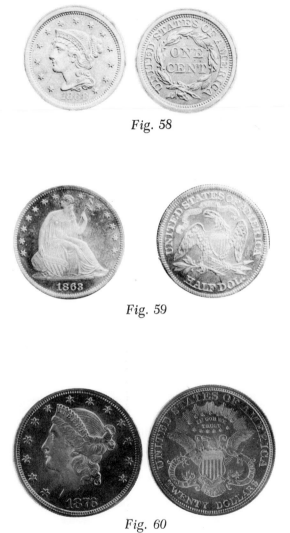

Fig. 58

Fig. 59

Fig. 60

Fig. 58. 1868 large cent. Eleven years after the series had ended—a surprise!
Fig. 59. 1863 half dollar with the regular motto of 1866; Fig. 60. Unique 1876
twenty-dollar gold pattern, ex Haseltine, Idler.

which had heretofore been a subject of esoteric amusement ceased at once to titillate.

One of the most famous altercations ensued over the Standard Dollar Patterns of 1878. In an article in Ed Frossard's *Numisma* (Dec. 7, 1878), S. K. Harzfeld writes:

> *These patterns form but another disgraceful story of the management of the United States Mint. In other countries, the Mint is the center from which Numismatic knowledge emanates. In this country the Mint abhors numismatic interests. It serves to coin money, to be run as a political machine, and to be abused by a certain class of its officials. It is a rule of the Mint that patterns shall be sold only during the year of issue, but this year the sale of the Barber-Morgan dollars was refused by the Mint while the officials, in a clandestine manner, sold these patterns at enormous prices. Patterns forming a part of the numismatic progress and the history of coinage of a country should be sold by the Mint to numismatists in limited numbers. As long as this is refused, there will be fraud and disgrace.*

In a later article entitled "U.S. Pattern Coins—Their illegal issue and sale, and the ineffectual efforts of numismatists to check it," Harzfeld refers to the above article thus:

> *When the attention of ex-governor Pollock, then Superintendent of the Philadelphia Mint, was called to this note, he fell into considerable passion and instructed the (then) Chief Coiner, Major O. C. Bosbyshell, to call upon me and ask for a formal public withdrawal of my charge, threatening in case of refusal, with legal proceedings.*

Whether or not Harzfeld complied is debatable. The "retraction" went only so far as to explain that the word "official" did not necessarily refer to the Superintendent and the Chief Coiner but could be taken to include anyone connected with the institution.

In the meantime Pollock's attention was being diverted by new assaults. An article which appeared in the *Philadelphia Times*, Jan. 6, 1879, openly stated that the best counterfeits of U.S. coins were not the production of unscrupulous coin dealers but those which had been fraudulently struck by the Mint itself!

In the midst of the new hostilities, Pollock was replaced by Archibald Louden Snowden, the erstwhile Chief Coiner from whom we have already heard. Before long, however, a new altercation ensued over the distribution of the metric patterns. Harzfeld writes:

> *My surprise may be imagined when I learned shortly afterwards that besides these 120 sets, 300 additional sets had been ordered and struck:— that they were officially offered to members of Congress and personal friends on payment of the intrinsic value ($6.10);—that the clerks of the Washington*

Departments had severally three, six or more sets which they openly offered for sale;—that sets were found in the hands of boarding house keepers and that the Stella gold coins may already be seen—pierced—as ornaments in possession of women of the "demi-monde" at Washington. During all this the respectable coin dealers and collectors could not get any of the sets at the Philadelphia Mint and were forced to negotiate for them with parties "who knew how to get them."

Fig. 61. $4 gold piece or "Stella." According to Harzfeld, they were available to everyone but the coin collectors.

As a result of the article, Harzfeld was granted an interview with the new Superintendent wherein, it must be admitted, the latter generally exculpated himself in regard to the metric coins. The increase from twenty to four hundred and twenty had been dictated by the Congressional Committee at the request of W. W. Hubbell, whose goloid dollar was featured in the sets. Snowden added that no pieces had been issued, retained or sold by himself nor could any other Mint official be justly held responsible for the issue. Harzfeld concludes his summary with the statement: "My interview with Colonel Snowden was highly satisfactory."

So satisfactory, in fact, was the meeting that *Numisma* magazine, formerly the most voluble of all the Mint's critics, was transformed, in the wink of an eye, into its arch apologist.

Thus, when rumors began to circulate upon the discontinuation of the Trade Dollar, *Numisma* leapt to the rescue. In an article in the March edition, 1884, the editor writes:

Our critic at the Sandham sale recently, almost openly, insinuated that Trade Dollars have been quietly manufactured at the Mint during the past year; in other words, not withstanding the positive assertions of the Mint authorities to the contrary, a Trade Dollar with the date 1884 does exist.

We hold that the plain but positive statement of the Mint officers on this point should be considered conclusive evidence, and they say that no Trade Dollars have been issued in the Philadelphia Mint, or in any Mint of the U.S. during the past year, or dated 1884.

But as doubts on this point may still exist in the minds of those who heard the report, we are authorized to make the following offers: $100 cash each for any number of United States Trade Dollars of 1884, coined at the Philadelphia or any other U.S. Mint; $25 cash down to anyone who will show us such a dollar.

*It is time that absurd and untruthful if not slanderous statements about
so-called "deals" at the National Mint should cease. The present management
has proved itself most honorable, impartial and just, and no one has unusual
facilities to obtain pattern pieces and proof sets, all collectors in this respect
being treated alike, i.e., what is obtainable by one at the Mint is obtainable
by all . . .*

In the light of history, the defense is rather amusing. In 1908,

Fig. 62. 1885 Trade Dollar, a slight omission from the annual Mint Report.

with the marketing of the Idler collection by John Haseltine, no less
than six of the non-existent 1884 Trade Dollars, together with a few
dated 1885, turned up among the regular proof sets for those years!
In addition to these, an all-copper proof set, complete with the
Trade Dollar and dated 1884 was sold with the collection of A. M.
Smith in 1936.[1] The set had as fine a pedigree as one could require.
It was obtained directly from the Superintendent of the Mint!

We may assume that a part of the purchase price of these coins
was a vow of eternal silence. Today, in their infrequent appearances at public sale, they are among the most talked-about of U.S.
coins.

Towards the end of 1885 a minor incident occurred which, but
for the uncommon probity of Director James Kimball, would have
passed like so many others into the quiet limbo of forgetfulness. Instead, it caused a revolution which shook the old Mint building to
its foundations. In his annual report of 1887, Kimball writes:

1. M. H. Bolender, the *A. M. Smith Collection*, Feb. 8, 1936. The coins included
in the set, and struck from regular dies in copper, were the standard silver dollar,
Trade Dollar, half dollar, quarter dollar, gold dollar, quarter eagle, three dollars,
half eagle, eagle and double eagle. There was also a duplicate 1884 Trade Dollar in
copper, uncirculated, and proof silver specimens of 1882 and 1883.

Within the experience of the present administration of the mint at Philadelphia, and also of this bureau, nothing had occurred previous to the last half of the fiscal year of 1887 to raise a question as to the legality and propriety of certain precedents and practices, so far as these were then believed to have been duly authorized, in the matter of the production and disposal for numismatical purposes of pieces to which the term 'pattern' has been colloquially, commonly, and as it has since proved, indiscriminately and erroneously applied. One trial dime of 1792 and one experimental 20 cent piece of 1874 found in duplicate in the coin cabinet of the mint at Philadelphia, were therefore suffered as late as December 1885, to pass beyond the walls of that mint, in exchange for a certain rare gold coin much coveted for its coin collection. This transaction which was upon the formal recommendation of the curator, for many years in charge of that cabinet, passed unquestioned on grounds no further than simple expediency.

It should be remembered that the Director was now situated in Washington, the actual management of the mints being left to the Superintendents. It is not therefore impossible that Kimball was ignorant of the past misdemeanors of the Philadelphia officers which were, by and large, confined to and promulgated within their own city. Thus, the sale of two duplicate patterns—by comparison to all that had gone before, a trifling affair—loomed suddenly as a major irregularity. An inquiry into the subject, moreover, disclosed that several of the older officers of the institution were suffering from a partial amnesia which rendered them incapable of providing any useful evidence. Kimball writes that, "Neither the official records or books of that institution, nor the personal statements of several of the present officers whose services date back beyond the passage of the Coinage Act of 1873, afford at present any knowledge of the public sale or general issue of other than patterns of adopted, and proofs of current, coins."

Other sources were fortunately more communicative. When Kimball had finished collating his notes in 1887, a most extraordinary Mint report was in the making. Indeed, the day of reckoning had come!

In a section entitled "IRREGULAR PRODUCTIONS OF THE UNITED STATES MINT: Cabinet coins, trial pieces and experimental coins, properly known as Pattern pieces," Kimball writes:

Section 5460, Revised Statutes, provides a severe penalty for debasing, by officers of the Mint, any of the gold or silver coins, or making them worse as to the proportion of fine gold or fine silver, or of less weight or value pursuant to law. This law was originally enacted March 3, 1825.

The denominations, standards, and weights of coins are declared by section 3516, Revised Statutes; the devices and legends provided by section 3517. The designs, as distinguished from devices, are fixed by the Coinage Act of 1873, section 3510, Revised Statutes, as those found in the original dies already authorized at the time of its enactment (Feb. 12, 1873).[1] The same section provides for new designs when new coins or devices are authorized. No change in design or devices of existing coins is at present provided by law.

Coins cannot be issued under the coinage laws of the United States by any mint, except as specifically prescribed as to weight and fineness (and incidentally as to diameter and size);[2] and also as to devices, designs and legends.

Yet it is a well-known fact that, since the enactment of the present coinage laws, as before, numerous pieces known as cabinet coins have been in circulation among numismatists, coin collectors and coin dealers, for even the permanent existence of which pieces no justification can be found in mint practice, nor authority of law for their manufacture—much less for their issue or escape from the mint. Such pieces may generally be described as follows, under the terms by which they are popularly known:

1. Mule-pieces or hybrids—pieces struck from a regular coinage die or dies of which the obverse or reverse or both, is other than authorized by law for coin of the same denomination, or other than employed in the regular coinage of the same denomination of the same date.

2. False-metal pieces—or replicas or copies of coins in a metal or alloy or of a weight and fineness other than prescribed by law.

3. Trial pieces—or impressions in a soft metal to test a die or dies, and not destroyed as required by regulation.

4. Experimental pieces—struck for mint purposes from regular coinage dies in experimental metal or alloy.

'Restrikes,' often a subject of question among coin collectors in the case of rare coins, possible only by a most flagrant violation of the coinage laws and mint regulations, involving not only failure to deface obverse dies at the expiration of the year of date, but in the act of reproduction falsification of dates, are not here scheduled among the well-recognized unauthorized cabinet pieces, as in no case of alleged reproduction of certain rare American coins

---

ORIGINAL FOOTNOTES OF ANNUAL REPORT OF MINT DIRECTOR

1. The adoption of new designs in the case of the silver dollar in 1878 and of the five-cent nickel piece in 1883, was not in accordance with the original act (February 12, 1873, section 8) from which section 3510 was codified.

2. The limitation of diameter and size follows from section 3510, which provides that "all working dies required for use in the coinage of the several mints" shall be prepared "from the original dies already authorized"—that is, from such as were employed at the time of the passage of the Act (February 12, 1873).

from perpetuated or restored dies, so far as I am aware, has any such charge ever been proven against any of the mints of the United States.[1]

That the present subject is not a new one is evidenced by reference to almost any important numismatical work published in the United States, or to the files of such special publications as, notably the American Journal of Numismatics, The Coin Collector's Journal, and even trade lists and catalogues of private collections. Such a reference cannot fail to show that the irregular productions of the United States mint have been recognized, not without grave apprehension on the part of the public, as involving operations at least not imparted to the public, and under any circumstances open to serious objection. This appears from criticisms and animadversions found in numerous writings, from which it is unnecessary to furnish citations.[3]

But it will be here proper to remark that no little difficulty presents itself in a review of popular references to the subject in hand for want of agreement with mint usage in the employment of technical terms.

1. It is difficult to understand what Director Kimball means by "proven" in this instance. We have already seen why mechanics render it impossible for any of the 1804 silver dollars to have actually been struck in that year. The Eckfeldt restrike, or overstrike, had at the time of Kimball's report, in fact, been in the Mint cabinet for nearly three decades.

Other examples abound of which a few may be cited: The 1839 restrike half dollars (with the reverse of 1838) used planchets of 192 grains as were not authorized until 1853. The second group of restrike half-cents, which date from 1840 to 1852, were struck from a reverse die of 1856. The *Standard Catalogue of United States Coins* which lists nearly a hundred authenticated restrikings, states: "Many U.S. items now accepted as part of the regular coinage belong in this category, and will be included upon the completion of the present research."

In addition to these irrefutable examples, many official and unofficial statements acknowledging the practice of restriking have been preserved in the archives. We can only assume that these were somehow withdrawn from Director Kimball's notice during the time of inquiry.

ORIGINAL FOOTNOTES OF ANNUAL REPORT OF MINT DIRECTOR

3. "The whole business of mint patterns," says a writer in *The Nation* in 1879 (using the term *pattern* in the popular sense), "has been singularly managed, and to some extent, is so still. It has been estimated that in 1859 and 1860, $50,000 worth of patterns were struck and disposed of at the mint, without any benefit to the Government at whose expense they were coined. During Mr. Lincoln's administration these abuses stopped, but of late years they have begun again. For example, numerous pattern dollars, struck between 1869 and 1874, have since then turned up and passed into the hands of collectors, none of which appear in the Government Collection." (*American Journal of Numismatics*, XIII, 1879, p. 55.)

An estimate of the value of irregular pieces issued in two years from the mint at Philadelphia, as large as $50,000, must, in the absence of specific explanation, be taken as numismatic or trade value apart from intrinsic value, of which it is no measure.

There is, indeed, no reason to believe that the mint has at any period sustained loss of precious metals from irregular issues, their intrinsic value, as it is safe to assume, having in all cases been made good to the special department of the mint from which they took source.

And it may be considered that, whatever on the part of a few persons outside of the mint in a quest of the "Unique" has been the encouragement of the production of irregular compositions at the mint, it is scarcely conceivable that any encouragement would have been found but for the employment in mint regulations and circulars of an undefined, if not indefinite, terminology of a technical character in respect to at least the issue of cabinet coins. But the same extenuation does not suggest itself in favor of persons in the mint service, responsible for these compositions, especially in the failure of official evidence to show that their production has been regarded otherwise than of a personal or privileged character.

The condition of "fraudulent intent" has often been supposed to qualify the first clause of section 5460, as well as the second which refers alone to such acts as the defacement, increase, or diminution of weights used at the mint. It is obvious that only under such a mistake on the part of all who have been engaged in the production of so-called false-metal pieces for cabinet purposes and for tokens, could impunity from the severe provisions of this section have been found for its violation in such instances—as if in the extreme departure from the letter of the law were to be found security against violation of the spirit and intent.

The attention of this Bureau having been directed to the production in times past, and to the present circulation among coin collectors, coin dealers, etc. of unauthorized and unlawful pieces, more or less in semblance of regular coins of the United States; or of irregular impressions from coinage and experimental dies, alleged to have been struck since the date of the Coinage Act of 1873 and subsequent mint regulations prohibiting their issue, the following circular was printed for the information of the public:

TREASURY DEPARTMENT, BUREAU OF THE MINT
Washington, D.C., July 1, 1887

The emission of impressions of experimental dies, whether in soft metal or in metal of the same weight and fineness proper to coins of the same denomination, is unlawful except in the case of pattern pieces of such denominations of coins as are coined for general circulation during the calendar year of its date.

All impressions taken in copper, bronze, or other soft metal from an experimental die, are required to be destroyed as soon as the purpose for which it was struck is subserved.

The above provisions, prescribed by the "General Instructions and Regulations in relation to the Transaction of Business at the Mints and Assay Offices of the United States" approved by the Secretary of the Treasury, have been in force since May 14, 1874.

The striking of a piece in the semblance of a United States coin in a metal or alloy, or of a weight or fineness, other than prescribed by law, is a violation of section 5460 of the Revised Statutes.

The emission or offer for sale or exchange of an impression from any die of a coin of the United States, or of a proposed coin of the United States, but with a device or devices not authorized by law, whether such die has been prepared at the mint of the United States or elsewhere, is contrary to the provision of sections 3517 and 5461, Revised Statutes.

No impression from any coinage die of the United States struck in other metal than that authorized by law or of a weight and fineness other than prescribed by law (Revised Statutes 3513, 3514, 3515), or pattern piece bearing a legend of a coin of the United States, and bearing a device or devices not authorized by law (Revised Statutes, 3516, 3517, vide Mint Regulations) should be in existence longer than required for the lawful purpose for which it was authorized to be struck.

Any emission, for private or personal use or possession, from the mints of the United States of pieces of the character above specified has been in violation of the coinage laws of the United States.

James P. Kimball
Director of the Mint

Approved:
   C. S. FAIRCHILD
      Secretary of the Treasury

It would be difficult to imagine any hearts stout enough to defy this thunderous declamation. For over two decades, in fact, there were none. Then, in 1912, the small annual appropriation which had been granted to Robert Patterson at the inception of the Mint Cabinet was suddenly revoked. According to Director George E. Roberts in 1913, the Mint officials had managed to make both ends meet by selling the rarer date gold coins which had accumulated in the vault. Today we are acquainted with another explanation which the Director failed to mention, one which went undisclosed for nearly seven years.

In December 1919, a small advertisement appeared in *The Numismatist* magazine offering to buy . . . 1913 Liberty Head nickels. What a strange request! The Liberty Head nickel coinage had ceased as of December 13, 1912, and thereafter the Indian Head-Buffalo design was adopted for the denomination. No record of any 1913 Liberty Head nickel coinage, or of dies for such a coinage, appeared in the official coinage register of the Mint. Yet, six years later, one Samuel W. Brown of North Tonawanda, New York, was not only convinced of the existence of such coins, but was offering to pay $500. each to obtain them! In January, 1920, Brown "upped the ante" to $600., and with this figure the advertisement was repeated through March of that year. Four months later, at the annual convention of the American Numismatic Association, Samuel Brown showed a few of his friends a matched set of coins he had acquired—five 1913 Liberty Head nickels!

The second surprise occurred in January 1924, when a Philadelphia dealer named August Wagner offered for sale the identical set of nickels advertising them as "the only Five-Cent Liberty Head coins of this design and year in existence." The set was subsequently purchased by Col. E. H. R. Green, son of the eccentric millionairess Hetty Green. When the Green estate was settled in 1942, the five coins were consigned to B. G. Johnson who sold them individually. Two of the nickels were, at different times, owned by King Farouk, in whose Palace Collection many other great rarities were known to reside.

One rather obvious question with regard to the foregoing is how August Wagner could be sure of the exact number of 1913 Liberty Head nickels in existence, when no record of any such coinage was ever made. Is it possible that he obtained his information from the man who had the issue struck?

It is also of interest that Samuel W. Brown, the first man to *publish*, *set a price on*, and *display* all five 1913 Liberty Head nickels, was Assistant Curator of the Mint from 1904 to 1907, and Clerk (Storekeeper) at the time when these coins were struck. Since Brown joined the American Numismatic Association in 1906, we can assume that he was, even at that time, actively interested in rare coins. Since Brown *displayed* all five pieces just a few months after offering to purchase them, there is the further suggestion that he may have possessed the set all along, and merely been trying to establish a price.

Like the 1804 dollars and 1884-85 Trade Dollars, the 1913 Liberty Head nickels have not been without their apologists. It has been suggested that the delay in completing the new Buffalo nickel hubs occasioned the manufacture of dies of the old design, and, thus, that the striking of proof 1913 Liberty Head nickels for collectors during the period from Jan. 1 to Feb. 19, 1913 (when the new coinage was authorized) was legal and proper.

In answer to such arguments we would like to point out the following facts made available to the author by the present Director of the United States Mint.

In a letter dated December 13, 1912, the then Director George E. Roberts, specifically instructed the Superintendent of the Philadelphia Mint, John H. Landis: *"Do nothing about five cent coinage for 1913 until the new designs are ready for use."*

Fig. 63. Story of an unauthorized coin—the 1913 Liberty Head nickel.

On December 26, 1912, reductions (i.e. hubs) for the Buffalo nickel coinage were received by the engraver at the Philadelphia Mint.

On January 18, 1913, Director Roberts further instructed the Superintendent of the Philadelphia Mint as follows: "Replying to yours of the 17th instant I beg to say that you will not forward any working dies for the new five-cent nickel piece to the other mints until instructions to that effect are given. *Do nothing about any coinage at Philadelphia until you receive formal instructions to that effect.* The new design has not been formally approved."

On Feb. 19, 1913, formal authority for the commencement of Buffalo nickel coinage, together with directions for the distribution of the issue, was forwarded by Director Roberts to the Superintendent of the Philadelphia Mint.

Thus, not only does the official Mint register reflect no production of 1913 Liberty Head nickels, but we have the specific injunction of the then Director *forbidding* the production of any such coinage.

An official statement to the author by the present Director of the Mint, Miss Eva Adams, has further confirmed the fact that *no Liberty Head nickel coinage was authorized for the year 1913!*

The summing up

Some forty years have passed since the revelation of the 1913 Liberty Head nickels. The men who made the little issue the most talked about of all American coins—Max Mehl and Colonel Green—have departed, and, as the saying goes, a lot of water has passed under the bridge. As for the status of the so-called "cabinet coins," there is little that can be added to the remarks made by Director Kimball in 1877. We should only mention that the confiscation of a 1933 twenty-dollar gold piece on the grounds that it was issued without authority (a decision upheld by the courts), clearly sets the precedent by which 1804 dollars, 1884-85 Trade Dollars and 1913 Liberty Head nickels could likewise be seized without compensation. Whether collectors, once informed of this all too patent fact, will continue to pay four and five figure prices for such "fancy" productions, only time will tell.

V

NEW DIES FROM OLD—A POSTSCRIPT

IN January 1816, the Mint caught fire and much of its heavy machinery was destroyed. Some time later, as men were clearing away the debris, a small subterranean vault was unearthed and its contents, consisting of several old dies, were sold to a worker in scrap steel.[1] The dies were then resold to the budding numismatist J. J. Mickley, in whose possession most of them remained for over half a century, before being reappropriated by their original owner.

After Mickley's death, a great many of his coins were sold at public auction (November 1878) by Moses Thomas and Sons, of Philadelphia, the catalogue having been prepared by the well known dealer Ebenezer Mason. Although the collection consisted mostly of foreign coins, lots 905 through 918 are of considerable interest to us. They are described under the heading "*U.S. Steel Dies, Hubs, etc.*", and include no less than seventeen obverse and reverse dies for U.S. coins! Lot 912 reads "1811 2-Hubs [2] obv. and rev., United States half

---

1. Related by M. W. Dickeson, in an undated, unsigned MS., No. 10 in the bibliography, ANS.
2. These were not hubs, but dies.

cent; rev. slightly damaged on edge." The reverse was actually Gilbert Variety 1 of 1802, and from this muling, Mickley had struck off six pieces on bright red copper planchets, the dies having first been retooled and carefully polished in order to produce "proofs." [1] (*Fig. 64*)

An editorial in the *American Journal* of *Numismatics*, Vol. XIII No. 3, January 1879, describes the incident for us:

> *The statement that the dies, hubs, etc. of U.S. Coins, advertised for sale with the Mickley Collection, were seized by the United States authorities, has given rise to a great deal of comment. We have received from a gentleman in Philadelphia the following account of the affair.*
>
> "*A few days previous to the sale, the United States authorities claimed the above, viz: some 20 obverse and reverse dies of the U.S. coinage, mostly in damaged and corroded condition, the same having been condemned by the Mint authorities above 'half a century ago,' and as tradition says was the custom in those days, 'sold for old iron.' Since then, we have grown more artful, and it has been deemed politic under existing laws, that the whole multitude of dated dies should be annually destroyed in the presence of three designated officers of the Mint. In the above described lots in the catalogue, there was not a complete pair of obverse and reverse. Even the obverse die of the half-cent of 1811 was muled with a reverse die of a different year. We cannot conceive by what authority the government, after making sale of its 'refuse material,' could seize upon the same property without tendering some compensation. There is scarcely a numismatist in the United States, but who is aware of the existence and whereabouts of similar dies, and who is also aware of the many 're-strikes,'—known to be such,—being made from the dies say of the 1804 cent, the 1811 half-cent, and of the 1823 cent, outside of the Mint.*"
>
> *Philadelphia, December, 1878.*
>
> "Coulton" [2]
>
> *From what we have seen in the public prints in reference to this matter, we infer that the government authorities were somewhat hasty in their action, and claimed the property without first satisfying themselves as to the ownership. No one would for a moment suspect Mr. Mickley of any wrong doing in the matter. The affair was settled, we believe, by a payment to the family of the estimated value of the dies, which were then presented to the Mint, and subsequently destroyed.*

Among the dies that never returned home was an odd pair (obv. 1823, rev. 1813) for striking large cents. Mickley had sold the dies, in cracked condition, to Dr. M. W. Dickeson who, after taking several impressions, resold them to J. W. Haseltine. The few silver impressions extant are thought to have been struck by Haseltine in 1878

---

1. One of these curiosities eventually found its way into the "Dupont" collection and was sold in 1954 for $275.
2. R. Coulton Davis, the early specialist in patterns.

or 1879. Sometime prior to 1907, Charles Steigerwalt (the official counterfeit detector of the A.N.A.) discovered the dies in Haseltine's store and defaced them. They are believed, however, to still be in numismatic circulation. *(Fig. 65)*

The peculiar ease with which discarded dies could be removed from the Mint in the early days is described by Charles K. Warner, the veteran Philadelphia medallist, in a letter to *The Numismatist* magazine, December 1910. Warner writes:

> I have at times in the past promised to write you something regarding my boyhood days around the old mint building, which still stands on the east side of Seventh street and which was pictured and featured in the January and February *Numismatist* of this year.
>
> My father, the late John S. Warner, who from 1823 to 1868 was the oldest established medallist in the United States, was well acquainted with a certain William Sellers who for many years conducted the business of a silversmith in the old mint building. He occupied the entire first floor and a greater part of the basement. In the latter part of 1857, Mr. Sellers gave to my father a larger number of old coin dies which were a part of a great lot of both obverse and reverse dies for all the silver and copper denominations that Sellers found in the old building when he first occupied it years before. It was stated at that time that these were found among general rubbish when the basement was cleaned. Most of the dies were considerably rusted, chipped on the edges, or cracked across the face. My father having no use for the old dies gave them to a particular friend of his, the then Chief Coiner of the mint, which was then located in Chestnut street near Broad.
>
> As a lad I frequently visited the old mint building on errands to Mr. Sellers for my father and often played about the building with a son of Sellers, who was about my age. I well remember the old vault. I could easily have explored the vault, and no doubt could have found many things which, if preserved, would be of great interest today, but lad that I was, I had no interest in such things.

So carelessly were the old dies housed that when, on occasion, they turned up outside the Mint, it was seldom in pairs.[1] R. Coulton Davis states that of the twenty obverse and reverse dies seized from the Mickley estate, no two were found to match. For this reason, many of the out-of-the-mint restrikes are mulings of a rather unusual character, as, for example, the 1806 half dollar, shown here, which has for its reverse a twelve-cent postage stamp! The stamp is from

1. These should not be confused with the dies preserved by Franklin Peale and George K. Childs, for the "benefit of the Mint collection," all of which were carefully labeled with their date and maker.

an embossing die that had been used on postal envelopes between 1874-76. *(Fig. 66)*

We should mention here that the 1804 and 1810 large cents with the reverse of 1820 were, in all probability, struck outside the Mint, despite Proskey's assertion to the contrary. The 1804 obverse has been crudely altered from S-261 of 1803 by means of a graver (not a punch) and both pieces are much inferior to the standard set by J. R. Snowden's productions. *(Fig. 67)*

A recent example of out-of-the-Mint muling was provided us by a young New York City dealer. The reverse die of an 1814 dime (the "error" reverse with STATESOFAMERICA as one word) was used, together with an original obverse inscribed GOD PRESERVE PHIL-ADELPHIA AND THE LORD'S PROPRIETERS 1869. M (in honor of Joseph Mickley), to strike five hundred and thirty-six impressions in platinum, gold, silver and bronze. Distribution, however, was terminated prematurely by Government confiscation of all the coins and both dies.

Possibly the most famous of all American restrikes was made in 1879 from the die of a then unknown Confederate half dollar. In re-issuing the historical piece, J. W. Scott disclosed, for the first time, the story of the short-lived rebel coinage. *(Fig. 68)*

When the Confederacy took possession of the New Orleans Mint, one of its objectives was the establishment of an independent coinage. But though plans were drawn up and designs furnished, the feasibility of ever striking the coins slowly dwindled under the hard exigencies of war.

Only one die was ever cut—a reverse [1] showing the Confederate Seal, and in a muling of this with a U.S. half dollar obverse, four patterns were struck on an old screw press.

When, at the close of the war, the Federal government regained possession of the Mint, it confiscated the obverse die, but allowed the Confederate reverse to remain with the erstwhile Chief Coiner of the C.S.A., Dr. B. F. Taylor. In 1879, Taylor sold the die, together with one of the half dollars, via Ebenezer Mason, to Scott & Co. of New York, for what seems today a trivial sum of $310.

---

1. According to Scott, the Confederate Seal was intended as the obverse device, the U.S. obverse being forced to serve as reverse for lack of time and skilled labor. Modern numismatists, however, conventionally refer to the seal as the *Confederate Reverse.*

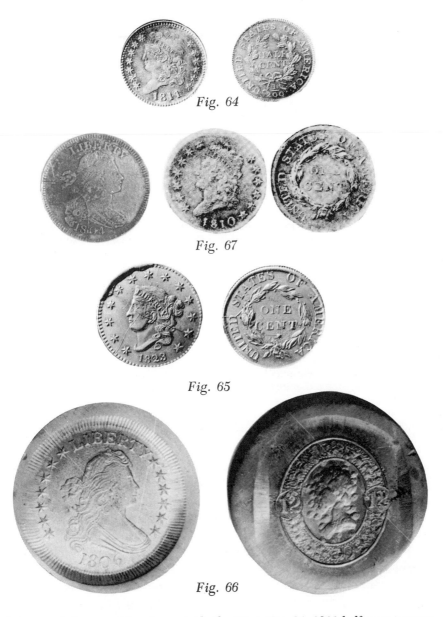

Fig. 64

Fig. 67

Fig. 65

Fig. 66

Coins struck from genuine dies *outside the Mint*. Fig. 64. 1811 half cent, reverse of 1802. The Mickley restrike; Fig. 67. 1804 and 1810 restrike cents, with reverse of 1820! Fig. 65. 1823 restrike cent, reverse of 1813; Fig. 66. Half coin, half postage stamp, from a die that got away. (Enlarged)

Scott, with the help of the numismatist-dealer David Proskey, obtained five hundred 1861 half dollars from the New Orleans Mint, shaved the reverse from each and restruck them with the Confederate die. The entire episode has been fortunately preserved for us by a pair of the original advertisements.

It may be asked whether Scott's avowed intention to overstrike five hundred U.S. half dollars with the emblem of a hostile provisional government did not evoke a few choice comments from his fellow colleagues. In the November, 1879 *Numisma*, Ed Frossard tells us:

It is said that the Fulton St. postage stamp dealers intend using the reverse die of this piece, at present in their hands, to restamp the reverse of genuine 1861, Orleans half dollars. A copy of the obverse die, which is, in fact, the identical obverse of the 1861 O halves, could not be manufactured with perfect safety, because of certain clauses of a well known U.S. law, which bear rather heavily on these points, but the wonderful fertility of resources of the head of the firm led him to adopt the clever dodge of simply restriking the reverse of genuine 1861 O half dollars with the so-called Confederate States half dollar reverse die, thus producing exact facsimilies of the originals. Unfortunately for the scheme there is another clause which forbids the wilful defacing, altering, etc., of United States coins, and the plan of thus increasing the number of Confederate States Half Dollars will moreover meet, as soon as known, with the marked hostility of the mint authorities, the numismatic societies and the collecting fraternity. The mint authorities should take immediate steps to recover this reverse die, which being made in a government building, with government tools, and by workmen paid with money stolen from the United States, clearly and unmistakably belongs to the United States, and place the same on permanent free exhibition in the mint cabinet, instead of allowing it to become the means of misleading and of deceiving collectors, in the hands of present or possible future speculative individuals.

In one respect, at least, Frossard was mistaken. Scott *did* overstrike the five hundred U.S. half dollars without government interference, and the mutations have been in numismatic circulation ever since. The cancelled Confederate die was last traced to Sanford Saltus who acquired it in 1918. Efforts to confirm Proskey's contention that Saltus presented the die to the Louisiana Historical Society have proved unsuccessful.

Of the four original Confederate half dollars, three can now be accounted for. The Taylor coin, which is the only one never to have seen circulation, now resides in the American Numismatic Society. Its weight is 192 grains. The other two pieces are owned by Eric P. Newman and John J. Ford Jr., and weigh 190.5 and 189 grains respectively. Ford, a well known numismatist, acquired his specimen under rather amusing circumstances. For many years he had avidly sought the great rarity, though without any real hope of ever acquiring it. To his friend Paul Franklin he once confided that he would even mortgage his house to obtain the fabulous piece! Then one night in May 1961, when Ford was attending an eastern convention, a dealer suddenly walked onto the floor and offered him a Scott restrike. It was 10:30 p.m. and Ford, who had been at his bourse table for some thirteen hours, scanned the piece with blood-shot eyes. It was only Fine plus and the owner wanted a rather high price, but after lengthy negotiations (known colloquially as "horse-trading") the coin was purchased. Paul Franklin, who had witnessed the transaction, then offered Ford a profit and, for the second time in five minutes, the piece exchanged hands. A few weeks later Ford prevailed upon Franklin to sell the coin back to him at a very substantial increase. The "restrike" had turned out to be not only an *original Confederate half dollar*, but is believed to be the identical specimen taken from Jefferson Davis at Fortress Monroe!

FOR SALE.
PRICE $1000.

CONFEDERATE HALF DOLLAR

SCOTT & COMPANY are pleased to be able to announce to Collectors, that they have purchased the celebrated Confederate half dollar, together with the die from which it was struck. They are therefore enabled to make the following offers to Amateurs who may wish to possess a re-strike of this interesting Coin :——

500 Coins will be struck from the original die, in *silver* of the weight and fineness of the original, after which the die will be destroyed. These 500 will be supplied to Numismatists at the rate of $2.00 each, and to insure a fair distribution, the following rules will be followed.

1. The Coins will be ready for distribution on the 15th of October, 1879.

2. Names of Collectors desiring to purchase, accompanied by the cash will be received up to the 10th of October.

3. No more than two of the coins will be supplied to any one person.

4. If the number of subscriptions received exceed 500, the names will be written on slips and Five hundred names drawn to whom the Coins will immediately be sent; while the money will be returned to those remaining.

5. In the event of the die breaking before the requisite 500 Coins have been struck, we shall immediately stop subscriptions and send out the number coined in the order in which the names were received.

6. As we consider this Coin to be the most interesting one ever struck in America, and have no doubt of its value as an investment, we pledge ourselves to re-purchase all offered us within one year from date at $2.00 each or at any time during the year 1881 at $3.00 each, in 1882 at $3.25 or in 1883 at $3.50 each; but they will in all probability be selling at $5.00 each before this year has expired.

The original Coin, (one of four—the other three being lost) can be had for $1,000 a written guarantee of genuineness and surrender value, accompanies the piece.

The die, damaged so as to prevent restriking can be purchased for $50.

While offering this valuable Coin for sale, a short account of it will prove interesting to purchasers, our remarks will necessarily be brief as we prefer to introduce sworn documents in preference to our own speculation.

On the 4th day of February, 1861, a party of conspirators organized an armed rebellion to the government of the United States and having taken possession of the U.S. branch Mint located at New Orleans on the 28th day of February, 1861, ordered the Superintendent, Mr. Wm. A. Elmore, to prepare dies for striking silver coins for use in those parts of the United States which were in rebellion; the time being short and skilled labor scarce, he economised both by using for a *Reverse* the die which had been heretofore employed in striking the *Obverse* of the U.S. half dollar of that year, making an entirely new Obverse die, which was engraved by A. H. M. Patterson—under the superintendence of Chief Coiner, B. F. Taylor, from these dies four (4) coins were struck which were disposed of as follows:

Jefferson Davis, President of the Confederacy.
Prof. Biddle, of the University of Louisiana.   one to each.
Dr. E. Ames of New Orleans.
Dr. B. F. Taylor, Chief Coiner of New Orleans Mint.

All the parties connected with the mint, are now living in New Orleans; they have made affidavits to the facts, as has been stated and are willing to verify them when desired. Thus it will be seen that the coin is genuine and fully authenticated beyond all doubt, and also it must be considered as one of the U.S. Series, for it was struck at the U.S. branch Mint by U.S. Officials with one of the regular U.S. dies, and from Government silver, the fact of the states being in rebellion, does not alter the facts of the case; for if we are to exclude this piece from the series, we must also strike out either the Siege pieces of Charles I or the coins of the Commonwealth from the English series; to say nothing of the vast array of Roman coins issued under similar circumstances; but we doubt if there is any Numismatist bigoted enough to affirm this, therfore, it must be placed at the head of the American series, being much rarer than the 1804 dollar of which at least eight are known, while this is unique. For historic interest there is only one other in the series which has any history attached to it, we refer to the "Franklin cent" which heralded the birth of a Nation: while the Confederate Half dollar shows the attempted destruction of freedom on the American Continent; and its rarity will show to distant ages the futility of the attempt.

This is the way the original Scott & Co. advertisement offered for sale the first known Confederate half dollar.

146 Fulton St., New York City,

October 17th, 1879.

Dear Sir:

It is with great pleasure we present you with the re-strike Confederate Half Dollar, subscribed for on the .... ult., and hope it will meet with your approbation. We regret the delay in forwarding, which was caused by the die breaking on the first trial, it then had to be set in a heavy steel band to prevent further damage; before risking the die again on the hard silver, we thought it advisable to strike the requisite number (500) in white metal, with the following inscription for a reverse: "4 originals struck by order of C. S. A. in New Orleans 1861. * * * * * * * rev. same as u. s. (From Original Die . Scott)." These will be sold in any quantity to those who subscribe to the Silver Confederate piece ; at 50 cents each. It was with difficulty we procured the 500 Half-Dollars of a special mintage, on which the pieces have been struck by a new method over genuine 1861 N. O. mint U. S. half-dollars, and in consequence they must rank high above ordinary re-struck coins.

The die (damaged only sufficiently to prevent re-striking,) is a very valuable and interesting relic, and is now for sale. Price, $50.

Up to the 10th inst. we received orders for 567 pieces; the odd 67 subscribers have been supplied from a like number of patrons who ordered two copies; this we concluded would be the more equitable plan for all parties concerned. Amateurs who ordered two will please remember that by this plan they certainly get one, whereas if they had drawn for chances they might have been left without any. We have received quite a number of orders since the 10th inst., all of which we are unable to fill, unless some of our subscribers, who get two, will kindly return one, for which we will be pleased to pay $2.50.

Respectfully,

SCOTT & COMPANY

A copy of this Scott & Co. letter accompanied each Confederate half dollar restrike to its new owner. According to David Proskey, Scott not only failed to sell out the issue, but had a plentiful supply for thirty years thereafter.

As a corollary to the above incident we should mention that specimens purporting to be "originals" are frequently offered for sale, though these are, of course, mere Scott restrikes. There are a few simple ways of differentiating between the two which every collector should know.

1. The weight of the restrike is about 185 grains, a loss of seven grains having occurred in shaving off the first reverse. The heaviest specimen seen weighs 186.9 grains, and is practically uncirculated.

2. The restrike shows die breakage along the beading opposite to the letters ER in AMERICA and L in DOL.

3. The obverse side of the restrike is buckled or flattened, an effect of the hard, plain brass plate which supported it. This feature varies from coin to coin, being most pronounced on the earliest pieces.

4. The reeding is almost completely obliterated, an effect of the plain edge collar used during the restriking.

It seems a little ironic that the dies for the Confederate cent should have been prepared by a Northerner. Yet, early in 1861, Bailey & Co., Philadelphia jewelers, agreed to provide a minor contract coinage for the "Southern Republic," and chose the well-known engraver Robert Lovett Jr. to execute the work. A year previously, Lovett had issued a store card showing a beautiful turbaned bust of Liberty, and the piece enjoyed extensive circulation. He now utilized the same punch for his Confederate cent, adding an equally lovely reverse in which a wreath of cotton, sugar cane, and tobacco enclosed the words "1 CENT." On the cotton bale at the bottom of the coin he placed a small initial L. *(Fig. 69)*

After striking twelve copper-nickel impressions, Lovett grew suddenly apprehensive over the nature of his assignment and, on his wife's advice, he hid the coins and dies in his cellar. A dozen years later one of two cents, which he had carried as pocket pieces and inadvertently spent in a tap room, reached the hands of Captain J. W. Haseltine who at once recognized it from its similarity to Lovett's store card. Haseltine paid several visits to the engraver, in the hope of obtaining the coins and dies, but could never draw him out until, one day, Lovett "slightly in his cups" pulled out a drawer in one of his cabinets, revealing a row of the little Confederate cents. Lovett then related the whole incident to Haseltine and allowed the Captain to purchase both the dies and the remaining ten coins. Haseltine, together with J. Colvin Randall, subsequently restruck a total of

Fig. 68

Fig. 69

Fig. 68. The Confederate half dollar; Fig. 69. The Confederate cent and dies. In 1961 the Robert Bashlow Co. made transfer dies from the originals and restruck more than 30,000 pieces in various metals. To the many collectors who could not previously afford this rarity, the restriking comprised the most important numismatic event of the year. At the completion of the issue, Bashlow presented both the original and the transfer dies to the Smithsonian Institute.

seventy-four pieces, consisting of seven in gold, twelve in silver and fifty-five in copper, all of which were offered for sale on April 2, 1874.

Soon afterwards, Henry Chapman (who was to become the doyen of American coin dealers and author of some of the most magnificently inaccurate catalogues ever compiled [1]) began his apprenticeship with Haseltine. Inventive by nature, young Chapman began to experiment with Haseltine's dies, and, before long, he struck a unique muling from the Confederate reverse and a Washington medalet obverse die, the latter of which had also been cut by Lovett.

From Haseltine, the Confederate dies passed successively to Judson Brenner, Virgil Brand, John J. Ford Jr., Q. David Bowers and Robert Bashlow. In 1962, Bashlow, using transfer dies, restruck more than thirty thousand impressions in platinum, silver, goldine, and bronze. The dies were then presented to the Mint collection now at the Smithsonian Institution.

The most interesting possibility, however, with respect to the Confederate cent was never realized. It is amusing to contemplate what might have happened if this little coin had actually been adopted, and the "Southern Republic" one day awoke to find its beloved Liberty Head adorning a Northern trade token!

1. In his catalogue of the celebrated Jenks collection Chapman, true to form, erroneously attributes the Confederate Cent dies to George H. Lovett, brother of Robert R.

CIRCULAR TO COLLECTORS

PHILADELPHIA, April 2, 1874.

Having succeeded in discovering and purchasing the dies of the Confederate Cent, we, the undersigned, have concluded to strike for the benefit of Collectors a limited number, and in order to protect those gentlemen who had the nickel pieces, originally struck in 1861, we determined to strike *none* in that metal. Our intention was to strike five hundred in copper, but after the fifty-fifth impression the collar burst and the dies were badly broken. They are now in the possession of Mr. Haseltine, and may be seen at any time at his store, No. 1343 Chestnut Street, Philadelphia.

The history of this piece is probably known to most Collectors, but, for the information of those who are ignorant of the facts, we will state that the dies were made by Mr. Lovett, of Philadelphia, in 1861, who says that they were ordered in that year for the South, and that he struck but twelve pieces, but probably thinking that he might have some difficulty in reference to them (having made the dies for the South), he mentioned the matter to no one until a few months since, when he parted with ten pieces, struck in nickel which he stated were all he had, having lost two pieces. One of the said lost pieces was the means of the dies and pieces being traced. Although the Southern Confederacy did not adopt this piece, it will always be considered interesting as the only coinage designed for the said confederacy.

Description.—Obverse, 1861; head of Liberty; inscription, "Confederate States of America;" reverse, a wreath of ears of corn and wheat, with a cotton bale at the bottom; in the centre, the words "1 Cent." The restrikes were struck by Peter L. Krider, No. 618 Chestnut Street, and we now offer them at the following prices:

Gold, only seven struck, each, ... $30 00
Silver, only twelve struck, each, ... 15 00
Copper, only fifty-five struck, each, ... 4 00
Nickel, originals struck in 1861, only four left, each, . . 20 00

All orders to be addressed to J. W. Haseltine. No 1343 Chestnut Street, Philadelphia.

Respectfully, J. COLVIN RANDALL,
JOHN W. HASELTINE.

PHILADELPHIA, April 2, 1874.

We, the undersigned, do hereby certify that the following is the exact number of pieces restruck from the dies of the Confederate Cent mentioned in the forgoing circular, and that the dies are now broken,

Seven in Gold,
Twelve in Silver,
Fifty-five in Copper,

J. COLVIN RANDALL,
JOHN W. HASELTINE,
PETER L. KRIDER.

An advertising circular by J. Colvin Randall and John Haseltine on the restriking of the Confederate cent.

VI

"PEDIGREED" FORGERIES

M ANY sonorous words have been written in praise of the numismatic pedigree, and there is little doubt that a coin which can be traced back to the cabinets of Matthew Stickney, J. J. Mickley, Charles Bushnell, or some other of the "favorite sons" of numismatics, will command its premium. Without seeking to disparage the wisdom of such sentimentality, we should point out, however, that the *value* of a pedigree lies, in the last analysis, in the appealing old-world ambience which one finds in a "special personality," and not in some extrinsic quality that is magically conveyed to the coin.

The finest of pedigrees, therefore, can only guarantee of a coin that *it is what it always was,* and not that *it is what it purports to be.* To illustrate this simple point, we are going to describe a number of very famous fabrications, all of which were, at one time, pronounced genuine by persons who, it seems to us, really should have known better.

The Wyatt counterfeits are perhaps the poorest examples of this thesis since they were exposed almost immediately following the notorious Chelsea "windfall," but the circumstances surrounding their manufacture and "distribution" are sufficiently provocative to warrant their inclusion here.

No attempt will be made, however, to cover the struck copies of Robinson, Idler, Dickeson, etc.,[1] which were obviously intended as "souvenir" productions, and would require an extreme ignorance, on the part of both dealer and collector, to be sold as genuine coins.

THE 1650 PINE TREE SHILLING

It was the autumn of 1854, just two hundred and two years after John Hull struck off the first New England shilling, and the spirit of the old Boston Mint House still lingered on in the hearts of collectors. In a day when numismatics had not yet come into its own, the silver Massachusetts shillings and their fractions retained a peculiar charm which kindled the imagination of young and old alike. Take the story of Getchell and Dr. Brown.

Getchell was a young man who knew very little about numismatics, though he possessed a curious and unaccountable passion for the coins of ancient Rome. Dr. Ammi Brown, on the other hand, was a prominent Boston collector who specialized in the Massachusetts series, a field in which he was considered to be very astute. Getchell had come to Dr. Brown seeking Roman coins, only to be told that the Doctor reserved his duplicates for trading purposes. Undaunted, Getchell declared that he had at home some 1650 and 1652 Massachusetts shillings which he had obtained from an elderly man in Boscawen, New Hampshire.

"1650 shillings?" The words reverberated in the Doctor's heart. Every Massachusetts shilling he had ever seen or heard of was dated 1652. If this young man actually possessed coins of an earlier issue, they must, perforce, be patterns—possibly the only ones in existence! Suppressing his emotion, Dr. Brown took a deep breath and replied that he would be interested in the coins, although he suspected that the informant was mistaken with regard to the 1650 date.

1. Bolen's copies are more deceptive, especially when rubbed, and a list of these, together with the identifying features of each, can be found in Richard Kenney's *Struck Copies of Early American Coins.*

Nevertheless, in about a week's time, Dr. Ammi Brown received by mail a large Pine Tree shilling, the date of which was indeed 1650. With bated breath, he wrapped up a duplicate 1652 shilling and a Roman coin from his own collection, and posted them for Getchell's approval. A few days later, his young correspondent replied that he was entirely satisfied with the transaction, and a short time thereafter, he re-appeared with four more 1650 shillings, three of which were struck on small flans. By trading off some more of his own pieces, Brown purchased the entire set, as well as several regular issue Massachusetts coins. Not knowing, as we do today, that the Pine Tree design did not originate until 1667, and the small flan type until 1675, he accepted the 1650 shillings as early Mint patterns. The crudeness of the workmanship, instead of arousing his suspicion, thus seemed natural and convincing of genuineness.

Fig. 70

Fig. 70. The 1650 Pine Tree shillings, large and small flans.

In 1858, Brown disposed of most of his collection, and three of the 1650 shillings, purchased from Getchell for next to nothing, were sold to the eminent collector J. J. Mickley, for $100 each, a very high price in those days. Another shilling went to a Mr. Brooks of Salem, and was afterwards sold to the Reverend Joseph Finotti.

In the meantime, news of the unique "patterns" had been bruited about the New England numismatic circles where it finally reached the ears of impressionable young Getchell. Ruing his impetuosity (and ignorant of the fact that Brown had already disposed of the coins), Getchell devised a scheme by which to regain them. He wrote to the Doctor, "confessing" that all the pieces he had sold to him were counterfeit, and avowing that, through the grace of the heavenly host, he had suffered a conversion, and now wished to make amends. Getchell enclosed a Massachusetts twopence obtained from Brown, and requested the Doctor to return one of the 1650 shillings, and to let him know how much money he should send for the other pieces, as he had parted with the coins received in trade. Brown, somewhat prejudiced by the favorable circumstances under which he had both purchased and sold the shillings, perceived that Getchell was lying, and in order to test him, he cut up one of the genuine 1652 shillings received from the young vendor, and enclosed it with a letter saying that it would take some time to obtain the other coins as they had passed from his hands. Brown added that he would mutilate these pieces also, to prevent their being used to perpetrate another fraud, and requested Getchell to reveal the identity of the counterfeiter. When Getchell failed to reply, Brown construed this to mean that the 1650 shillings were, after all, quite genuine.

For all practical purposes, our anecdote ends here. In 1857, a year before Brown disposed of his collection, the diary of John Hull was published, and from the scattered entries given, a chronology of the early Massachusetts coinage was slowly reconstructed. Sylvester Crosby, in his *Early Coins of America, 1873*, published Brown's account, but condemned the 1650 shillings as spurious. No one has since found cause to reverse the decision.

THE GOOD SAMARITAN SHILLING *(Fig. 71)*

In addition to its including two 1650 Pine Tree shillings, the Charles I. Bushnell collection was graced with the presence of another unusual specimen of early Massachusetts coinage called the "Good Samaritan shilling." This coin, which was unknown to numismatists until 1859, when it was purchased by Bushnell from the English dealer Charles Richard Taylor, was described by the Chapman Bros., in their catalogue of the Bushnell collection, 1882, as "known to be unique for over two hundred years."

Another Good Samaritan shilling, of somewhat different fabric, had been acquired by the Earl of Pembroke prior to 1730, and in 1848 it was purchased by the British Museum. This was a cruder variation of the same theme, except that it showed the words "Fac simile" above the device. The Chapmans interpreted this inscription to mean that the coin was a fabrication, probably copied from the Bushnell specimen, which they were offering for sale (without pedigree) as genuine. The sale of the "Bushnell shilling" to Lorin

Fig. 71. The "Good Samaritan" shilling: 1) Original seal of the British Commission of Sick and Wounded; 2) Pembroke specimen; 3) Bushnell specimen.

Parmelee for $650, touched off a controversy which continued until 1959, when Eric P. Newman published his classic monograph "The Secret of the Good Samaritan Shilling."

Newman discovered that the Pembroke specimen was actually a rubbed down Pine tree shilling (Noe 25), which had been counterstamped with the seal of the British "Commission of Sick and Wounded," a seventeenth century precursor to the American Red Cross. The cryptic words "fac simile" also appeared in the seal, in which context their meaning was quite clear. "Fac simile" was an abbreviated form of "fac similiter" which means "do likewise." These were the words which Jesus spoke to his listener in the Latin Vulgate version of the New Testament after telling the parable of the Good Samaritan. Newman goes on to show how the "Bushnell shilling" was copied from a 1769 drawing of the Pembroke fantasy, by Thomas Snelling, a British coin dealer (who had never seen the original, but himself had copied the earlier and unrealistic illustrations of Martin Folkes and the Pembroke catalogue plate), and how the counterfeiter, misconstruing the meaning of "fac simile," thus omitted the motto. The story is much too complex to be told in detail here, nor would doing so serve much purpose. We recommend, instead, that those who would like to curl up with the slickest true detective story in numismatics read for themselves Mr. Newman's monograph, which can be obtained from the American Numismatic Society in New York.

THE COUNTERFEITS OF THOMAS WYATT *(Fig. 72)*

Newman describes Thomas Wyatt as a self-styled professor who, in addition to being an active numismatist, edited and compiled "books on such varied subjects as conchology, French history, religion, natural history, poetry, geology and American military data."[1] In 1854 Wyatt published a book on American military medals, and by 1856, he had progressed sufficiently in his studies to give vent to his creative aspirations. In this year he ordered struck a dozen "sets" of early Massachusetts coinage which were subse-

1. Eric P. Newman, *The Secret of the Good Samaritan Shilling*, 1959.

quently distributed in and around Boston.[1] Each set consisted of a New England shilling and sixpence, an Oak Tree shilling and twopence, a Pine Tree sixpence, threepence and "penny," and a Good Samaritan shilling. An examination of these fabrications is very fruitful since it reveals 1) that the N E shilling and sixpence were copied from the engravings of Felt [2] (which in turn had been copied from those of Folkes), and that they show the horizontal striations which Felt added to illustrate the fields of these coins; 2) that the Oak Tree twopence was dated 1652 (instead of with the correct date of 1662) apparently on the authority of Folkes; 3) that a non-existent Pine Tree penny was made on the authority of Felt, after the original error of Folkes; and 4) that the words "fac simile" were omitted from the Good Samaritan shilling because of their earlier omission by Felt who had misunderstood the meaning of the motto.

The distribution of the Wyatt counterfeits, and their subsequent detection, are revealed to us through a series of contemporary reports collated by the *American Journal of Numismatics* in July, 1872. The first article, from the *Boston Journal,* is dated June 16, 1856.

Relics of By-Gone Days.—We had the pleasure of seeing today some of the Pine Tree money of Massachusetts, which was dug up some time since at Chelsea.
There were a shilling, sixpence, threepence, and twopence, dated 1652, in almost as good preservation as if they had been coined one year (ago) only, every letter and figure upon them being perfectly clear and distinct; they probably have been entombed for more than one hundred and fifty years. The bottle in which they were found, and several of the coins, were purchased by a gentleman to be presented to the British Museum.

The editor of the *American Journal of Numismatics* then comments:

The day after the appearance of the above we made diligent inquiry as to the finder of the coins. No one at the office of the Journal, *in which it appeared, could give any information in relation to the matter. The "oldest inhabitant" in Chelsea had never heard of it, not even "Mrs. Parkington," who resided there, of whom we made inquiry.*

---

1. In a letter dated July 11, 1856, Wyatt wrote to the Boston numismatist Jeremiah Colburn: "I can obtain the whole series, viz.: 12-6-3-2-1, five pieces, by making an exchange with some of my medals; if you wish it, I will do so. . . . I will have in my possession, shortly, a fine specimen of the Good Samaritan."
2. Joseph B. Felt, *An Historical Account of the Massachusetts Currency,* 1839.

But, on August 19, 1856, the *Boston Transcript*, in an article entitled "The Counterfeit Pine Tree Money," reported:

It is remarkable to observe how many different means unprincipled people resort to to replenish their empty purses. Too proud to work for an honest livelihood, and too indolent to engage in some legitimate pursuit, their wits are constantly at work devising new ways to fatten themselves upon the industry of others. Their craving thirst for lucre must be satisfied at all events, even though it be at the sacrifice of every sense of honor and principle. The most novel example of this has lately come to our knowledge. A few weeks since a paragraph appeared in several of our papers, stating that a large number of pine tree coins had been recently dug up in this vicinity. No sooner had this announcement been made than complete sets of this coinage poured into our city. "N.E." shillings and sixpence, before so rare, together with some other pieces never before seen, were to be found exposed for sale in this city. The extraordinary appearance of such a number of coins before held so rare, naturally attracted considerable attention from every one, and called for the investigation of the curious in such matters as to the cause of this great and sudden windfall. Some few of our most credulous and superstitious citizens were pretty well settled in their own convictions that the spirit of good old John Hull had entered among us once more, and some even fancied that at certain times of night, distinct sounds of an old rusty, creaking screw press could be heard from the quarter where the old mint house once stood.

It has, however, turned out that all these pieces are counterfeit, and made by a man in New York City, who represents them to be originals, and has disposed of numbers of them to our antiquarian friends, at exorbitant prices. Such a piece of rascality is seldom revealed, and it would be well if some of those who have been victims of this extortion, would ferret out and bring to justice the fellow who would resort to such a contemptible mode to replenish his empty purse.

"NOVUM BELGIUM."

In May, 1864, a small but "select" offering of American colonial coins was sold at public sale by a young Yale sophomore named C. Wyllys Betts. Preceding the description of the lots, a rather curious notation advised that:

Very many of the pieces here offered, are struck from excessively rare dies, recently engraved, all of which are destroyed, and every piece being the best in existence, it is the sincere wish of the owner that they meet with satisfaction.

The following coins were then listed.

   1. *N.E. Sixpence (not Wyatt's); silver, unique.*
   2. *Pine Tree Shilling, 1653. "Massachusetts in." "New England, Anno 1653, XII;" silver, very fine, unique.*

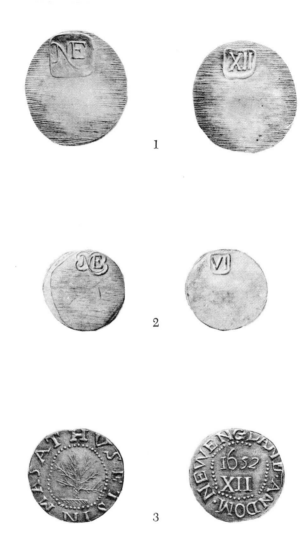

Fig. 72. The counterfeits of Thomas Wyatt; 1) N.E. shilling; 2) N.E. sixpence; 3) Oak Tree shilling;

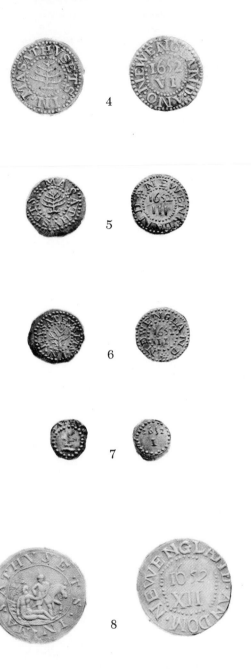

Fig. 72 (Continued). 4) Pine Tree sixpence; 5) Pine Tree threepence; 6) Oak Tree twopence; 7) Pine Tree "penny"; 8) "Good Samaritan" shilling.

3. *Connecticut Shilling. Obv.: grape vine, "Connecticut in." Rev.: "New England, An.Do. 1662 XII." Struck over an unique N.E. Shilling (not Wyatt's); silver, very fine, excessively rare, and in respect to the N.E. Shilling, unique.*

4. *Lord Baltimore Shilling; silver, very fine, unique.*

5. *Lord Baltimore Sixpence; silver, very good, unique.*

6. *Lord Baltimore Penny. Engraved, unique.*

7. *Obv.: Goddess of Liberty facing left. "Colony of." Rev.: bust in armor facing right. "New Yorke;" excessively rare in lead. This specimen is in silver, and unique.*

8. *New York Piece. Obv.: Beaver on Shield (old coat-of-arms of New York under the Dutch government), "Novum Belgium, 1623." Rev.: Crown "Peter Masuit" (first Gov.): lead.*

9. *Rhode Island Piece Obv.: "Rhodia Orsula, 1779." Rev.: "Nova Brittania, 1." Copper, very fine, excessively rare.*

10. *Annapolis Sixpence, 1783; silver, very fine, unique.*

11. *Auctori Plebis 1785; very fine, unique.*

12. *"Nova Constellatio," Rev. "Immune Columbia, 1785." Obv.: "Genuine." Very fine, unique.*

13. *"Immunis Columbia, 1786." Rev.: Shield "E Pluribus Unum. "Rev. Genuine; good, unique.*

14. *"Non vi virtute vici, 1786;" fine, unique.*

15. *"Nova Eborac." Rev.—"Immune Columbia, 1786;" very fine—excessively rare.*

16. *"George III. Rex." Rev.: Immune Columbia, 1785; very fine. Obv. Genuine; excessively rare. (All the dies of "Immune Columbia" are different).*

17. *New Hampshire Cent. Obv.; Bust in armor, facing right, "Nova Hamps." Rev.: Figure of Liberty, seated facing right; "Libertas, 1787;" very fine; two struck.*

18. *"Liber Natus Libertatem Defendo," Indian standing. Rev.—Eagle, "Neo Eboracus, 1787, Excelsior;" very fine, unique.*

19. *Obv.: The same, Indian standing, Rev.: coat-of-arms of N.Y., "1787, excelsior;" very fine, unique.*

20. *"Non vi virtute vici." Rev.—Eagle. "Neo Eboracus, 1787, Excelsior;" fine, unique.*

21. *Washington medal. Obv.: Bust to right. "Washington." Rev.: Five-pointed star, "Commander of the Armie of Virginia;" copper, very fine; very slightly double struck; unique.*

22. *Washington medal. Obv. Two ships sailing, "George Washington," Rev.: Payable to John Kerdrig. T.O.O.E.W.T.T.W.N." Silver, very fine, unique.*

Such a piece has (sic) to have been issued in 1794, but no original is in existence.

We should add, for clarification, that the name Peter Masuit, mentioned in lot No. 8, was intended to read Peter Minuit, and that this piece, properly called "Novum Belgium," sold to a Mr. Nixon for forty cents.

After a thirteen year silence we again hear of "Novum Belgium," this time from Edouard "Ed" Frossard's newly founded Journal *Numisma*. In the November 1877 issue, Frossard writes:

*DISCOVERY OF A COLONIAL COIN RELATING TO NEW NETHER-
LANDS. On the 19th of September last, and while awaiting the opening of the
Balmanno coin sales at Bangs & Co., in Broadway, Captain Wilson Defendorf,
a well known New York collector, submitted to our inspection a copper coin
of which the following description will suffice for the present:*

*Obverse, Earl's crown, PETER MINUIT. Reverse, Triangular shield with
slightly curving border, and beaver in field of rippling waters, NOVUM
BELGIUM 1623; border serrated, size 18. In condition this coin can be
described as a somewhat weak impress, especially in certain parts of the
legends, but not to any extent abrased or circulated.*

*Of the meaning of the words "NOVUM BELGIUM" we had previously
communicated to Capt. Defendorf our opinion that they were to be translated
by "NEW NETHERLANDS," an assertion which we offered to prove by
referring to various historical works; nothing remained therefore but to
examine the coin critically, and our impression after a thorough and minute
inspection that the piece bore on its face the testimonials of age and authenticity
was shared by Mr. David Proskey, though dissented from by Mr. Cogan; these
two gentlemen, Captain Defendorf and ourself being the only ones who took
part in the discussion.*

For the next two pages, the reader is inflicted with a rambling
dissertation (based on Brodhead's and Dunlap's histories of N.Y.),
in which he is told of the founding of New Netherland under the
Dutch West Indian Company, of the Governor Peter Minuit, and
other luminous accounts proving the historicity of fabulous "Novum
Belgium," which the editor has "the honor of bringing . . . to the
notice of the American collectors . . ."

Fig. 73. "Novum Belgium."

Of the journals that wisely doubted *Numisma's* findings, none
were so vociferous in their reaction as the rival *Coin Collector's
Journal* of J. W. Scott. In the December, 1877 issue, the editor writes:

*THE LAST DISCOVERY. The illustration given above is one of a class
of coins which have been common in all ages, and we suppose will continue to
appear 'til the millennium, as they are usually conceived by cupidity, brought
forth by lies, and adopted through ignorance. Novum Belgium is an exception
to this rule only in the fact that it was made by a young man to pass away
time, and sold at public auction as a fraud, so that no one could offer any
excuse for being taken in by it, much less the editor of a numismatic paper,*

unless that the difficulty of acquiring the English language offers obstacles so insurmountable to the average foreigner as to prevent him from attaining a useful knowledge of it, or as he has lately shown himself incapable of even understanding such a classical (?) work as a coin sale catalogue, for we cannot suppose that any respectable person, much less one who devotes his life and talents to the education of the young, would knowingly descend to falsehood.

The coin of which we propose to give the history may be briefly described as follows:

Obverse, *Beaver on shield, NOVUM BELGIUM, 1623.*

Reverse, *Crown, PETER MINUIT.*

It is the property of Capt. Defendorf, a well-known and highly esteemed collector of this city, who became possessed of it many years ago; having purchased it along with a lot of old coins, he has kept it from that day to this without ever attaching any importance to it. On looking over a lot of his coins, he thought he would try to find out something about it. He, accordingly, carried it with him to a coin sale, and asked the opinion of a few collectors concerning it. The general opinion was that it was a fraud, which was concurred in by the writer for reasons given below, and probably would have never been again noticed had it not been for the fact that a young editor had his acutely reasoning, historical and critical faculties terribly mixed by the bewildering anticipation of being the first to have "The honor of bringing out the coin to the notice of the American collectors and numismatics." (Sic.) Whatever this curiously constructed sentence may mean, it really is amusing to think how pathetically he must have pleaded with the owner for all the credit, and we certainly shall not be cruel enough to rob him of one particle of the renown which his excellent judgement and deep historic learning entitle him to receive from all well-informed numismatists.

Our reasons for not believing in the authority of the coin were:

1st. The style of engraving did not correspond with that of the period in which the coin as professed (by the date) was made.

2nd. We know of no person connected with New Amsterdam of the name of Peter Minuit, and if it was intended for Peter Minnewit we think it quite probable he knew how to spell his own name, even if his English contemporaries preferred to call him Minuit or Minuits.

3d. We thought it scarcely probable that the then (1623) Governor of New Amsterdam, Jacobson May, would have coins struck with the name of one of his successors on them. These trifles, however (although he was not ignorant of them), were not allowed to bias the judgement of our critic.

4th. Mr. Cogan, a gentleman of excellent judgement, who has grown gray in the study of numismatics, said that he knew it to be false, and gave the name of the probable maker; we never allow our opinion to stand in the way of obtaining facts, when a few hours' investigation would settle the matter.

Again, regarding the manufacture of the coin, we will show how easy it is to get up a fraud that will deceive some people. A young gentleman (we do not give his name although it is an open secret), finding time hang heavily on his hands, amused himself by engraving dies in imitation of rare coins; afterward he branched out and designed some altogether fictitious, a list of which together with his counterfeits, we subjoin.[1] His mode of work was simply

1. The May 1864 auction sale.

to take two large U.S. cents, and file one side perfectly smooth, and then sitting at his desk, dig out the designs with his penknife, an operation requiring great labor, but not more than has been accomplished by mere school boys in cutting out the heads on pennies. After both sides were finished, he would take another cent, and file both sides smooth, and placing this between his dies, hammer it until he obtained a pretty fair impression, which our contemporary justly described as a "somewhat weak impress, especially in certain parts of the legends, but not to any extent abrased or circulated!"

But, like Goldsmith's famous schoolmaster, the dauntless *Numisma*, "though vanquished, argued still." In the January 1878 issue, Frossard replied:

In regard to the "Novum Belgium" coin described in our last, we reiterate our opinion, shared by several of the most prominent coin collectors in the United States, that the piece owned by Capt. Defendorf is an original coin issued in Holland sometime between the years 1625 and 1632. Of the base imitations so accurately described by our contemporary, we know nothing whatsoever except that they undoubtedly exist. The fact, however, that counterfeit coins, postage stamp restrikes, and other abominations are in the market, only gives proof of the existence of the originals.

At a future time we hope to present our readers additional data concerning the coin in possession of Captain Defendorf; in the meanwhile we decline further controversy with the publishers of the C.C.J. We view the personal attacks they have made upon us with the same indifference as we do their opinions on coins, but we are ready at any time to enter into a friendly discussion of the subject with any other numismatic publication or with individuals.

True to its word (though in a more penitent mood), the March 1878 issue of *Numisma*, presents us with the following additional data. Under the title of "FABRICATION," Frossard writes:

If the so-called Novum Belgium copper described in the December number of this journal, had by any possible chance fallen into our hands eighteen years ago, we do not think that, even with the most mediocre abilities, it would have taken us well nigh a quarter of a century to discover its true nature! The error of supposing that the discussion relates not so much to the origin, as to the meaning of the legend, coat of arms, etc., led us into the further error of adopting the coin as genuine, because, when we studied the subject, we found that it harmonized with historical facts relating to the period to which it was described.

We overlooked the fact that the same chain of historical items which enabled us to place the coin and to describe it correctly, had, by a sort of priori reasoning, been the very cause of its birth. In other words, the Novum Belgium copper, and in fact most of the coins related to it, were manufactured for the purpose of illustrating some definite event, either in history or in the life of the designer, his friends or business acquaintances. When, in an interview with the gentleman who so successfully and ingeniously, yet innocently, imposed upon the credulity of his numismatic friends by his original productions, we enumerated the facts that had led us into a belief of the authenticity of Novum Belgium, he informed us that the same passages in the works we had consulted had suggested to him the making of that coin. In describing to us some other coins with like historical reference, Mr. —— drew in ink a most beautiful design of the clever "Masa: Plym: Con: New Haven, United Colonies of N. England," 1643, with pine tree in center, piece, which struck in silver, he presented some fifteen years ago to Mr. C. I. Bushnell, author of several numismatic works. The facility and elegance with which this coin was drawn from memory, after so many years during which the author had not given the slightest attention to the subject, convinced us that from such hands the Novum Belgium, after all, was only a bungling piece of work! It was indeed fortunate that the remarkable gifts possessed by this gentleman should never have been urged with a sinister motive, or for the purpose of gain! The majority of the coins thus manufactured, sometimes as many as two in one evening, and numbering altogether nearly two hundred types were eventually placed into the Yale college collection, where, after lying dormant for a long time, they may in future years again become the subject of learned (?) and heated discussion! But few found their way into the cabinets of collectors, and these mostly described in the interesting letter we append. It is the earnest desire of the originator of these coins, who years ago gave up all interest in fabrications, and regrets that anybody should ever have been deceived by them, that they should be returned to him for final cancellation, and we promised to do our utmost to assist him in this object.

The following letter, from C. Wyllys Betts to Frossard, is appended:

Dear Sir:

I have been away from home for some time or your request would have been earlier remembered.

It was in 1860 that I made my first attempt at die cutting and the occasion was the receipt of a quantity of coins and medals from some New York dealers for inspection. After selecting those which my collection lacked, I sold the rest to various collectors in New Haven, and thereupon in commemoration of this business enterprise I struck a medal with this obverse: CONNECTICUT, with three pine trees in the center, and on the reverse my own name, with the words, "Coins and Medals, New Haven, 1860."

About half a dozen were struck in lead and one in copper. The latter is in the Yale college collection, and is a very good impression. The die is altered to 1861.

My next attempt at coinage was a leaden token with the inscription, "Colony of New Yorke," the latter words being on the obverse surrounding a head. One of these tokens I sent to Mr. Mickley of Philadelphia.

It was some time before I acquired sufficient skill to make impressions in any metal but lead. The dies were cut in copper or sometimes brass, and were so soft as to be often destroyed in the attempt to stamp upon copper or silver. I believe that my first successful impression upon copper was from dies having the obverse of the "Nova Eborac," and the reverse, "Immune Columbia."

The dies were cut upon coins of the halfpenny size, either worn smooth or filed away on one side. My only tools were an awl for cutting the letters and the outlines of the figures, and a knife for gouging out the broader parts of the designs. When the cutting was finished each die was heated white hot and dipped into cold water. A third smooth copper of the half-penny size was then heated and placed between the dies, and the three, being quickly rolled together in sheet lead, from a tea box, to prevent them from slipping, were pounded upon an anvil with a six-pound dumb-bell. The heating process gave an air of antiquity to the pieces. . . .

Unfortunately some one, about 1862, presented me with a set of letters (i.e. punches) and several engraving tools, and in learning the use of them I made a great number of store cards and medallets, most of which are unique, and all, I think, in the Yale College collection.

The earlier ones I look upon with some interest because they used to afford me a great deal of amusement, not only in the making, but in the astonishment of collectors when looking over my cabinet.

Yours truly,
(C. Wyllys Betts)

THE 1665 XII PENCE

The discovery, by Frossard, of C. Wyllys Betts, soon led to a reappraisal of nineteenth century counterfeit-detecting techniques. Thus, when David Proskey inquired about an unpublished "Immunis Columbia" cent he had discovered, Frossard replied: "We suggest that Mr. P. pursue the same course that we did with the Novum Belgium. If our nameless correspondent rejects the coin at sight as not of his fabrication, then it is undoubtedly genuine; but if he recognizes in the piece an old friend, then only one more illusion will be dispelled."

Nevertheless this sort of thing can be carried a little too far, as evidenced by the July 1881 issue of *Numisma*, where Frossard, still the champion of lost causes, describes his latest "find."

The 1665 XII Pence. Obverse. COL°M°N.E. Star or sun with long rays in centre. Rev. XII PENCE 1665. Milling triangular or rounded; size 16, silver.

The above described piece was originally purchased at $3.00 by Mr. John C. Schayer of Boston, Mass., of a countryman from the vicinity of Concord, N.H. who declared that he had known of its existence many years, and that the former owner possessed a VI pence of the same design.

Mr. Crosby, who saw the piece, we are informed, neither rejected, nor adopted it as a genuine Colonial coin, but thought that further investigation might throw more light on its true character and history.

In the meanwhile, Mr. Woodward, who had purchased the piece of Mr. Schayer, for $5, placed it in his sale May 6-7, 1880, where it was purchased by *us at $11. From careful inquiries made by us, we can positively state that the piece is not of recent manufacture. The designer of the Novum Belgium and other coins, as will be seen by the letter following this article, disclaims this piece and knows nothing of its existence, and a few well informed numismatists share our opinion in ascribing its origin to the year 1665. In general design, metal, weight and execution the piece is a close imitation of the New England and Massachusetts shillings, and there is nothing modern in the appearance of the coin. We are almost forced to the conclusion that the piece was designed and issued by a private individual, in imitation of the regular coinage of the Colony of Massachusetts, and intended for circulation. It is well known that the Massachusetts coinage was never authorized but only tolerated by the English government, and it is quite possible that a private individual may have conceived the project of a private mint, as a private venture, with the supposition that the Colonial authorities, themselves the issuers of an unauthorized coinage, would offer no opposition to the undertaking. Such was however not the case, and the bold innovator must have discovered at his cost that there was after all a marked difference between the acts of an organized Colonial Government and those of a private individual. If these surmises be correct this coin may be considered as the first of American tokens, preceding the issue of the celebrated Granby coppers by nearly seventy years. The discovery of other shillings from the same dies or of the six pence would conclusively establish the claims of this coin to be ranked among the "Early Coins of America."*

The following letter is appended to the above: "Mr. Ed. Frossard. Dear Sir:—The token of 1665, "XII Pence, N.E. COL.M.," is not of my manufacture. You must feel at liberty at any time to ask such questions. Please do not forget my request that all such pieces of my work as you may discover may be returned to me. Yours truly, C. Wyllys Betts."

Fig. 74. The "1665" XII Pence.

This time, however, it was dealer Ebenezer Mason who led the assault. In his September, 1881, *Coin Collector's Herald*, Mason writes:

Numisma (Bi-monthly) for July, received and scanned with considerable interest. The quarrel, or rather "unpleasantness" between the editor and our Roxbury friend, W.E.W., continues, to the amusement of the lookers on. W., it seems, inserted in one of his recent catalogues a detailed story of one Ichabod, in the Rip Van Winkle style, leaving the reader to form his own conclusions as to the party hit. Numisma *hits the author of the pleasant little bit of satire in numerous spots; and the fun continues. The main editorial in the current* Numisma *is devoted to the recent fabrication entitled by the editor, "THE 1665 XII PENCE." We "Si still and say nix." (This is meant for a foreign expression, only appreciated by the French); but we smile as we think of one individual in New England who will read the description of the unique (?) coin, and, as he reads it, will "giggle" right out. We are led to suppose this exuberance of humor on the part of the N.E. gent, by various circumstances which are not exactly facts, or references of a positive nature, concerning what we believe to be a recent manufacture in a numismatic way, but having had duplicates of the aforementioned coin (?) we feel like the man that knew something. . . . The idea that C. W. Betts made the 1665 shilling is ridiculous, and did not require a contradiction, which appears in* Numisma, *from the distinguished originator of the greatest numismatic frauds ever perpetrated in this country. Oh Betts! Betts! You have much to answer for, and it appears that your contrition over the subject of making the Colonial (?) pieces is genuine, and the boys are willing to forgive you, but who pays the cost? . . .*

To this wise if whimsical refutation we need only add the following article from the November 1881 issue of *Numisma*. Frossard writes:

In his remarks about what he is pleased to call our "unpleasantness" with Dr. Woodward, Bro. Mason loses sight of the fact that all Numisma *has published under that score have (sic) been really only fair, honest and truthful criticisms of certain coins offered by the Dr. in his sales, while thus far the Dr.'s replies have been simply of personal abuse and vituperations. The 1665 XII pence was purchased as stated in July number of* Numisma, *and if of recent manufacture, the fact, if proved, would certainly add another feather to the Dr.'s cap, who is responsible for its introduction at a sale to the purchasing public. It is true that at the time of the sale several buyers, whom we can name, publicly announced it to be spurious, but our faith in the Dr.'s statements made to us at the time was so unbounded that we actually bid against the Dr. himself up to $11, at which price he kindly let us have it. What we now want to see is not so much a duplicate of the piece, which would prove nothing, as a statement printed by Bro. Mason, or sent us by him, or anyone else, giving the full history of the piece, its origin, where manufactured, etc. Give us facts Bro. Mason, not simply innuendos and we shall cheerfully acknowledge that like the boy in Franklin's Almanac "we have paid dearly for our whistle."*

In answer to the above, which we privately submitted to Brother Mason, he sent us the following information, which we add with comments.

"In regards to the 'XII pence,' I may be in error, and prefer not to say too much. I saw two duplicates and purchased them, receiving $5 each for them when sold. We do not know positively that the pieces are of recent manufacture but from the price, the man, and other circumstances I presumed the piece was "a catch." I think yours will fetch $10 or more at a sale, for I do not believe any more can be had at any price, as I subsequently to my first purchase offered $4.50 each for two more, and the answer was "have none." I was led to think they were bogus, because I secured from the same source 2 copper bar cents having similar rude workmanship."

THE WASHINGTON HALF CENT *(Fig. 75)*

From the terse descriptions usually given of the 1793 "Washington half cent," we should have little idea of the storms of controversy which once raged over this quaint fabrication. Two original specimens, as well as several electrotypes exist which, appearance-wise, may be described as follows: obv. military bust of George Washington facing r.; rev. the regular half cent die of Breen B, Crosby A.

One of the originals can be seen in the Mint collection, now at the Smithsonian Institute. It was first published, without comment, in J. R. Snowden's "Washington and National Medals," 1861, and thereafter, in the 1914 Catalogue of the Mint collection compiled by T. L. Comparette.

The other piece was first recorded in the 1882 Bushnell sale where it was described by the Chapmans as "A fabrication of the period with genuine rev. as is the Mint specimen; only two known. A pattern?" Although the wonderful alchemy by which a fabrication could be transformed into a pattern was never explained, the Washington half cent, so described, was bid up to $21, presumably by William S. Appleton who subsequently presented the piece to the Massachusetts Historical Society.

As early as 1869, however, Ebenezer Mason had wisely doubted the authenticity of the Washington half cent, and Elliot Woodward, in his Holland Sale, Nov. 11, 1878, described an electrotype copy as an "Electro of the imaginary Washington Half Cent of 1793." In an all-out assault on that anomalous superstructure, the *Bushnell Catalogue,* Woodward further tells us: [1] ". . . the Washington Half Cent of 1793 is stated to be 'a fabrication of the period,' a statement wholly unsupported, if 'by the period' is meant 1793. Those persons who commenced the study of American Numismatics several years ago, are aware that this coin is referable to the 'period' when Mr. Edwin Bishop, an ingenious mechanic, kept his shop in Dutch Street, New York City."

Nevertheless, time has a peculiar way of reviving old myths, and in the July, 1897 issue of the *American Journal of Numismatics,* we find no less an authority than Sylvester Crosby writing: "It is impossible to state with certainty that this (the Washington half cent) was

1. *The Montreal Sale,* July, 1882.

intended as a pattern, but as it has every appearance of a genuinely struck piece, with reverse from a die used with the Half Cents of the regular issue, I am inclined to believe it to have been so intended, and therefore give it a place upon the plate as a pattern."

Then, in 1912, thirty years after he had described the Bushnell piece as a "fabrication of the period," Henry Chapman, in one of his proverbial moments of wool-gathering, wrote to Edgar Adams, the authority on pattern coins: [1]

> In regard to the article, on page 213, in regard to THE UNITED STATES HALF CENT, a fourth paragraph states "It is remarkable that no pattern has been made from the half cent at the United States Mint." I beg to draw your attention to the half cent of 1793 with bust of George Washington, in place of the usual head of Liberty, which is spoken of in Baker's work on Medallic Portraits of Washington, under No. 27, page 21, and in Crosby's work on 1793 Cents and Half Cents, letter A, plate III, page 33 and 34. Frossard also mentions it in his Monograph, and Appleton describes it in his Description of Medals of Washington. In the Bushnell collection it is described on page 24. It is also spoken of in Snowden, page 39.

It is interesting to note that while Chapman refers to the works of Baker, Snowden, and Appleton, he fails to mention that none of these writers attributed the Washington half cent as a pattern, and that Baker specifically denied it such a status. Furthermore, the reference to Frossard is entirely in error.

In 1951, nearly forty years after Chapman's classic pedigree, Walter Breen examined the Mint specimen which Crosby had described more than a half century before. Breen observed that not only was the reverse of the coin genuine, but that the word LIBERTY, and the first three date punches were identical to those on the regular 1793 half cent. This precluded the possibility of muling, and called for a closer scrutiny of the Washington device. A faint circular line around the bust told the story: The Washington half cent was, after all, no more than a genuine 1793 coin on which the Liberty Head had been ground down, and replaced by brazing on a new design! The top of the 3 had been retooled to make it round, and the whole coin recolored to disguise the fraud.

It is amusing to contemplate the possibility that the "ingenious mechanic" Edwin Bishop made the first of these fabrications for

1. *The Numismatist* Magazine, November 1912.

the purpose of trading it to Director Snowden, who was avidly seeking new Washington pieces for his pet collection. Considering the sum and source of Snowden's numismatic material, the swap would have been, no doubt, an equitable transaction.

THE EDWARDS 1796 HALF CENT *(Fig. 76)*

Whether the responsibility for striking this fabrication lies with Dr. Frank Smith Edwards of New York, or with the notorious British counterfeiter "Singleton" (alias Dr. James Edwards) cannot now be determined. In the first recorded sale of this forgery (lot 944 of the Hoffman collection, April 1866), Elliot Woodward tells us: "One of the Edwards counterfeits; as fine as when it fell from the die; this piece is found in no other cabinet in the country; the dies were destroyed since the death of Dr. Edwards, together with all the pieces struck from them,[1] with the exception of twelve purchased from him, his statement being that they were bought in London. It now appears that the dies were made to order in New York City." A notation in the catalogue at the American Numismatic Society tells us, incidentally, that the above coin was purchased for $5.50 by Sylvester Crosby.

The only occasion, to the writer's knowledge, when an Edwards half cent has been inadvertently sold as a genuine coin was the June 1951 sale of the late Max Mehl, where the fabrication was described as simply "an entirely different variety." Actually, the Edwards copy is comparatively crude, and can be easily identified both by its light weight and general appearance.

THE 1848 SMALL DATE, SMALL STARS, LARGE CENT *(Fig. 77)*

A comparison of this cent with any of its contemporaries struck at the U.S. Mint reveals that 1) the device, stars and circumscription are all crude, and could not possibly have been produced by a hub in use at the Mint, and 2) the date is not aligned, and therefore

---

1. Reference to the James E. Root sale, Dec. 16, 1878, lot 391, where Edward Cogan states: ". . . I believe about twelve (Edwards half cents) were circulated, and I destroyed all that were in the possession of the late Dr. Edwards, at the time of his death."

does not reflect the use of a logotype with which all dates on Mint-made cents were punched from 1840 on.

A history of the 1848 small date, small stars, large cent shows that the first of the half dozen pieces now known appeared in lot 1431 of the 1865 Levick sale, where Edward Cogan described it as simply a "Peculiar type." The same piece was resold by Cogan on Nov. 13, 1871, and later realized $4 (despite its being described as unique!) in the sale of the great Parmelee collection. It was not until 1940, however, that the dissenting if somewhat cautious voice of Howard Newcomb expressed the belief that the 1848 small date large cents were, after all, contemporary counterfeits. Subsequent cataloguers, not wishing to disturb our timorous hearts with so bold a truth, have paused in their effusions only long enough to whisper "not of Mint workmanship," a phrase calculated to be soon forgotten amid the endless encomiums of "rare," "splendid," "pedigreed," etc. How long collectors will permit themselves to be deceived by such gobbledygook, we shall have to wait and see.

THE 1787 HALF DOLLAR (*Fig. 78*)

On April 27, 1962, a Pensacola, Florida collector announced "one of the greatest discoveries in American numismatic history, a 1787 half dollar." The article received almost an entire page in *Coin World*, a tribute which bespoke the magnitude of the discovery. An enlarged photograph of the half dollar, which was *dated seven years prior to any heretofore known*, appeared together with a caption stating that the coin had been authenticated in every respect.

Collectors not fortunate enough to behold this rara avis for themselves could only marvel; for our part we felt that the promoter had expressed himself in too modest terms. The 1787 half dollar was not merely *one* of the greatest discoveries in numismatic history . . . It was *the* greatest . . . since the 1650 Pine Tree shilling!

From the above mentioned article it appears that the coin was authenticated on the grounds that it showed no signs of alteration from a known variety. Yet, one look at the bizarre workmanship should have indicated that any discussion of altering was utterly irrelevant.

Nevertheless, having once labored to prove that the coin was from an original die, it never occurred to its promoter that the poor

Fig. 75

Fig. 76

Fig. 77

Fig. 78

Fig. 75. The 1793 Washington half cent; Fig. 76. 1796 half cent with pole to cap. Genuine specimen and Edwards counterfeit. Note that the Liberty Head on the Edwards piece is larger and closer to the word LIBERTY; Fig. 77. 1848 large cent. Genuine specimen and "small date" counterfeit; Fig. 78. Counterfeit 1787 half dollar.

workmanship might betoken a counterfeit piece rather than an early pattern, or that the designs shown on both sides of the coin, which were obviously copied from the 1794-5 designs of Robert Scot, had not been so much as dreamed of in 1787!

It might also be pointed out that the 1787 half dollar is not a new discovery. The coin is listed as a fabrication in the appendix of Judd's *U.S. Pattern, Trial, and Experimental Pieces*, and it was thoroughly discussed by John J. Ford, Jr., in the November 1950 issue of the *Coin Collector's Journal*. More than a decade ago, Oscar Schilke of Beaver Falls, Connecticut, discovered a similar coin with fourteen stars, and a little research soon disclosed other examples or "die varieties." Ford also described and illustrated these in his 1950 article. The Schilke "discovery coin" was owned by an elderly man who claimed that it had been with his family for many years. The coin was wrapped in a piece of stained and yellowed paper which was beginning to crumble at the crease marks. An almost illegible inscription on the paper read:

"LIMPSTEN (?) WEDNESDAY, MAY 19, 1813—THIS DAY REC'D OF JOHN CRAM OF UNITY, ONE HALF DOLLAR PIECE —OF THE UNITED STATES COIN DATED 1787—AND IN-CLOSED (sic) THE SAME WITHIN THIS PAPER —FRANCIS CHASE & CHS (Charles) WAY PRESENT AT THE TIME—ATTES —ABNEIL CHASE."

The above note, if genuine, would indicate that the manufacture of these coins took place some time between 1794 and 1813. And yet, the omission of any 1787 dies from Riddell's extremely inclusive list of counterfeit half dollars [1] would seem to preclude this possibility. The alternative is that they were made around the third quarter of the last century, along with the 1650 Pine Tree shillings, the Washington half cent, and other such fancy productions.

The "1787 half dollar" was also noted as being a fabrication by Henry Chapman and Farran Zerbe, in the May 1916 issue of *The Numismatist*, and before that by W. E. Woodward. The impossible date of 1787 was undoubtedly chosen because of the production of Fugio cents in that year.

1. Riddell, J. L. *Monograph of the Dollar* (1845).

THE 1804 HALF DOLLAR

According to the Mint report of 1804, a total of 156,519 half dollars were coined during that year, a staggering figure considering that no genuine specimen has ever been found. The answer to this "paradox" is, of course, the same as that which accounted for the 19,570 silver dollars also coined during 1804: the coins in question were all struck from earlier dies. It is true that two dies were originally punched with an 1804 date, and subsequently over-punched with one of 1805, but whether these were actually intended for striking 1804 coins and then brought up to date during the following year, or whether they represent mere errors in die punching, perpetrated and corrected during 1805, is mere conjecture. Nor is it, in fact, of any consequence since *no coins are known to have been struck from either die before the corrections were made.*

Nevertheless, in his 1859 *Manual*, Montroville W. Dickeson affirms the existence of an 1804 half dollar, comparing its rarity to that of the silver dollar of the same year. During the early 1880's, this unique coin appeared several times in the Woodward sales, and was illustrated in the collections of Ferguson Haines (Nov. 1880), and Winslow Lewis (May 1883). In cataloguing the Ferguson Haines collection, Woodward gives us the following sales pitch to prove that the piece is genuine:

> *This half dollar was believed by its former owner, a distinguished numismatist and collector, to be a genuine coin of the date. That a die was cut for 1804 is known to all collectors, and the wonder is not that a specimen has been discovered, but that more have not been found. I have given to the piece a most thorough and careful examination, and have no reason to doubt that it is original and genuine; if genuine, we all know it to be* the rarest coin in the American mint series.

It should be pointed out that Woodward's implication that the 1804 half dollar is from a known die of that year is manifestly untrue, as the illustration of the coin shows a "plain" 4 in the date, entirely unlike the "crosslet" 4 punches of both 1805/04 obverses, or any other punches used during that year.

In the Winslow Lewis sale, a more knowledgeable, and somewhat less confident, Woodward tells us:

> *This piece, purchased in the Haines collection for $45, bears every mark of genuineness so far as appearance shows; it was struck from a die; the figure is not formed by throwing up the surface, by indenting the reverse; the piece*

has been thoroughly scoured with pumice on the end of a blunt stick around the figures for the purpose of bringing to light any indication of tooling or soldering, but, with the aid of a powerful glass I fail to discover that the piece has in any way been tampered with since it was made. All numismatists know that not only one but several (?) dies were made for the half dollar of 1804, but the coin itself having never been discovered; of course it is easy and natural to decide that this piece is an alteration; but if an alteration, as it probably is, the workmanship finds no parallel in any other job of the kind I have seen.

It is amusing to note that Woodward's scouring of the metal with pumice "for the purpose of bringing to light any indication of tooling or soldering," undoubtedly produced the opposite effect of eliminating whatever tell-tale marks remained.

Fig. 79. A) 1804 (altered date) half dollar; B) close-up of genuine 1805/4 half dollar. The genuine 4 has a crosslet on the end of it.

Thus, after a fifty-year obscurity, the nonpareil 1804 half dollar was rediscovered and published by the dean of twentieth century American coin dealers, B. Max Mehl. On the strength of Mehl's article (Nov. 1933 *Numismatist*) the fabulous coin was subsequently included in Green's "Mint Record and Type Table" and the *Guide Book* (1948-57 editions). Today it reposes in the collection of Eric P. Newman where, at last, it is correctly described . . . as an alteration of 1806!

THE 1804 AND 1805 SILVER DOLLARS *(Figs. 80 and 81)*

In an article which appeared, during June, 1961, in the nation's four leading numismatic journals, Alfred J. Ostheimer, 3rd, an-

nounced the authentication of an 1804 and an 1805 silver dollar as
genuine coins struck in the year of their date. These two dollars, so
attributed, and authenticated by a well known silver dollar specialist,
would have represented the rarest of all regular issue U.S. coins, and
been worth, individually, far in excess of the $28,500 brought by the
sale of a so-called 1804 dollar (circa 1858) a few months earlier. Mr.
Ostheimer announced the purchase, by his wife and himself, of
both coins from the New York dealer Louis Werner. The 1804 and
1805 dollars were stated as having been "known to Spink & Son, Ltd.
of London," and purchased, in 1940, by Farran Zerbe who sold
them, in the following year, to Werner. Zerbe was reported not to
have guaranteed the pieces, but to have stated simply that "they
may be false or genuine." It was also maintained that the St. Louis
dealer, B. G. Johnson had concluded that the coins "could not be
genuine because they did not resemble the then known 1804
dollars." Johnson's opinion, the only dissenting one mentioned, is
thus shown to be founded on an erroneous conception regarding the
existing 1804 dollars.

Two months after the publication of the Ostheimer article, Eric
P. Newman, speaking before the annual convention of the American
Numismatic Association, proved beyond the shadow of a doubt
that both the 1804 and 1805 dollars sold by Mr. Werner to Mr. and
Mrs. Ostheimer had been fraudulently altered, in exactly the same
way, from coins of earlier years. With the exception of the final
digit and certain diagnostic stars, the two coins were identical
to the 1802 over 1, Bolender 4 variety, and the 1803, Bolender 6
variety, respectively. They were identical not only with respect to
their punch relationships (which in itself would have been conclusive, since each element was individually punched into the early
dies), but even to the existence of *minute die defects*. Furthermore,
the diagnostic stars were not *intrinsically* different, but had merely
been re-aimed by shaving away and tooling part of the ends and
sides, which resulted in their rays being imperfectly aligned. *Only
the stars which were critical for die variety determination had, in
each case, been molested.* The two coins were, in Newman's words,
"masterpieces of deception."

In Chapter IV, we gave reasons for believing that the 19,570
silver dollars coined during 1804 were struck from dies of earlier
years. Of course a die-hard might contend that since our arguments

Fig. 80

Fig. 81

Figs. 80-81. The Zerbe-Werner-Ostheimer 1804 and 1805 dollar alterations.

are based on the supposition that no genuine 1804 dollar is known to exist, they are, technically at least, inconclusive. As regards the silver dollars of *1805*, however, there is not left even this small refuge for the credulous, as evidenced by the following statement made by Mint Director J. R. Snowden, as early as 1860:

There is much dispute among numismatists in regard to the coinage of dollars in the year 1805. It is contended that 321 pieces were struck; and, in fact the Director's Report of that year is the authority for the statement. In 'Bullion Journal A,' we find the following entry on page 363, under date of June 28, 1805. We give the entry as it stands upon the Journal:—
"Silver Coinage . . . Dr. to Chief Coiner his account of silver received from him in pursuance of a warrant of the Director No. *349*
"*34,000* Quarter dollars.
"*321* Dollars, being found amongst Spanish dollars brought to the Mint."
This entry settles the question, that the issue *of that number of pieces took place; and also, that they were* not *dollars of 1805, but of previous dates.'*

The history and pedigree of the Zerbe-Werner-Ostheimer dollars of 1804 and 1805, in so far as they can be determined, are as follows:

The first record is to be found in a letter written by Samuel Friedenberg to *The Numismatist* magazine (Page 799), October, 1939. Mr. Friedenberg writes:

I was in London a short time ago and while there visited the Coin and Medal Department of the British Museum. In conversing with the men in charge, they asked me whether I had any knowledge of United States coins. I told them that while my knowledge was limited, I had a fair idea of standard coins minted by the Federal Government from 1793 to date.

I was shown an 1804 U.S. silver dollar. Knowing that this date is extremely rare, I asked for a reading glass. I examined the dollar, and it looked to me as though it was an unaltered date. Then they showed me an 1805 dollar. I expressed my amazement, for this dollar is even rarer than the 1804. I asked them whether these U.S. dollars were given to the British Museum, and they replied in the negative, stating that the dollars were sent to them by someone in the West Indies with the request that they put a valuation on them. I was further informed that these two dollars were being sent to Messrs. Spink & Son (London) with instructions that they be sold on a commission basis.

That night I kept thinking about these two dollars and came to the conclusion that I was a little hasty in looking at them through a glass. The dollars were fairly worn, but I failed to note whether the dates were equally worn with the coin. It was my intention to go back to the Museum, but I was so pressed for time and as my stay in London was limited I did not get back.

If this letter is of special interest, I wish you would publish it in the hope that some of your readers may know something of these two particular dollars and further in the hope that this letter will be read by the two gentlemen who conversed with me at the British Museum. I am curious to know whether the dates have been altered or whether they were originals.

Shortly after Samuel Friedenberg's visit to the British Museum, the 1804 and 1805 dollars were sent by Spink & Son to a Miss M. A. Dunne of Brooklyn, with the suggestion that the two coins be shown to the famous numismatist and dealer B. G. Johnson. Johnson announced that the pieces were alterations, and wrote Miss Dunne to that effect. Arthur B. Kelley, who saw them while they were in Johnson's possession, was of the same opinion.

In November, 1939, Farran Zerbe, then Curator of the Chase Manhattan Bank's Money Museum, purchased the debunked 1804 and 1805 dollars for his private collection. He purchased them as alterations, paying fifty dollars for the pair.

In January, 1940, Johnson's appraisal of the coins was recorded in the following letter from Spink & Son to *The Numismatist:*

> With reference to Samuel Friedenberg's report in the October issue of The Numismatist *that he had seen two United States silver dollars of 1804 and 1805 at the British Museum, these were subsequently sent on to us, and we feel that your readers would no doubt be glad to hear a little more about these coins.*
>
> *We were originally asked by the owner to buy them from him, or sell them on a commission, but when they came into our hands we were not entirely satisfied that they were all they should be, particularly as they had a somewhat convex appearance, and we therefore submitted them to one of the foremost coin experts in the United States for his judgement. His report, not altogether unexpected, was as follows: ". . . both are altered dates, the 1804 from an 1801,[1] of which we have a piece in stock struck from the exact die, even to the minute diebreaks. The 1805 is altered from an 1803, of which we have a specimen in stock struck from the exact die, even to the tiny die break above the letter D of UNITED, and another more severe die break at the end of the eagle's wing on the left. Furthermore the die break on our specimen is worse, or in other words has gone farther than on the 1805. It is a very clever piece of work, but done simply by lowering the surface of the coin all around the rim through the stars and the word LIBERTY, as well as the date. Under a high-powered glass you will find the coin much sunken at the edge as compared with the centre, and there can be no question about both of these being altered dates. I have seen a good many alterations of the 1804, but never one of an 1805 before, but it did not take me five minutes to find the original coins in stock from which these alterations were made. Of course, the die break on a worn 1803 we have, being more pronounced than that of an 1805 from the same die, would condemn the piece by itself.*

It is obvious from the above letter that B.G. Johnson rejected the 1804 and 1805 silver dollars because he *saw* that they were alterations, and not, as erroneously stated, "because they did not resemble the then known 1804 dollars."

1. A scrivener's or typographical error for 1802/1.

Furthermore, Johnson not only identified the die varieties of the original coins, but described what he believed to have been the method used to perpetrate the fraud. This technique, which is called "chasing," differs from soldering in that it involves neither heat nor the use of any foreign substance to effect a fusion. Instead, the artisan works on an annealed surface with a semi-polished blunt instrument, squeezing out the metal to form a new figure, or reshaping the one which is already there. In the present instance, the formation and contours of the numerals are so perfect, and the tool marks have been removed so skillfully, that we can only assume the operation was performed under high magnification.

In 1951 Werner let it be known that he owned an original 1805 dollar, although he did not then make mention of the 1804. Walter Breen states that he recalls seeing the coin at club meetings and convention bourses, and that he identified it at that time as an alteration from an 1803 large 3 (Bolender 6) variety. When, however, M.H. Bolender, himself, pronounced the two coins genuine, on the assumption that the position of the stars differed from all other known dies of the period, Werner decided to submit the coins to laboratory tests for confirmation. In the first test, the coins were examined under a metallographic microscope at magnifications ranging from 25X to 1150X, and no evidence of alteration, removing, or retooling of the metal could be detected. The laboratory technicians, not being numismatists or familiar with the appearance of early silver dollars, could hardly be expected to detect a few minutely misaligned star points, and they thus based their conclusions solely on the visual appearance of the metal. A magnification of 1150X no doubt sounds very authoritative, but for detecting alterations, anything above 75X serves little purpose. It might also be mentioned that the second test, in which the two coins were etched to determine whether or not replacement figures had been soldered on, was even more pointless, since almost all alterations of this kind are wrought by chasing. If the etching had at least been prolonged, the original numerals might have been "brought out," but as such an experiment would have been slightly destructive to the metal, it was not attempted. Thus, the one and only effect of the etching was to obscure any traces of tooling which might have remained!

The 1804 and 1805 silver dollars will live forever. They have taken their place alongside the great forgeries of the past, and their example should alert all of us to the danger of similar forgeries in the future. It is hoped that the facts disclosed in this chapter will not, however, dim the faith of numismatists in "final verifications," but engender a desire for numismatic knowledge, which is, in itself, the surest safeguard against such false and contemptible productions.

VII

PRIVATE COINS BY NECESSITY

WHEN the thirteen original colonies united, they recognized that the right to regulate and coin money (one of the highest prerogatives of sovereignty) could no longer be entrusted to individual states, but must henceforth reside in the Federal government alone. In the early days, however, a shortage of bullion (aggravated by the melting and hoarding of specie) often prevented the government from successfully exercising its "prerogative." On a few occasions, at least, when the shortage of coin became acute, private companies issued their own emergency pieces, relying on judicial good sense to forgive the infringement of Federal authority.

The first era of the "hard times tokens" (1834-1844) coincides with the latter part of Jackson's presidency and, indeed, the two are inseparable. The tokens, for the most part, contain political lampoons directed against Jackson and, after the suspension of specie payments in 1837, they were made to do service for regular coins.

The bitter controversy which raged between Jackson and his opponents centered around the privately owned but Federally sponsored Bank of the United States. The Bank was the largest institution of its kind and it exerted a powerful influence on the national economy. In the midst of a great industrial revolution, the young nation was just coming into its own, and expansion and speculation were in its blood. The big Bank understood all this, but it knew also that such eras were not without dangers. Whenever money became too loose, it tended to depreciate with the rise of prices, and to prevent this, the Bank restrained its loans, a practice considered by its opponents to encroach upon private enterprise. Jackson called the institution monopolistic and antithetical to the ideals of a democracy. In 1832 he vetoed its recharter and, a year later, transferred the public deposits to local banks which were incorporated under state law. This was the famous "experiment" by which he hoped to prove that the latter could act with equal responsibility as fiscal agents of the government. The experiment was not a success. The restraint which had characterized the big Bank was now thrown to the four winds, producing for a time a tremendous surge of business activity and feverish land speculation. Before long it became clear that the state banks had overextended themselves. They had come to regard the deposit of the public funds as a permanent loan, and when these funds were withdrawn the banks collapsed. The blow came just as Jackson was leaving office, and the brunt of it fell upon his successor, Martin Van Buren.

Virtually all of the satirical tokens of this period allude to the famous controversy and the effect of Jackson's experiment. One of the earliest pieces depicts Jackson as a wild boar whose sentiments are expressed in the legend: PERISH CREDIT. PERISH COMMERCE . . .MY victory . . . down with the BANK. The reverse side continues with MY SUBSTITUTE FOR THE U.S. BANK. MY experiment. MY currency. MY glory. (Fig. 82)

In another celebrated piece, Jackson has become a jackass standing on the word "veto." On his saddle blanket appear the letters L.L.D. The president had received an honorary doctor of laws degree in 1833, a distinction which won him more ridicule than respect from his opponents. The legend reads: THE CONSTITUTION AS I UNDERSTAND IT. ROMAN FIRMNESS. The other side shows Jackson emerging out of a treasure chest, brandishing a sword in one hand and a bag of money in the other. The legend reads: I TAKE THE RESPONSIBILITY. This was the "union of the purse and the sword" which the opponents of Jackson and Van Buren believed would bring ruin to the nation.(Fig. 83)

Jackson, who rose to fame as a result of his brilliant defeat of the British at New Orleans, was always thereafter associated with the military uniform, and though he actually wore the plainest of clothes, his opponents have depicted him, on an early die, complete with epaulets and sword, the latter awkwardly brandished. The legend (which is derived from Jackson's own speeches) reads: A PLAIN SYSTEM.''VOID OF POMP.'(Fig. 84)

It has been said that the election of Van Buren was a greater victory for Jackson than for the incumbent. It is certainly true that Jackson had primed him for the job, and Van Buren, in his inaugural address, proclaimed: "I follow in the footsteps of my illustrious predecessor." The phrase was avidly seized on by caricaturists who depicted the new president cautiously stepping into the footprints of a jackass. On the tokens Van Buren has been eliminated and the jackass alone remains. The reverse shows a tortoise carrying the sub-treasury on its back. This is the new fiscal agent and the legend reads: EXECUTIVE EXPERIMENT. (Fig. 85)

The "ship of state" was another pet theme of the lampoonists. A famous token depicts the ship, marked "experiment," smashing to pieces upon large reefs. The legend reads: VAN BUREN. METAL-LIC CURRENCY. 1837. On the reverse, the ship, now marked "constitution," is restored. The legend reads: WEBSTER. CREDIT CURRENCY. (Fig. 86)

Webster was regarded as the great upholder of the Constitution and he believed that it provided for the U.S. Bank. Thus, although he was not personally disposed towards the institution, he was pre-pared to accept it. On the Gibb's tokens his position is less sympa-thetically portrayed by a bellicose steer and the circumscription: A FRIEND OF THE CONSTITUTION. (Fig. 87)

The suspension of specie payments by the "broken banks" was a bitter pill to swallow, and the occasion was aptly commemorated on various tokens and storecards during the nation's convalescence. With the demise of the Federally backed Bank of the United States, the government disavowed all responsibility for its currency. Thus, when the state banks went broke they stayed broke, and their paper money remained worthless. (Fig. 88)

The nation was still licking its wounds when the "wildcat banks," as they were now called, began once more to pour out large sums of paper currency. The result was another panic in 1857. Then, four

Figs. 82-88. Jacksonian or "Hard Times" tokens.

years later, the Civil War broke out, plunging the nation into its darkest hour.

In order to meet the tremendous expenditures of war, the Federal government issued a series of demand notes (the famous greenbacks!) but no sooner were these circulated than the wary citizens, having suffered twice from failure of the paper currency, took them to the banks for redemption in coin. Since this defeated the entire purpose of the issue, which was to alleviate the shortage of metal currency, the banks countered in December, 1861, by suspending further specie payments. The Treasury quickly followed suit. As a final measure, the demand notes were made legal tender and had to be accepted for all debts. Despite this fiat, however, the notes remained unpopular and sharply declined in value.

The suspension of specie payments led to the hoarding of silver and gold coins, and merchants, in order to maintain their businesses, were forced to pay a premium for whatever small amounts they might obtain. Anticipating a similar rise in the value of copper, people took to hoarding even one-cent coins with the result that the most menial transactions became now a formidable task!

For a time it was thought that postage stamps might serve in place of the coins, but when it was found that they were too fragile and easily soiled, other experiments were undertaken. In August, 1862, John Gault patented a small protective frame, made of brass and fitted on one side with a transparent mica window, to encase individual stamps. By now, however, the supply of postage stamps was exhausted, and after two months of ambitious production inventor Gault was forced into retirement.

Fig. 89. Necessity money: a ten cent encased postage stamp.

In the autumn of 1862, a New York saloon-keeper named Lindenmueller struck the first series of Civil War tokens, numbering a million pieces. This was followed by the famous Knickerbocker strikings, also in great quantities. The idea, once implemented,

spread so rapidly that, by the end of the war there were no less
than twenty-five million "copperheads" [1] in circulation, of which
present day numismatists list over eleven thousand varieties!

Fig. 90. These are the famous copperheads or Civil War tokens. Over eleven
thousand different varieties are known.

Like the earlier issues, these were primarily of two kinds, i.e., the
patriotic token which replaced the political-satirical type, and the
storecard. Either no denomination was given, or it was cleverly
preceded by the word "not" so as to read "not one cent." It was thus
maintained that the copperheads were not coins at all, but merely
tokens.

Owing to the obvious disparity between their intrinsic and "tacit"
face values—the former being only about one fifth of the latter—
people began to fear lest the parties issuing the copperheads choose
ultimately not to honor them. These apprehensions were, in fact,
soon borne out when Lindenmueller, in an altercation with the
Third Avenue Railroad of New York, scornfully repudiated all
responsibility for his issues. The railroad, having no redress for the
amount, doubtless appealed to the Federal authorities; for just two
months later Congress resolved "that if any person or persons shall
make use of, pass, or cause to be passed, any coin, card or token, or
device whatsoever, in metal or its compounds, intended to pass or

1. The term "copperhead" by which the Civil War tokens were generally known,
was also employed in a derogatory sense for members of "the Knights of the Golden
Circle," a secret society composed of Northerners whose sympathies lay with the
South. These persons identified themselves by means of a cut-down copper large
cent which they at first wore, obverse up, in their lapel, but later carried in the
pocket and only flashed surreptitiously.

be passed for a one-cent or a two-cent piece, such person or persons, shall be deemed guilty of a misdemeanor and shall, upon conviction thereof, be punished by a fine not exceeding one thousand dollars and by imprisonment for a term not exceeding five years." The approval of this bill on April 22, 1864, put an end to the afore-mentioned abuses and in so doing, closed one of the most colorful chapters in the history of numismatic America.

An amusing postscript to the story of the copperheads was provided by the following curiosity which appeared in the *Detroit Free Press*, Nov. 14, 1879, just fifteen years after the expulsion of the tokens from circulation.

COUNTERFEIT COINS IN DETROIT

In making change, one of the most prominent banks in Detroit was yesterday victimized to the extent of three cents. The new coins are a first class imitation of a small cent of the issue of 1863, and are perfect, with the exception that the "head side" bears thirteen stars in place of the words "United States of America." The coins are not moulded, but pressed out with a lever die, and it is thought that they are not of copper, but of the glass and metal mixture, with a copper wash. In the upper portion of the wreath which surrounds the words "one cent" is stamped in small letters the word "not" so that the face reads "not one cent." This however, would not be observed except by a close observer.

As one might expect, such ardent journalism did not go long unrewarded. In a facetious editorial, the *Coin Collector's Journal* replied:

We are of the opinion, not without cause, that the author of the above article must have been a new arrival from the lumber country and had mistaken his vocation. Nature possibly intended him for a cigar store Indian, and only in that capacity would his fully developed block-headedness have been appreciated. When he speaks of a "prominent bank" being victimized to the extent of three cents, the fact becomes perfectly alarming, for if the great banks suffered to such an extent, what must be the losses of the lesser ones, or of the bootblacks whose main currency consists of cents, or of the press reporter who deals in nonsense? The simple thought of the consequences makes us shudder.And when we read of the "new coins" being a perfect and first class imitation of the 1863 cent, except that they are totally unalike in every particular, we are inclined to think that a bull from Hibernia was intended; certainly the piece mentioned could scarcely be more unlike the nickel cent of 1863, in colour, thickness, design or inscription. He indeed must be youthful who has not before seen the "copperhead" currency which circulated throughout the country during 1862-1864 and particularly in the west. The information volunteered that the coins are not moulded, is invaluable to those who thought coins and bullets were made in the same manner; but the shrine of the Temple of Wisdom is attained when we read that glass and metal, washed with copper, is the composition on which these dangerous counterfeits are struck.

The aforesaid reporter evidently considered not the cost of producing such pieces, which would be at least one cent each and thus the object for which they were intended would fail entirely.

"Necessity coins" have enjoyed a long, colorful history and there are few countries in which they have not, at one time or another, been employed. The copperheads were also necessity coins despite the legal technicality by which they maintained their token status. On the other hand, the California gold issues made no such pretense, and many of them were obviously imitative of U.S. coins. In this respect they are unique, and their alternate acceptance and rejection by the State legislature clearly defines the economics of bullion currency, a concept which has now fallen into disuse.

The presence of gold had long been known to the native population of California. It is said, in fact, that the Franciscan monks helped the Indians in assaying the gold dust and nuggets used to purchase supplies from the traders. But for all that, the treasure of the Sierra Madre remained concealed until one fateful morning in January, 1848, when James Marshall, a worker in Sutter's Mills, suddenly "struck it rich." The bonanza that followed Marshall's discovery literally changed the face of California, ushering in one of the most feverish periods of American history. Men from every walk of life, residents from neighboring towns and travellers from distant states and territories—all intoxicated with the dream of sudden wealth—crowded into the county of El Dorado to stake their claims. Those who had made fortunes wanted to live high and, almost overnight, an extravagent economy sprang up to accommodate them. Often, however, the fortunes were swiftly lost in the gambling dens and, in this bacchanalian atmosphere, a thousand murders were committed from 1849 to 1856 with but a single conviction.[1]

Despite the outer chaos, an inner economic stability was evolving which would ultimately establish the entire nation on a firm financial basis. The backward territory which, two years previously, had belonged to Mexico and which "had known no other representatives of value than its hides and cattle, whose imports were so limited as to afford employment to only a dozen vessels annually, at once be-

1. R. H. Burnie, *Small California and Territorial Gold Coins.*

came the resort of all unemployed vessels on the Pacific, and when the stimulant of so important a discovery was communicated to our Atlantic and the European cities, a thousand vessels entered the port of San Francisco the year succeeding, freighted with valuable cargoes, to supply the host that had embarked for the theatre of profitable labor." [1]

For the time being, however, the "important discovery" posed a severe mercantile problem. According to law, all duties had to be paid in coin, neither gold dust nor nuggets being accepted by the Custom House, although they passed freely in circulation.[2] The shortage of actual specie, however, made the fulfillment of this law virtually impossible. The closest mint was then in Philadelphia, some three thousand miles away, and currency could be obtained more easily from many South American and even European countries.

By the summer of 1848, a great deal of import had gathered up in the Custom House, the merchants being unable to secure it for want of appropriate currency. In this impasse they requested the military governor, R. B. Mason, to accept gold dust at its intrinsic value in lieu of the unobtainable coined money. The governor at first agreed, but then, thinking better of it, revoked his permission. By way of a concession, Mason allowed the merchants to deposit their gold dust at the Custom House at ten dollars per ounce, as a bond for future payment. In the event that the requisite duties could not be raised within sixty days, the gold dust was to be auctioned off, and the money received applied towards their payment.

Instead of solving anything, the new measure only brought the situation to a head. Those who still had some coined money either hoarded it to pay their own duties or used it to speculate in the un-

---

1. From a communication between San Francisco businessmen and Secretary of the Treasury, Thomas Corwin, September, 1852.

2. The value of gold was computed, at the official rate of $20.67 per troy ounce. According to assay tests taken by Eckfeldt and DuBois in 1850, the gold found in different regions of California varied little in fineness and (when unadulterated), was usually assayed at between 860 and 900/1000 pure, the flat spangles panned from the rivers averaging about 1% over other grains. The smallest denomination in use was the "pinch," i.e., the amount of gold dust one could raise between his thumb and forefinger. Equal to twenty-five cents in silver coin, the pinch soon gave rise to a spirited competition between purchaser and vendor. The former would add a quantity of ground brass to the gold in his satchel, and the latter moistened his fingers and dug in until his adversary really "felt the pinch!" Rigged scales were another convenience and these, of course, served both sides impartially.

redeemed gold dust. In desperation the merchants asked that they be allowed an extension of six months to meet their pledges. The petition, though granted, failed to save most of the deposits from being ultimately auctioned off at six to eight dollars per ounce. What little coin still remained was soon "absorbed by the Treasury" and the merchants had thus to resort to the importation of foreign currencies.

French francs, Spanish pesetas, and Pieces of Eight, all of which were acceptable at the Custom House, now swelled the meager circulation. But once again the unfortunate merchants had to sustain a loss. The silver five-franc piece, for example, could only be obtained on a parity with the dollar, although its actual value was ninety-three cents. Moreover, the one-franc coin, worth only about eighteen-and-a-half cents, was made to pass for a quarter, the denomination most nearly resembling it in size!

Consequently, on July 27, 1848, the businessmen once more petitioned Mason, this time for nothing less than the right to issue their own coins. The vacillating governor at first agreed, but fearing lest he offend the Federal authority, once more revoked his permission. But this time it was too late. The miners and businessmen at a mass meeting fixed the value of gold at a prudent sixteen dollars per ounce and drew up plans for their historic coinages.

On May 31, 1849, an Alta California newspaper described what may have been the first of the territory's pioneer gold pieces, a five dollar coin which "has been struck at Benicia City, though the imprint is San Francisco." The initials N.G.N. stamped on the reverse remained an enigma until 1902 when they were identified as representing the firm of Norris, Grieg and Norris. (*Fig. 91, p. 177*)

In June, the firm of Moffat & Co. began to issue small rectangular ingots and, thereafter, five- and ten-dollar gold coins. Of all the firms born during this period, none outlasted Moffat which was singularly trusted for its integrity.

The pioneer companies functioned primarily in two ways. As coiners, they purchased dust and nuggets at less than intrinsic value, wrought them into coins and sold them at a premium, thus compounding their profits. As assayers, they converted into ingots the dust and nuggets *of their depositors,* stamping each piece with a denomination and design. The usual fee for this service ranged from 2½ to 5 per cent of the value of the ingot.

Among the most prominent newcomers were the Miner's Bank, the Pacific Co., Ormsby & Co., and the Cincinnati Mining & Trading Co. In addition, gold pieces from other territories, including the famous Mormon issues, now poured into the motley circulation. As the weeks rolled by, a veritable avalanche of private coin rescusitated the moribund economy and business thrived as never before.

In the midst of the boom the citizens received a rude shock. A series of assay tests, taken by Eckfeldt and DuBois at the Philadelphia Mint, revealed that almost all of the coins in circulation were debased. The Mormon gold, whose coining was supervised by none other than Brigham Young, was found to be wanting by as much as twenty per cent, and that of the Pacific Co., by even more. The assay report stated: "Ten and five-dollar pieces of the "Pacific Company," 1849; very irregular in weight, and debased in fineness; a ten-dollar piece weighed 229 grains, a five-dollar, 130; assay of a third, 797 thousandths. At those rates, the larger piece would be worth $7.86, the smaller $4.48; but the valuation is altogether uncertain." (*Fig. 92, p. 177*)

In the panic that followed the publication of Eckfeldt and DuBois' findings, the debased issues quickly depreciated, and those holding them suffered severe losses. One by one the firms were driven out of business, and at the end of 1849 Moffat & Co. alone survived.

At the risk of spoiling what might otherwise seem to be a perfect moral, we should mention the ultimate fate of the two controllers of the Pacific Co., David C. Broderick and Frederick D. Kohler. Broderick was elected State Senator in 1850, and with the admission of California to the Union, he served in the United States Senate. In April of the same year, his equally high-minded partner, Frederick Kohler, was appointed to (of all things) the office of State Assayer!

Fig. 93. Soft metal die-trial splashers for five-and ten-dollar Dubosq coinage.

During the year 1850 Moffat was joined by several new companies, including the well known Dubosq and Baldwin firms. Theodore Dubosq had been a jeweler in Philadelphia at the time when J. P. Longacre was Chief Engraver for the United States Mint. It is of interest to note that two die trial splashers of the Dubosq coinage figured among the effects of the Longacre estate—and of *more* than interest, that the representations on both pieces are virtually identical to Longacre's own designs for U. S. coinage. Is it possible that in addition to its various other extracurricular "activities," the Mint was taking orders for dies from its competitors in sunny California? The suggestion is inescapable . . . *(Fig. 93)*

But to return to our story. Despite the establishment of several new companies, public resentment against the pioneer gold pieces was mounting, and their legality was now seriously challenged. The use of designs imitating those of U.S. coins further elicited the charge of counterfeiting, and only an eloquent appeal by J. L. Moffat prevented passage of Senator Woodworth's bill of Jan. 21, 1850, calling for the abolition of private coinage. Nevertheless, on Feb. 6, a second bill was introduced which would prohibit the coining of gold in amounts of less than four ounces, that is, less than the size of about four $20 gold pieces. The point got across!

But, as the saying goes, a blind uncle is better than none at all. With passage of the bill, March 7, the shortage of coin at once resumed, recreating conditions of the previous year.

Finally on April 9, 1850, a number of prominent businessmen petitioned Governor Peter Burnett to establish the office of State Assayer. A bill providing for the office was passed by the Senate and the Assembly, and signed by the Governor on the 20th. Frederick D. Kohler was appointed Assayer, and authorized to refine and assay gold dust, and cast it into bars of not less than two ounces each. These ingots, which bore the state name, as well as their weight, value and number of carats, were made payable for all "State and county dues, taxes, and assessments, at the value expressed thereon in dollars and cents." *The authority thus assumed is that of a provisional State Mint*, and it is, in fact, only because California had not yet been formally admitted to the Union (though she had already adopted a state constitution and elected senators and congressmen to serve in Washington), that a violation of the Federal constitution did not result. *(Fig. 94, p. 177)*

Yet the need for an assay office had been very great. The gold ores were not only variable to some extent, but were frequently adulterated, whether the medium was dust, nuggets or coin. Some contemporary techniques were described by Eckfeldt and DuBois in their *Coins, Coinage and Bullion*, 1851:

The manufacture of mammoth lumps has been carried on to some extent in California, and apparently for different purposes. At first, the genuine California gold, being taken fluid from the melting-pot, was ingeniously mingled with broken bits of quartz, producing a specimen which at once astonished the beholder and commanded an extra price. But this was legerdemain in the golden age. They have since found a method of imposing upon traders with a base mixture, about half gold, the rest silver and copper, which, being cast out among stones, and afterwards pickled, certainly presents quite a native appearance, very likely to deceive. Several such have been offered at the mint. They can always be detected, however, by one of the surfaces (the bottom one) showing marks of previous fusion. A little cutting, also, soon betrays the hardness and redness.

Another technique involved "quicksilver," or "sponge," gold, a rather porous extraction resulting from the use of mercury in the refining process. A large nugget of this gold looked very impressive to the uninitiated, especially when weighed on the owner's scale.

Oddly enough, the most remarkable feature of Kohler's Assay Office bars was that they were always worth *more* than their expressed value. Eckfeldt and DuBois write: "We find a slight undervaluing in his (Kohler's) basis of calculation, and generally an error of assay in the same direction; so that on the average his bars are worth at the mint one per cent, perhaps one and a half, more than the value stamped upon them."

On September 30, 1850 three weeks after the admission of California to the Union, a second provisional mint was established in San Francisco, this time federally backed by the first session of the 33rd Congress of the United States. Contract for the coinage was given to Moffat & Co., and Augustus Humbert, a New York jeweler, was appointed assayer. The Act providing for the (now illegal) California State Assay Office was repealed on January 28, 1851, just two days before Humbert arrived to take up his position. Soon afterwards, the first of the famous Moffat-Humbert issues appeared—a fifty dollar gold slug.[1] *(Fig. 96)*

1. The status of the Humbert slugs was clearly defined in a statement by the Secretary of the Treasury, February, 1851, which ordered that they be received for customs duties and other dues to the United States Government. Thus, for all intents and purposes, they served as regular United States coins.

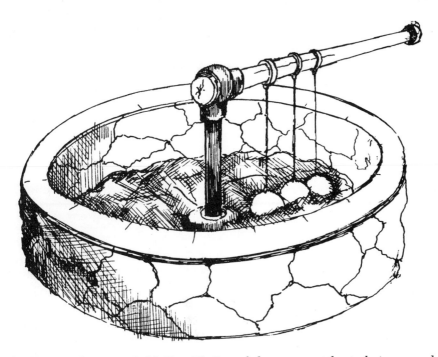

The Genesis of Sponge Gold. Fig. 95. One of the most popular techniques used by the early Californians to refine gold made use of mercury or quick silver. The gold ore was strewn on the cement floor of a three-foot-high circular brick construction called an arrester. In the center stood an iron pole fixed with a pivot and a long horizontal beam. Several large rocks were suspended from the beam which was usually turned by means of a mule. In this way the gold ore was crushed and finally reduced to a powder. Mercury (which has a great affinity for gold) was then added to separate the gold from its dross, and the new alloy was moistened until viscous, removed, and heated in a retort. The mercury vapor was funneled out, cooled and allowed to deposit, drop by drop, in a cast iron flask, leaving the gold pure but porous. Some of the less prudent miners refined small amounts of gold dust by heating the mercury-imbued grains in open pans. This method, while simple enough, was very dangerous, and the toxic effect of the fumes resulted in many deaths.

One would think that with the establishment of the United States Assay Office in San Francisco, the citizens' pecuniary problems would have been solved. Yet this was far from the case. To begin with, the smallest denomination the treasury would permit Moffat to strike was fifty dollars! For a time these unwieldly slugs were gratefully received, as at least a means of paying the customs duties, even though they did little to alleviate the general shortage of coin. Gradually, however, as the smaller private issues (most of which had been discredited) disappeared from circulation, the slug became eminently unpopular, the more so as it could only be changed for a 4 per cent fee. Finally, on March 25, 1851, the State Legislature, in sheer desperation, repealed the injunction of Feb. 6, 1850 against private coinage. Thus we witness the return of Baldwin & Co., as well as the appearance of several new firms, including Dunbar & Co. and Shults & Co. Once again, however, the issues proved to be debased, this time from thirty to sixty cents per twenty dollars. For the Legislature this was the last straw. Acting on the refusal of banks to accept the issues, it now, for the second and final time, abolished the private coinages.

Meanwhile, Moffat was continually importuning the Treasury for permission to issue smaller denominations. In the absence of any positive reply by as late as January, 1852, the Assay Office proceeded on its own to strike a series of ten- and twenty-dollar coins. A month afterwards the belated permission arrived! It is not generally realized that when these two issues (both bearing the Moffat name) were actually struck, John Little Moffat had already been separated from the U.S. Assay Office for several weeks. The firm was thereafter known as "The United States Assay Office of Gold," but it retained the right to use the Moffat name.

On September 4, 1852, the Customs collector at San Francisco was suddenly informed by the assistant Secretary of the Treasury, William Hodge, that he could no longer accept the Assay Office slugs (in spite of the fact that they contained a full $50 worth of gold) because their fineness was slightly less than the official 900. (The same authorities, however, accepted the gold coins of other nations, regardless of their fineness.) After a lengthy correspondence, it was finally conceded that if the Assay Office would issue its ingots at the desired fineness, their legal tender status would be restored. In the interim, during which new dies had to be prepared, the Customs collector was prevailed upon to accept the old slugs on the condition that the merchants would indemnify him against any losses incurred.

The United States Assay Office of Gold continued to operate until December 14, 1853 when it was closed in expectation of the long-awaited San Francisco Mint. Owing to a delay in the Mint's opening, however, the shortage of coined money once more became acute and another crisis loomed. Consequently, in 1854, a quondam employee

Fig. 91 Fig. 92

Fig. 94

Fig. 96

Fig. 97

California "Pioneer Gold" coins: Fig. 91. Norris, Grieg & Norris half eagle; Fig. 92. Mormon half eagle. The legend G.S.L.C.P.G. means "Great Salt Lake City Pure Gold"; Fig. 94. Gold ingot coined by F. D. Kohler, State Assayer; Fig. 96. $50 slug struck by U.S. Assayer Augustus Humbert. An act of Congress provided for values of up to $500! Fig. 97. $50 gold coin struck by Wass, Molitor & Co.

of Moffat & Co. and the U.S. Assay Office, John G. Kellogg, together with G.F. Richter, a former U.S. Assayer, struck a twenty-dollar coin, under the name of Kellogg & Co. In 1855, in a new partnership with Augustus Humbert, Kellogg struck a fifty-dollar piece to assist production at the newly operating Mint. A few months later, Wass, Molitor & Co. issued denominations of ten, twenty and fifty dollars. There were only a few later private gold issues in California, most notably those of Blake & Agnell, otherwise Blake & Co. (1855-56). Gradually the San Francisco Mint obtained sufficient quantities of acids for refining gold deposits, coinage increased, and the private gold issues found their way into the melting pots. Further discoveries of gold in Utah and Colorado—regions not readily accessible to the Mint—stimulated a brief private coining activity by local assayers: Parsons & Co., J. J. Conway, Clark Gruber & Co. The last-named firm was the most active of these, and its coinage continued until 1862 when the Government purchased the plant for conversion into the Denver Mint and Assay Office. With this event the era of "pioneer" coins may be said to close.[1] (*Fig. 97*)

1. The final injunction which prohibited the private coining of gold was passed by Congress on June 4, 1864. Fractional issues of a quarter and half dollar, however, were permitted until 1882 and, in addition to these, ingots of various assayers in the remoter areas of the west continued to circulate until sometime around 1900.

VIII

A Comedy of Mint Errors
(And Epilogue)

IT is said that in the heart of every true collector there lurks a secret disposition towards the anomalous and the unique. Modern Mint techniques have left little scope for the acquisition of such pieces, and, as a result, a new school of collectors is growing up. With Jobian patience, these persons plod through bag after endless Mint bag, subjecting each of the shiny, virgin coins to a rigorous scrutiny. What are they looking for? Well, practically anything— that is, anything *different*.

To a moralist it must seem a trifle perverse to prey upon the errors of one's National Mint. But such errors! Is there a man who can resist coins that are square, or cup-shaped, or that have been struck double, triple, backwards or inside out? Besides, as almost all such errors result from some kind of mechanical failure, no aspersion can be cast on the efficiency of Mint personnel.

It should not be inferred, however, that the "Mint error" is a modern invention. Many phenomena which we today describe as errors—off-centering, double-striking etc.—were very nearly stand- ard procedure a few centuries ago. There are, of course, a few anomalies which may, with some justification, be called "products of our time"—just as there are others which have been eliminated by the streamlining of various techniques.

The process of coining, as we have seen, begins with the manufacture of hubs and dies. The earliest hubs could do no more than sink the device or central portion of the die, the remainder being cut thereafter by hand. Each letter and numeral had its own punch, or rather punches, since the engraver was working with dies which varied greatly in size. As for the actual selection of punches—it would appear that this was considered of little moment. Probably whatever was closest at hand sufficed, for we often find within different dies of the same date and denomination, several variations in a single character.

It is not difficult to understand how these early die cutters, working as they did eleven hours a day, six days a week, occasionally lapsed into forgetfulness, and produced an incorrect letter or numeral. Whenever this happened, they did not simply throw the die away, but tried as best they could to correct it. Unfortunately, welding had not then been invented, and the only method of repair was to punch over the error in the hope of obliterating the greater part of it.

One of the most flagrant of these errors resulted from holding the punch (which was four sided) either sideways or backwards. A case in point is the celebrated "LIHERTY" cent of 1796. The appearance of the H was actually caused by the sinking of a correct or "backward" B over an upside-down or forward one, the vertical, in each case, predominating. The 1844 and 1851 over inverted 81 large cents, and the 1865-S over inverted 186 gold eagle are examples of the same error in regard to the date. *(Fig. 98, p. 183)*

Another famous faux pas in the large cent series is known as the "three errors reverse." After punching the U of UNITED upside down (and correcting it to the appearance of II) the engraver then omitted the left stem from the bottom of the wreath and finally punched the fraction 1/100 as 1/000. *(Fig. 99, p. 183)*

A rare variety among the 1813 half dollars shows the letters UNI (for UNITED, which is properly situated in the legend at the top of the coin) peeking out below 50C. at the bottom. Evidently, the engraver, after giving one or two light taps to each of these punches, became dissatisfied, turned the die around and started over. *(Fig. 100, p. 183)*

Today, the only part of the working die which is not applied by hubbing is the mint mark. This is punched into each die separately, leaving the door still slightly ajar for the variety hunters. There are quite a few dates which show evidence of double-punched mint marks, and even a few with the first mint mark punched in sideways, but rare indeed is the coin which can boast that it was intended for two different Mints! The 1938 D over S Buffalo nickels are already history. Yet, the fact that two different dies, of the same date and denomination, were corrected in such an unusual manner would seem to preclude the possibility of error, at least in the usual sense. In all likelihood a 1938 Buffalo nickel coinage was then planned for San Francisco, although, as we now know, it never came off.

On the other hand, the 1875 S over CC Trade dollar, published here for the first time, shows every indication of being a genuine die-cutting error, and a unique one at that. If any collector finds another, the author would very much like to hear from him. (*Fig. 102, p. 184*)

By far the most popular type of recut coin is the overdate. It has been conjectured that our early Mint officials used to perpetuate the old dies by repunching them with the current date. Yet, of the scores of corrected dies from 1793 to 1836, we find only three, the 1806/5 quarter and quarter eagle, and the 1803 1/100 over 1/000 (Sheldon's rev. G), which can be traced to a previous use. This would seem strange if it were not for the enormous difficulties involved in reannealing and cutting dies that had seen long service and which (judging from their life span) were not of very good steel anyway. Besides, in a pinch, it was not considered objectionable to strike coins from the old dies just as they were. Take the case of the dollars of 1804.

How then did these early overdates occur? The inevitable conclusion is that they represent, by and large, mere errors in die cutting, corrected the best way possible under the prevailing technology.

There appears to be some confusion regarding the various kinds of date corrections, most of which is due not to real misunderstanding, but to a careless and inconsistent terminology. From 1793 to 1839, all dates were cut into the die with individual numeral punches. *An overdate* occurred when the engraver having first seized the wrong punch, had to utilize another to make the correction; the *recut or re-engraved date* occurred when the correction was made with the same punch. The latter terms, however, are only applicable when all four numerals of the date have been recut, or when a person is speaking in a general sense. Otherwise, it is more proper to say 1805, recut 5, than 1805, recut date. From 1840 on we have a new contestant called the *double-cut date*. This fellow was a result of the logotype, or multiple numeral punch, which rendered it possible to pervert most or all of the date with a single blow. The term *recutting* is henceforth used only to describe the re-tooling or repunching of an individual numeral. Even if all four figures are outlined, unless the outlines are those of the logotype, the correct term is *recut* (or *re-engraved*) *date. (Fig. 103)*

In distinction to the early overdates are a few of more recent vintage e.g., the 1909/08 twenty dollar gold piece, the 1918/17-S quarter, the 1918/17-D nickel and the 1942/41 dime. We know that every particular of a modern die (except for the mint mark) is impressed by a hub. Theoretically then there are two ways in which the modern overdate might occur. Take the case of the 1942/41 dime. It is generally believed that the die responsible for this fault was erroneously struck from a 1941 hub and thereafter corrected with one of 1942. This is improbable for the reason that had the error been discovered the die would not have been used. Each die is numbered and signed for, and the person responsible for the blunder would hardly have cared to enlarge upon it by allowing a faulty die to go into production. It is more probable that the error went undetected. This could happen if the die were first struck *correctly* with a 1941 hub and then, *incorrectly*, with one dating 1942. Since the production of dies is today an all-year-around job, this is entirely possible. Towards the end of 1941, when the production of 1942 dies was just getting underway, others were still being manufactured for the contemporary year.

In the modern coining press, the two dies (which operate as part of a single mechanical motion) are set to come within a certain distance of each other, which is represented by the thickness of the planchet. In the event, therefore, that the layer-on fails to advance a blank, there is, theoretically, no chance of their clashing and sustaining injury. Once in a great while, however, through malfunction-

Fig. 98

Fig. 99

Fig. 100

Fig. 103

Blundered dies: Fig. 98. 1865-S over inverted 186 gold eagle; Fig. 99. 1801 large cent, the famous three-errors reverse; Fig. 100. 1813 half dollar with inverted UNI beneath 50 C; Fig. 103. 1866 five-cent nickel with double-punched date.

*Fig.
101*

Fig. 102

Blundered dies (continued). Fig. 101. 1856 large S over small S quarter. Only
two pieces are known; Fig. 102. The unique 1875-S over CC Trade Dollar.

ing, the accident does occur, and then each die receives an embossed impression of the other. If coins are then struck, each side will show, in addition to its regular relief, an incuse or mirrored image of its complement.

The screw press had only a manual check, and, consequently, the accident used to happen very often. Half dollars between 1808 and 1820 frequently show the effect, and those of 1813 without any sign of incusing may be considered as something of a rarity. *(Fig. 104)*

Another type of error which sometimes occurs during the hubbing or die sinking process is that of doubling. Remember that it takes several blows from a hub to fully establish the detail in a die and that, between each striking, the latter must be reannealed to prevent it from becoming work-hardened and possibly breaking. The die is set against markers so that it may be replaced in the same position, but even then, one of the blows will occasionally be out of register, producing a doubled impression.

The most famous modern example of this error is the 1955 "doubled die" cent. A quick glance would suggest that only the date and lettering are doubled. With the aid of a glass, however, the phenomenon becomes apparent throughout. If you will draw a circle with two diameters just slightly out of register, you will realize at once why the effect diminishes as it approaches the center of the coin. *(Fig. 105)*

Among the most appealing relics of our early coinage are those curious configurations known as die breaks. True, in a parochial sense, they are not really errors, even though their presence on a coin may be considered as adventitious. And yet, no one can say how or where the break is going to occur, or in what form. A celebrated variety of the 1807 half dollar, for example, shows a crack extending down from the chin of Liberty, an effect which commentators have likened to a Van Dyke beard! *(Fig. 106)*

A more recent case is that of the 1955 "Bugs Bunny" half dollar. Here, Ben Franklin has become the proud possessor of a pair of fangs. This, of course, did not result from any malice on the engraver's part, but simply from a few minute chips that developed in the die. *(Fig. 107)*

Aside from their anomalous character, die defects serve a very important function in numismatics: they enable us, through a study of their progress, to form a chronology of dies despite frequent

Fig. 104

Fig. 105

Fig. 104. 1813 half dollar. Note the incusations above the date. The letters US UNUM (from the reverse motto) are clearly visible. Dies sustaining an injury from clashing with each other are sometimes called "leaved," blanked" or "clashed" dies.

Fig. 105. The famous 1955 doubled-die cent. It is estimated that some 20,000 pieces were placed into circulation.

Fig. 106

Fig. 107

Fig. 106. 1807 Bust Type half dollar. Liberty sports a Van Dyke beard.

Fig. 107. 1955 "Bugs Bunny" half dollar. Just a few chips out of the die.

alternation and muling. Occasionally, they serve us in other ways also, as was shown in the exposé of the "unique" 1804 and 1805 silver dollars. The most convincing proof of alteration on these pieces was the presence of certain small die breaks identical to those on coins of earlier years.

Cracks, chips and other die defects may be likened to diseases which plague some persons but leave others in peace. Attrition, on the other hand, like old age, spares none, and when a die becomes excessively worn and is not retired, its intaglio impression will eventually start to fill in. The tiny area of the mint mark is often the first to go, as we saw with the 1922 "plain" cent. Ordinarily it does not fill in all at once, but over a period of many thousands of coins, which is why we have numerous transitional examples of 1922 "broken D" cents. A similar, but less publicized, example is the 1916 "plain" half eagle. Since no coins of this date and denomination were struck in Philadelphia, the lack of any visible mint mark can only be the result of a "filled die."

From the manufacture of hubs and dies we may now proceed to the next step, which is the preparation of the coin blank or planchet. As we have seen, this operation begins with the refining of raw metals, and, should any impurity pass here undetected, it will inevitably be revealed later on. Let us say that a globule of talc is left in the metal. When the ingot is drawn through the rollers, the impurity, not being ductile, will be crushed, and separate from the strip, leaving in its place a small hole. If the impurity, however, runs for a distance beneath the surface, it will cause the entire area to separate or "peel" into layers. Occasionally, coin blanks punched from such imperfect metal make their way to the press and escape from the Mint. These "laminated planchets" are most frequently encountered among nickel coins, this metal being very difficult both to alloy and to melt.

But refining is only the first step. After the different metals have been separated from their dross they are then poured together according to the proportions prescribed by law. Occasionally, a bad mix will result, and when this happens the color of the coin will naturally be a little different than usual. Take the case of the Lincoln Head cent. This coin is normally composed of ninety-five per cent copper and five per cent tin and zinc, an alloy known as bronze. As the proportion of zinc to copper increases, the coin assumes a yellowish color until, at a ratio of 30 to 70 per cent, it becomes ordinary brass. Quite a few brass coins have, in fact, come into existence as the result of a poor alloy mix. Others resulting from the use of a foreign planchet will be dealt with presently.

While it is true that the actual separating or laminating of the planchet occurs during the rolling operation, the origin of the error must be placed at the time of refining. Nevertheless, the rolling is not without difficulties of its own. The action of the rollers is reversible causing the strip to move back and forth between them. But if they reverse prematurely a section of the strip will be left out and remain too thick.

The front of the strip tapers off like a blade in order to facilitate its entry into the last rollers. This section is supposed to be cut off prior to the blanking operation, but occasionally, through inadvertence, it is left on.

Thus we have the possibility of coin blanks being punched from metal either too thick or too thin for the purpose. Cents as thin as slivers are sometimes found and these will always be weakly struck, as they can receive no more than a very light blow from the dies. Thick cents are more scarce as they will jam the counting machines in the Federal Reserve and are thus discovered and returned to the Mint. Most of the "freaks" that we see or hear about have been found in mint-sealed bags obtained by interested persons from the reserve.[1] *(Fig. 108, p. 192)*

The *blanking operation* is one during which a great many errors are liable to occur. Here the strip is carried along a tread while a group of circular cutters punch out planchets from above. Now you can see that if the strip fails to advance properly, each punch will overlap the last, and the blank will appear to have a "bite" taken out

---

1. Genuine "thin planchets" are often simulated by unscrupulous persons, and sold as Mint products. These are no more than acidized coins which have had part of their metal eaten away. Whereas in a genuine thin cent the diameter will be equal to that of a normal coin, in the fabrication it will be reduced. In addition, the thin cent will have a smooth surface and the lowest part of its relief is apt to be missing altogether. The surface of the acidized coin, owing to the uneven action of the chemical, will be mottled and its relief approximately equal throughout.

Aside from the cult of shrunken pennies, one sometimes encounters coins that have been enlarged by being squeezed in a vise between two strips of leather. The author has seen some very excellent examples of this technique in which the detail has, in every respect, been faithfully preserved.

of it.[1] The same effect can also result when a partially used strip is reversed and not withdrawn in time. The following plate will give you an idea of the possibilities. *(Fig. 109, p. 193)*

Again, if the strip is used right down to the end, or moved too far over to one side or the other, a flat or edge clip will result.

A "clip to end all clips" was discovered a couple of years ago by a New Jersey collector. It is flat on not one side, nor two sides, but on all four! It is, in fact, the only rectangular Lincoln Head cent in existence! All of the journals which ran the discovery managed to avoid any explanation of its impossible third and fourth sides— and for a very good reason. The coin is not a "clip" at all! This is the way in which it came about. Visualize a strip as it is being punched out in gangs of four. If you draw a line following the *inner* contour of the four holes, you will arrive at a shape similar to that of a rectangle but with each of its sides pushed in.

This form exists potentially between every gang of four punches —only in the present instance it broke off and became mixed in with the normal blanks. Somehow, and in some way known only to Providence, it managed to survive all the intermediate operations and find its way into the coining press. Here it was struck along with its round brothers and, under pressure of the blow, swelled out to form an almost perfect rectangle. *(Fig. 110, p. 193)*

Our next example is a planchet which, having already been punched out, contrived to get back beneath the cutters a second time. As a result a part of it has been sheared away. This is a most unusual error since the cutter, as it punches out each blank, inevitably pushes it through an aperture directly below. Perhaps the man who emptied the receptacle dropped one of the blanks on the floor, and another person, equally careless, tossed it back onto the moving strip. *(Fig. 111, p. 193)*

Occasionally a blank will miss the next major operation, which is that of milling or upsetting, and when this happens its diameter will be too large to enter the collar. The bottom die (which is forced by the mechanism to come within a set distance of the top) will

---

1. Here again imitations abound. These are produced by punching out a bit of the coin with a round punch die. Such fabrications will show a flattened or buckled effect on the underside of the planchet from the force of the blow. Also examine the rim: On a genuine Mint error, it will begin to taper off as it approaches the clip due to the free flow of metal in this direction.

then push up, and the coin will be struck without its accustomed reeding. *(Fig. 112, p. 193)*

It sometimes happens that a blank, after traveling all this way, manages to circumvent the final operation of stamping. Collectors differentiate between blank planchets that have not been "upset" and those that have. These are generally referred to by the terms "first" and "second process," though unmilled and milled would doubtless be more precise. The verification of genuine first process planchets is a rather difficult task. It is easy enough to punch out a blank metal planchet of the correct weight. Of course one could have it assayed but that would cost more than the piece was worth. The best proof of all would be to find such a blank in a mint-sealed bag, but there are only a few verified instances where this has happened. *(Fig. 113, p. 194)*

We come now to the stamping itself. One might think that any coin which had weathered all of the previous ordeals ran little risk of a further misadventure. But, in actual fact, it is still far from the goal.

In this last section we are going to describe the so-called "classic errors," which are those resulting from some failure in the action of the press. Up to this point we have only been wading. Now it is time to venture into the deeps!

Let us assume, for example, that the layer-on fails to perform properly and that the planchet is left hanging against the collar, partly outside of the die. When this happens the result will be an off-centered coin. Such pieces are never entirely round and they are always a little more than a "whole" coin since the portion beneath the die expands under pressure of the blow.

Off-centered coins are second only to "clips" in frequency of appearance. Specialists sometimes collect them by date or in various positions, according to the dial of a clock. *(Fig. 114, p. 195)*

Another kind of partial impression is the half-reeded or railroad rim. In this instance the bottom die has not retracted all the way, and the coin is struck partly above the collar. This should make us realize, incidentally, that the collar is, in a very real sense, a third die. Coins struck completely outside the collar are fairly common and can be distinguished by their exceptionally wide rim. *(Fig. 115, p. 197)*

The next anomaly on our list is the double or multiple strike.

Fig. 108. Three Lincoln cents: thin, normal and thick.

Fig. 109

Fig. 110

Fig. 111    Fig. 112

Fig. 109. Clipped planchets: the second from the end is an edge clip; the last is a triple-clipped planchet which never got struck! Fig. 110. John A. Troyan's rectangular cent; Fig. 111. A "sheared" 1945 cent; Fig. 112. An unmilled Mercury dime. The broad rim is due to the fact that the coin was struck outside the collar.

Fig. 113. Blank planchets intended for striking silver dollar, half dollar, quarter, dime, nickel and cent.

Fig. 114. Off-center strikings of U.S. coins.

This is due to a simple malfunctioning of the ejector system whereby a coin which has already been struck is left in the collar to receive a second blow. It is interesting to speculate on how many coins of this nature pass through our hands undetected for the simple reason that both of their strikings are in perfect register. Double strikes, like off-centered coins, are valued (within their own denomination) by the extent of the deviation, the jackpot being, of course, a rotation of full one hundred and eighty degrees. *(Fig. 116)*

One of the most sought-after of all Mint errors is the double-struck, off-center coin. Here, a planchet which has been perfectly struck is partly ejected and then struck a second time, creating two separate and distinct impressions. *(Fig. 117)* Triple strikes resembling a clover leaf are extremely rare. *(Fig. 118)*

If we were to pick a single coin to crown this little group, however, it would be the unique overstruck specimen shown here. This remarkable piece, first struck in 1899, contrived to find its way back to the press in 1900, and was restruck upside down and half off center! *(Fig. 119)*

Occasionally, when a coin is partly ejected, a new planchet is brought forth and placed onto the die. Under pressure of the blow the overlapping area of the old coin will then dig into the blank, causing a big scoop, and forcing the metal to build up along the edge. *(Fig. 120, p. 200)*

Again, coins sometimes turn up which are double struck on one side only. When, in rare instances, this is not due to a doubling in the die, it is the result of the die rotating between the first and second striking. While we are on the subject of misaligned dies, we should mention that the normal relationship between obverse and reverse is always upside down, though, through a careless setting up of the press, other arrangements sometimes occur.

One of the most vexatious of the minor numismatic problems is the double profile. This is a very slight doubling (usually not more than one sixteenth of an inch from the original impression) which appears on the obverse of many coins struck between 1794 and 1835. At one time the phenomenon was attributed to a misalignment between blows in the hubbing process, an explanation which seemed reasonable since the early hubs contained no more than the device or central portion of the die. When Newcomb pointed out, however, that within the same die variety some coins showed doubling while

Fig. 116

Fig. 115. "Railroad rim" or partly reeded silver dollar. Fig. 116. 1807 half cent double struck after a full rotation of 180 degrees. Turn the picture upside down and you will be able to make out the first Liberty Head.

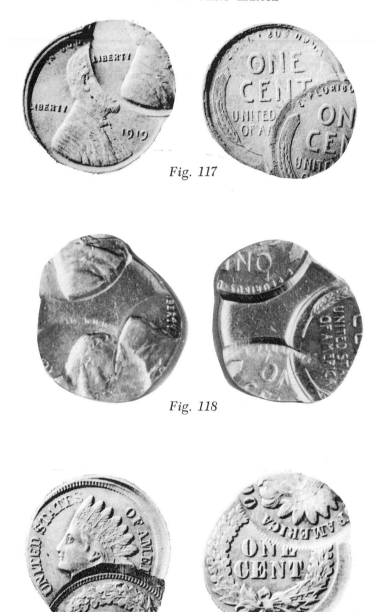

Fig. 117

Fig. 118

Fig. 119

Fig. 117. Double-struck, off-center Lincoln cent. Fig. 118. Extremely rare triple-struck, off-center Lincoln cent. Fig. 119. Unique inverted double-struck off-center cent. One side shows the date 1899, the other 1900!

others did not, the question was revived. If the doubling were not the result of improper die sinking, it must have occurred during the stamping. But why then should it be evident in the obverse device and nowhere else?

The answer is that double profiles result from rebounds of the upper (obverse) die on an *old* screw press. It should be noted that while this die was driven by the force of a rotating screw, the casing in which it was held moved straight up and down. After years of use (and possibly insufficient lubrication), the casing must have worn slightly and become loose, with the result that it did not always register the blow in exactly the same spot. Since the rebound lacked the momentum of the regular blow, it could do no more than impress the centermost part of the coin. The reverse die remained fixed to the foundation, which is why the doubling invariably occurred only in the obverse. *(Fig. 121)*

Another kind of doubling, or rather partial doubling, which is sometimes found among coins of smaller denomination, results from trying to correct an error in the wrong way. What happens is this: A pair of dies are set into the press inaccurately so that their faces are slightly oblique instead of being level to one another. The side on which the dies are further apart will appear weakly struck, and in order to bring up the relief, the attendant will increase the pressure throughout. This will cause the metal on the heavy side to squeeze out of the die which instantly fills up, giving the appearance of doubling.

There is one more type of partial doubling, and this occurs when the ring collar breaks, and the viscous metal is allowed to exude through the fissure. Such a coin will show a bulge and progressive doubling of the features (due to metal displacement) in the area of the break. Actually, the collar is thick and sturdy and the occasions on which it cracks are very few. Almost all of the coins offered for sale as broken-collar strikes are simply examples of faulty collar traction in which the coin is struck completely outside the mechanism. *(Fig. 122)*

We have seen how incusing can result from the contact of the dies with each other. The phenomenon also occurs however when a coin fails to eject properly and another is placed on top of it (or beneath it, as the case may be) in the die. A coin may not eject for numerous reasons. It may be that the bottom die has failed to

Fig. 121. 1824 Bust Type half dollar with double profile.

Fig. 120. A "scooped out" 1954-S Lincoln cent.

rise up through the collar. It can even happen that a coin is sucked up into the top die and held there by a speck of moisture. When, in the first instance, a coin remains in the bottom or reverse die, the second coin will receive two obverse impressions, a normal embossed one on its upper side and an incused one on the bottom. If, instead, the first coin becomes stuck in the top or obverse die, the second will be double-tailed, its underside normal, its top incused. (*Fig. 123*)

The principle of incusing is simple enough, but in actual fact it can become extremely complicated. Take, for example, the Lincoln Head cent shown here. While the reverse of this coin is perfectly struck, the obverse is, to say the least, an enigma. To begin with, there are two busts of Lincoln, one normal (though very faint), and another, considerably enlarged. The edge is very high (more so in fact than on a proof) and the surface depressed, showing that it has been struck under great pressure (*Fig. 124*)

Previously we described only the incused coin, which is the *second* of the two to enter the collar. Our present coin happens to be the *first*, and we shall see just how it fares during the process of incusing. We shall refer to these two pieces as A and B in order of their appearance in the dies. Our coin is A.

Coin A enters the ring collar, is struck, and then for some reason fails to eject from the bottom die. As a rule, when this happens, the layer-on will also fail to perform, and the coin will be struck a second blow. In the present instance, however, coin B was placed on top of it, and both coins (or rather the coin and blank planchet) were then struck together.

As we have said, the dies in a modern press are set to meet with only a certain distance between them. Thus, the presence of an additional planchet greatly increases the pressure of the blow, causing in each coin an excessive displacement of metal away from the center. Since the bottom coin is confined by the collar, the metal, after it has reached the edge, rushes upward, creating a sharp fin along the entire rim.

But as the collar is scarcely any higher than a single planchet, the underside of coin B (together with its incused impression) is thus free to spread out, carrying along with it the metal of coin A and leaving on the latter an enlarged, embossed head, in addition to its nearly obliterated first design.

As far as our present coin is concerned, the story ends here. But sometimes coin B will now get rolled up in the top die and stay there, and when this happens, it will register an enlarged obverse impression on every incoming planchet. With each blow it will spread a little more until it takes on a peculiar concave shape. Cupped coins of this sort have actually been found in mint-sealed bags, although they are, of course, very rare. *(Figs. 125, 6, 7)*

The incused coin shown here is actually a copper-nickel Indian Head cent of the 1860-64 period. Not only was the coin struck by another which lay on top of it, but at the time, neither piece was contained by the collar. It is the only example of this compound error which the writer has seen. *(Fig. 128)*

It might be asked why, of the two sides, only the incused design is subject to spreading. The reason for this is that whereas the incusing is *free* of the relief that causes it, the relief, which takes its impression from the die, is "gripped" by the incusing.

We shall describe one last example of the possibilities of incusing, this being the most unusual so far. The present coin has much in common with our earlier Lincoln Head cent. The surface is depressed and the edge built up in the same manner. Again, the reverse is perfectly struck. On the obverse side there is the same faint shadow of a normal embossed head of Lincoln. But predominate here is an enlarged incuse version of the reverse design, of which only a part could fit onto the planchet. This is indeed a puzzle! The presence of an embossed obverse and an incused reverse on the same side can only mean that both of the coins involved, prior to their contact with each other, had already been struck by the dies. But surely one of the two coins must have been a blank planchet, so what happened? The phenomenon becomes intelligible when we recall that modern coin presses operate on dual dies. These dies are very close to each other, and once in a while a coin from one of them will be improperly ejected and pushed over into the other. This is exactly what happened in the present instance, and it demonstrates the kind of errors possible through the simultaneous malfunctioning of more than one part of the press. *(Fig. 129)*

Collectors should beware of simulated incusations, and reject at once any coin that is sharply incused on both sides. Fabrications of this sort are made by placing one coin between two others and then hammering on it. Each side will thus show an incusing in

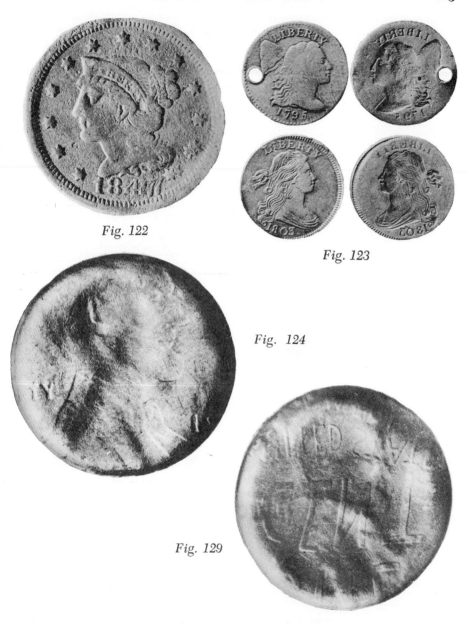

Fig. 122

Fig. 123

Fig. 124

Fig. 129

Fig. 122. 1847 large cent struck in a broken collar. Note the doubling of the 7 and the last two stars. Fig. 123. 1795 and 1803 large cents with embossed and incused obverses. These are usually called "brockages." Fig. 124. Lincoln cent with enlarged embossed head.   Fig. 129. Lincoln cent with enlarged reverse incusations over a faintly embossed obverse.

Fig. 125. Evolution of a cupped coin. No. 1. This is what happens when a coin, adhering to the top or obverse die, continues to be struck against incoming planchets. Since it is free of the collar, it expands with every blow, gradually wrapping itself around the die. The diffusion of the obverse impression indicates that after the coin dislodged, it was battered a few times against blank planchets.

Fig. 126. Cupped coin No. 2. If the layer-on periodically fails to operate during this process, the coin will again be struck with both dies, reinforcing the original impression. This is what happened in the above instance.

Fig. 127. Cupped coin No. 3. Here, so much metal has been forced outward that the extra-thin center has begun to give way. The reverse impression is practically effaced from its constant battering by blank planchets.

Fig. 128. Unique copper-nickel Indian Head cent with embossed and incused reverse.

addition to its regular impression. Blank planchets are subject to the same abuse, and are often found with simulated incusations on both sides. Most of these are patchwork jobs, but even when they are performed with care, they need deceive no one, for the simple reason that they cannot legitimately occur. Even if two coins become stuck, one in each die, the second one in will take an incusing, and should a third coin then come along, it will receive one incused and one embossed impression.

It should also be noted that any time two coins are present together in the die, the heightened pressure is going to obliterate most of the detail on the sides that meet. Whatever is conveyed in the exchange will be both larger and weaker than normal. In the case of an obverse incusing, the planchet, which has been struck outside the collar, will also be distended. In a reverse incusing, the presence of the collar around the coin will result in a depressed surface and a high-wire edge. Without machinery equal to that of the Mint itself, no counterfeiter can hope to duplicate these details.

Among the most coveted (not to mention controversial) of the Mint errors are off-planchet coins. These are of four kinds, to wit:

1. Coins struck on planchets intended for another denomination, but in the same metal.

2. Coins struck on planchets intended for another denomination, and in a different metal.

3. Coins struck on planchets intended for a previous issue of the same denomination, but in a different metal, e.g. 1943 bronze cents, 1944 steel cents.[1]

4. Coins struck on planchets intended for a foreign issue.

These are neither die trials nor "favor coins," but come about in the following way: we will assume that a press is engaged in stamping cents. After the run has been finished, the attendant will strike the "hopper" with a rubber mallet to insure that no blank planchets have loitered behind. But even then, one or two stragglers occasionally lodge in a crevice and are by-passed. Now the machine is again set up—but this time for striking nickels. When the new blanks are fed into the hopper, the odds are that one of them will dislodge the old planchet, causing it to be mixed in with the present company.

---

1. Two other undiscovered possibilities of this type are 1942 type II nickels struck in "nickel," and 1946 five-cent pieces struck in the silver composition. In used condition these would be apt to pass undetected.

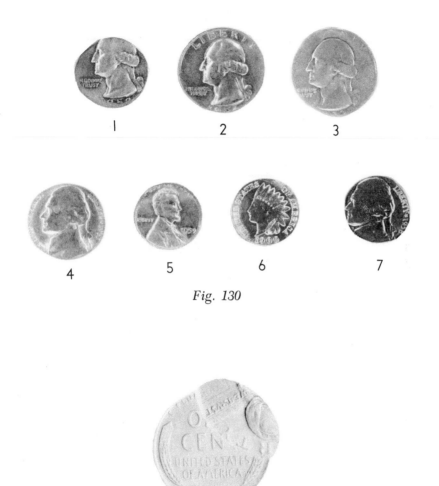

Fig. 130

Fig. 131

Fig. 130. Off-planchet coins: 1) 1958 quarter struck on dime planchet; 2) 1957 quarter struck on nickel five-cent planchet; 3) 1952 quarter struck on bronze cent planchet; 4) 1957 nickel struck on bronze cent planchet; 5) 1959 cent struck on dime planchet; 6) 1900 Indian Head cent struck on gold quarter-eagle planchet; and 7) 1958 nickel five cents struck on nickel planchet intended for a foreign coin. Fig. 131. Unique Lincoln cent overstruck with dies intended for striking Liberty Standing quarters.

Fig. 132. 1934 quarter struck over a 1916 dime. A Mint error?

When this happens, we end up with a copper "nickel," a nickel "quarter" or some other anomaly. Our Government also strikes coins for several foreign countries, and every now and then one of the planchets for these issues will likewise show up bearing a U.S. denomination. *(Fig. 130)*

From the same family, but a hundred times rarer, are the double denomination or overstruck coins. These can only result from great carelessness or caprice,[1] for a coin which has already left one press must find its way into another engaged in striking different coins. In the first instance it would mean that a person found a finished coin on the floor and didn't look where he threw it. This could possibly be alleged for the cent shown here which has been overstruck with the dies of a Liberty Standing quarter *(Fig. 131)*

On the other hand, it would hardly account for the next coin. Here is a 1916 Mercury dime which, eighteen years after its issue, contrived to land between dies intended for striking 1934 quarters! "Well," you will say, "someone who was passing through the Mint probably dropped the coin out of his pocket." Unlikely as this explanation seems, we might still accept it—were it not for one fact: judging from the relief of the earlier impression, it would appear that the dime was uncirculated or very close to it—hardly a coin to be jingled in one's pocket. Besides, the registry of the two strikings, which is exactly one hundred and eighty degrees apart, would indicate that the coin had been carefully fed into the collar to achieve the best possible effect. *(Fig. 132)*

Until recently, the existence of the above-mentioned "Mint error" was generally unknown. Its publication thus posed a problem of where to include it in the present work. Since the bulk of the manuscript (including Chapter IV) had already been completed, the writer finally decided to append it to the section on Mint errors, though not without explanation. Lovers of the ironic should appreciate this anachronism, for, having come all this way through the

1. Formerly this was not so. In the Colonies it was often found more expedient to overstrike the coins of a neighboring mint than to prepare blanks of one's own. This practice, which originated in ancient Greece, was also resorted to by our early Philadelphia Mint, as evinced by the number of 1795 half cents which are found struck over cut-down Talbot. Allum and Lee tokens. Large cents, overstruck with dies intended for striking silver dollars and half dollars also turn up occasionally. These no doubt served as handy die trials when no soft-metal blanks were immediately available.

official (and some not-so-official) boudoirs, it is only fitting that we take our leave by the same door. . . . Certainly the way is open.

Epilogue

Despite the Government's seizure of another silver cent, it is difficult to believe that the Treasury Department seriously intends to confiscate all numismatic errors which fail to conform to the Revised Statutes of 1873. And yet, the implications are obvious. If "off-metal" Mint errors are illegal, then what about coins lacking one or both of their designs (incused pieces and blank planchets), coins lacking their date, denomination or a part of their devices (off-centered or clipped pieces), coins above or below their weight tolerance (thick, thin and clipped planchets), and the multitude of other errors which fail to meet the requirements of the Revised Statutes? And what is the status of a modern date silver cent, in brilliant proof, still intact in its holder, as sold together with a proof nickel, dime, quarter, and half dollar as a specimen set, *and at a premium*, by the Philadelphia Mint?

The alleged basis for these arbitrary confiscations is that any coin failing to meet the specifications of the 1873 laws has not been legally issued, and therefore remains the property of the United States Government. We may inquire, however, whether the laws in question were framed for the purpose of seizing numismatic errors which occur through mechanical malfunctioning and are released at face value through the Federal Reserve, or whether they might not have been intended to cover such elaborate productions as the 1804 dollars struck in 1834-5 and again in 1858, and the 1913 Liberty Head nickel (to name but a few), which were made illegally and disposed of through "private" channels. The answer, we feel, was given by Director James P. Kimball in his annual report of 1887, from which we have quoted liberally in Chapter IV. And while we are on the subject, how is it that no attempt has ever been made to bring any of these extremely illegitimate black sheep back to the fold—and that even today, a dollar bearing the year 1804, but struck over a Swiss shooting thaler of 1857, adorns the Mint Cabinet?

Let the facts about unauthorized coins be aired and a status clearly defined for each of the series. Until this is done, such confiscations as are sporadically undertaken by Treasury agents can only be presumptuous and without regard for the due process of law.

APPENDIX

A RECENT discovery by the English numismatist and dealer, David Spink, has confirmed the existence of an eighth 1804 "original" dollar, as part of a proof set presented by the Mint to the King of Siam. The State Department order for this set, as well as for another to be sent to the Sultan of Muscat, is dated Nov. 11, 1834. It calls for "duplicate specimens of each kind (of U.S. coin) now in use." The then Mint Director, Samuel Moore, evidently opined that the silver dollar and gold eagle ($10) should also be represented, even though their use had been countermanded three decades earlier. Whatever his reasoning, the occasion would seem to furnish us with the specific reason why ante-dated dollar and eagle dies were originally made, and coins struck. It is interesting to note that while the weight of the 1804 restrike eagle (270½ grains) conforms to the standard of 1804, it does not do so with respect to the Act of June 28, 1834, which was passed prior to its striking. This makes this eagle a most illegal eagle, and a coin even more provocative than its notorious compeer, the 1804 dollar.

Suggested Reading

The Standard Catalogue of United States Coins, Ford-Breen-Taxay, Ford Numismatic Publications. 19th edition in process.

The Fantastic 1804 Dollar, Newman-Bressett, Whitman Publishing Co.

The Secret of the Good Samaritan Shilling, Newman, American Numismatic Society.

Struck Copies of Early American Coins, Kenney, Wayte Raymond Inc.

Monograph of the Dollar, J. L. Riddell (1845).

Electrotypes, Copies, Casts, etc., Kenney, *Numismatic Scrapbook Magazine,* July, 1955.

The Hundred Year Vendetta, Breen, *Numismatic Scrapbook Magazine,* Aug. 1962.

INDEX

Adams, Edgar H., 98, 149
Adams, Eva, 118
American Journal of Numismatics, 113, 120, 138
Appleton, William S., 148-149
Assaying, method of, 52

Bailey & Co. Jewelers, 128
Baldwin & Co., 173, 176
Barber, Charles E., 91
Bashlow, Robert, 129-130
Betts, C. Wyllys, counterfeits of, 139-147
Birmingham half-pence, 26-27
Bishop, Edwin, 148-149
Blake & Co., 177
Blanking, method of, 10, 189-90
Bolender, M. H., 110, 160
Bosbyshell, O. C., 90-91, 108
Boudinot, Elias, 95
Boulton, Matthew, 22
Bouvet pattern eagle ($10), 17
Bowers, Q. David, 130
Brand, Virgil, 130
Breen, Walter H., 68, 80, 99, 149, 160
Brenner, Judson, 130
Bressett, Kenneth, 84
Broderick, David C., 172
Brodhead, Richard, 99
Brown, Ammi, 133-135
Brown, Samuel W., 115-116
Buel, Abel, 24, 26
Burnett, Peter, 173

Burnie, R. H., 169
Bushnell, Charles I., 132, 135

Cast counterfeiting, 32-40
Centrifugal casting (see Lost Wax Method)
Cents:
   1787, Fugio, 26
   1795, Jefferson head, 17, 49
   1796, "LIHERTY" error, 180
   1799, alterations, 59-62
   1801, "three-error reverse," 180
   1803, corrected fraction, 181
   1804, alterations, 61-63
   —muling of, 122
   1810, muling of, 122
   1823, restrike, 120-121
   1844, over 81, error, 180
   1848, small date counterfeit, 150-151
   1851, over 81, error, 180
   1856, Flying Eagle, alterations, 63
   —, patterns, 82
   1861, Confederate, 128-131
   1869, muling with five-cent die, 16, 102
   1914-D, alterations, 63-64
   1922, "plain," alterations
   —, error, 188
   1943, "copper," alterations and counterfeits, 66-67
   1944, steel, 66
   1955, doubled die, 185
   counterfeit, 39, 49, 66-67, 150-51, 168
   pieces de caprice, 16, 100, 102
   Vermont, muling with dies for British half-pence, 27-28
Chapman, Henry, 83, 130, 135, 148, 149, 153

Chapman, Samuel H., 83, 95, 135, 148
Childs, George K., 80, 121
Chop marks, 74
Cincinnati Mining & Trading Co., 172
Clark Gruber & Co., 177
Clayton, P., 80-81
Clipped planchets, 189-190
Clipping, 23-24
Cobb, Howell, 80
Cogan, Edward, 82, 86, 150, 151
Cohen, M. I., 83
Coin Collector's Herald, 146
Coin Collector's Journal, 141-143, 153
Coining press (see Press)
Coin World, 151
Colburn, Jeremiah, 86-87, 138
Comparette, T. L., 148
Confederate cent, 128-131
Confederate half dollar, 122, 124-28
Conway, J. J., 177
Corwin, Thomas, 170
Crosby, Sylvester, 135, 145, 148, 150
Cupellation, 52
Curtis, John K., 80

Date logotypes, 8, 100
Davis, Jefferson, 125-126
—, R. Coulton, 91, 94, 105, 120, 121
Debasing, 21-22
Dickeson, M. W., 119, 120, 154
Die sinking, 4-5, 9, 180
Dimes:
  1814, "error reverse," muling of, 122
  1916, overstruck with 1934 quarter
    dies, 211
  1942, over 1, 182
Dollars:
  gold, counterfeits, 39-41
  goloid, 13, 109
  silver:
    1801, 1802, 1803, restrikes, 16, 84
    1804, 16, 82-95, 112, 116, 118, 212,
      213
    —alterations, 56, 155-161
    1805, alteration, 155-161
    1866, without motto, 16, 98-99
    1876, reverse of 1857-59, 100-101
    1877, experimental patterns in silver
      and copper, 104-105
    1878, Barber-Morgan patterns, 106
Double denomination coins, 211
Double Eagles ($20):
  1849, brass restrike, 105
  1876, patterns, 106

Driefus, W. Julius, 91
"Drop-in" electrotype (see Electrotypes)
Dubois, William E., 76-77, 82-83, 87, 94,
  170, 172, 174
Dubosq & Co., 173
Dunne, Miss M. A., 159

Eagles ($10):
  1804, restrike, 84, 213
  1865-S, over 186, 183
Eckfeldt, Adam, 77
—, George, 84
—, Jacob, 82, 170, 172, 174
Edge lettering, method of, 10
Edwards, Frank S., 150-152
Electroplating, method of, 32
Electrotypes, 48-51
Ellsworth, James W., 90-91
Elmore, William A., 126
"Evasions," 22, 25
Explosive impact copying, 48

False metal coins, 17, 99, 103-105, 110
Farouk, King, 116
Felt, Joseph B., 138
Filling of gold coins, the, 30-31
Folkes, Martin, 137, 138
Ford, John J. Jr., 12, 96, 124-125, 130,
  151
Franklin, Paul, 125
Friedenberg, Samuel, 158-159
Frossard, Edouard, 124, 140, 143-147,
  149

Gault, John, 166
Glaser, Lynn, 98
Good Samaritan Shillings, 135-138
Green, E. H. R., 116, 118
Guthrie, James, 78-79
Gyges, King, 3

Haines, Ferguson, catalogue of collection,
  87-88, 154
Half Cents:
  1793, Washington head fabrication,
    148-150, 152
  1795, struck over Talbot, Allum & Lee
    tokens, 17, 211
  1796, Edward's counterfeit, 150
  1840-1852 restrikes, 113
Half Dollars:
  1787 counterfeit, 151, 153

1804 alteration, 154-155
1805 over 4, 154-155
1806, muling with postage stamp die, 121
1807, Van Dyke Beard variety, 185
1813, 50C over UNI, 180
—, incused UNI above date, 185
1839, restrikes, 113
1844-O, doubled date, 183
1861, "God Our Trust" patterns, 88
—, Confederate, 68, 70-72
1866, without motto, 16, 98-99, 101
1922 Grant Memorial alterations, 68, 70-72
1955, "Bugs Bunny" variety, 185
struck counterfeits, 40-43
Half Eagle ($5), 1916 "plain," 188
Harmon, Reuben, 27
Harzfeld, S. K., 108-109
Haseltine, John W., 40, 91, 106, 110, 107, 120-121, 128, 130-131
Henry I, King, 21-22
Hill's engraving machine, 96
Hinge dies, 6
Hodge, William, 176
Hubbel, W. W., 109
Hull, John, 24
Humbert, Augustus, 174, 177-178
Hydraulic press (see Press)

Idler, William, 106, 107, 110
Incused coins, 184-185, 199, 201-202, 208
Ingham, S. D., 84

Jackson, Andrew, 162-164
Janvier reducing machine, 9, 48
Johnson, B. G., 156, 159-160
Judd, J. Hewitt, 98, 153

Kelley, Arthur B., 159
Kellogg, John G., 177
Kenney, Richard, 133
Kettle & Son, 73
Kimball, James P., annual Mint report of, 104, 110-114, 118, 212
Kohler, Frederick D., 172-174, 178
Krider, Peter L., 131

Laminated planchets, 188-189
Landis, John H., 116
Levick, J. N. T., 90, 151
Lewis, Winslow, collection of, 154-155
Lindenmueller tokens, 166-167

Linderman, Henry R., 88, 90, 94, 99, 100, 101, 105
Logotypes (see Date logotypes)
Longacre, J. P., 173
Lost Wax method, the, 33-34
Lovett, Robert Jr., 128, 131

Machin's Mill, 27-28
McClure, R. A., 91
McCulloch, Hugh, 96
Marshall, James, 169
Mason, Ebenezer L., 49, 84, 103, 119, 122, 146-148
—, R. B., 170-171
Matte Proofs (see Proof coins)
Mehl, B. Max, 118, 150, 155
Metallography, 56
Mickley, Joseph J., 83, 119, 120, 122, 132, 144
Milling, method of, 10
Miner's Bank, 172
Moffat & Co., J. L., 171-176
Moore, Samuel, 84, 213
Mormon coinage, 172, 178
Multiple impressions on coins, 185, 191, 196, 199

Nero, Emperor, 21
Newcomb, Howard, 151, 196
Newman, Eric P., 84, 124, 137, 155, 156
Nichols, C. P., 86
Nickel Five Cents:
  1869, muling with cent die, 16, 102
  1875, struck counterfeits, 43-45
  1913, Liberty head, 115-118
  1937-D, "Three-legged Buffalo" variety, alterations, 67-69
  1938 D, over S, 181
  1944 "plain" counterfeits, 39
Noe, Sydney P., 72
Norris, Grieg & Norris, firm of, 171, 178
"Novum Belgium" fabrication, 139-145
Numisma magazine, 90, 108-110, 124, 140-141, 143-147
Numismatist, The, magazine, 115, 121, 149, 153, 158

Off-centered coins, 191, 196
Off-planchet coins, 188-189, 208, 211
Opdyke, George, 103
Ormsby & Co., 172
Ostheimer, Alfred J., 155

Overdates, 181-182

Pacific Co., 172
Parmelee, L. G., 83, 135, 137, 151
Parsons & Co., 177
Patterson, Robert, 76-78, 115
Peach, Mr., 28-29
Peale, Franklin, 78-79, 100, 121
Pembroke, Earl of, 135
Peterson, A. H. M., 126
Platinum-filled gold coins, 30-31
"Plugging" of coins, the, 30
Pollock, James, 89-90, 95-99, 104-106, 108
Portrait lathe, 8
Press:
    hydraulic, 11
    screw, 5, 6, 185
    steam, 7
Pressure casting (see Lost Wax method)
Prime, W. C., 82
Proof coins, the manufacture of, 11-12
Proskey, David, 122, 124, 127

Quarter Dollars:
    1806, over 5, 181
    1856-S, large S over small S, 184
    1866, without motto, 16, 98-99
    1869, bi-metallic muling with two-cent die, 16, 102

Randall, J. Colvin, 128, 131
Ready, August, 49
—, Charles, 49
—, Robert Cooper, 49
Richter, G. F., 177
Riddell, J. L., 153
Roberts, George E., 115-116, 118
Root, James E., collection of, 150
Rosenthal, Isaac, 91

Saltus, Sanford, 124
Sandblast proofs (see Proof coins)
Sanford, E. H., 83
Schayer, John C., 145
Schilke, Oscar, 153
"Scooping" of gold coins, the, 30
Scot, Robert, 153
Scott & Co., J. W., 94, 122, 124, 126-127, 141-143
Screw press (see Press)
Sellers, William, 121

Sheldon, W. H., 76
Shillings:
    Massachusetts, 24
    —, 1650 fabrication, 133-135
    —, 1665 fabrication, 145-147
    Good Samaritan, 135-138
Shults & Co., 176
Smith, A. M., collection of, 110
Snelling, Thomas, 137
Snowden, A. Louden, 99-100, 108-110
—, James Ross, 79-82, 84, 89, 99-100, 122, 148, 150, 158
Specific gravity test, 51-52
Spectro-analysis, 53
Spink & Son, 158-159, 213
Sponge gold, 174-175
Standard Catalogue of United States Coins, The, 12, 113
Steam press (see Press)
Stearns, William G., 77
Steigerwalt, Charles, 121
"Stella," pattern four-dollar gold, 15, 109
Stickney, Matthew, 82-83, 132
Suckauhock (see Wampumpeage)
"Sweating" of gold coins, the, 30

Taylor, B. F., 122, 126
—, Charles R., 135
Thomas & Sons, Moses, 119
Thompson, Walter, 88
Tour a Portrait de Contamin (see Portrait lathe)
Trade Dollars:
    1875-S, over CC, 181
    1884, 1885, 16, 109-10, 118
Two-Cent pieces
    1865, bi-metallic, 16, 202
    1869, muling with standard silver quarter, 16, 102

Upsetting, method of (see Milling)

Van Buren, Martin, 163-164

Wagner, August, 116
Warner, Charles K., 121
—, John S., 121
Washington half-cent fabrication, 148-150, 152
Wass, Molitor & Co., 177-178
Webster, Daniel, 164
Weights of U.S. coins, 36-37

Werner, Louis, 156, 160
Weyl, Adolph, collection of, 83
Wharton, Joseph, 99
William III, King, 23
Window tax, 23
Witch pieces, 72
Woodin, William H., 98
Woodward, Elliot, 87-88, 94, 146-148, 150, 153-155

Wyatt, Thomas, counterfeits of, 132, 137-139

X-ray diffractometry, 53-55
X-ray spectography, 55-56

Young, Brigham, 172

Zerbe, Farran, 106, 151, 156, 159